0055925

D0777196

KOHYKWT99

AZ
999
K64
1990

Kohn, Alfie.

You know what they
say-.

$17.95

© THE BAKER & TAYLOR CO.

YOU KNOW WHAT THEY SAY...

BOOKS BY ALFIE KOHN

You Know What They Say . . . :
The Truth about Popular Beliefs

The Brighter Side of Human Nature:
Altruism and Empathy in Everyday Life

No Contest:
The Case against Competition

YOU KNOW WHAT THEY SAY...

THE TRUTH ABOUT POPULAR BELIEFS

ALFIE KOHN

HarperCollins*Publishers*

FIRST EDITION

Designed by Cassandra J. Pappas

Library of Congress Cataloging-in-Publication Data

Kohn, Alfie.
    You know what they say : the truth about popular beliefs / Alfie
Kohn. — 1st ed.
        p. cm.   Includes bibliographical references.
    ISBN 0-06-016040-3
    1. Errors, popular.   I.Title.
AZ999.K64   1990   89-46541
001.9'6—dc20

---

90 91 92 93 94 CC/RRD 10 9 8 7 6 5 4 3 2 1

CONTENTS

Introduction   *1*

Don't swim for an hour after eating   **9**

Women want sex for intimacy; men want sex for
pleasure   **11**

Chocolate causes acne   **15**

People become more conservative as they get
older   **17**

Lemmings commit mass suicide   **20**

Capital punishment is a good way to keep the murder
rate down   **21**

Beauty is only skin deep (or You can't judge a book by
its cover)   **25**

Catherine the Great died from horsing around   **27**

Lots of people are just tone-deaf   **28**

No two snowflakes are alike   **30**

Rewards motivate people   **31**

Spicy food is bad for the stomach   **35**

Couples should beware The Seven-Year Itch   **36**

The rich get richer and the poor get poorer   **38**

Familiarity breeds contempt   **40**

Women's moods change at "That Time of the Month"   **41**

When college teams win, the bucks roll in   **46**

Absence makes the heart grow fonder vs. Out of sight, out of mind   **48**

Salt raises your blood pressure   **49**

The full moon makes people crazy   **50**

The squeaky wheel gets the grease   **53**

Abused children grow up to abuse their own children   **54**

Time flies when you're having fun   **56**

If the Atomic Bomb had not been dropped on Hiroshima, the war would have continued and even more lives would have been lost   **58**

Boys are better at math than girls   **63**

Laughter is the best medicine   **64**

Reading in the dark will ruin your eyes   **68**

Humans are naturally aggressive   **69**

Watch out for subliminal advertising   **72**

Breakfast is the most important meal of the day   **75**

Actions speak louder than words   **78**

After the baby comes the blues   **79**

Competition builds character   **81**

An elephant never forgets   **84**

Great minds think alike   **85**

Carrots are good for your eyes   **88**

Plead insanity and you can get away with murder   **88**

Playing hard to get makes one more attractive 91

You can catch cold from being chilled—and cure it with chicken soup 94

Picking up babies every time they cry will only spoil them 99

Power corrupts 102

Boston drivers are the worst 104

You're never too old to learn vs. You can't teach an old dog new tricks 106

Don't marry your cousin 109

Female praying mantises eat their mates 111

Beauty is in the eye of the beholder 112

Expressing hostility gets it out of your system 113

Fright can turn your hair white overnight 118

Nearsighted people are smarter 119

He who lives by the sword, dies by the sword 123

No pain, no gain 124

Laugh and the whole world laughs with you; cry and you cry alone 126

Most homeless people are crazy 127

Religious people are more altruistic 129

Women reach their sexual peak after age thirty; men, in their teens 131

Spare the rod and spoil the child 135

Cracking your knuckles will give you arthritis 138

Basketball players shoot in streaks 141

More people commit suicide during the holidays 143

Firstborns are different from other children 144

Marijuana today, hard drugs tomorrow 148

Creativity requires a touch of madness 150

People are starving because of overpopulation   **154**

Like father, like son   **155**

Kids don't read because they're addicted to television   **157**

Women are more empathic (and intuitive) than men   **161**

Grouping students by ability allows them to learn better   **163**

. . . Mondays always get me down   **166**

Marry in haste, repent at leisure   **168**

Don't have sex before the big game   **170**

Adoption cures infertility   **171**

Blind people are blessed with supersensitive hearing   **174**

Adolescence is a time of turmoil and alienation   **176**

There's safety in numbers   **178**

Stress is bad for you   **180**

Birds of a feather flock together vs. Opposites attract   **182**

. . . A woman's work is never done   **184**

Blondes have more fun   **186**

Necessity is the mother of invention   **188**

Ignorance is bliss   **190**

Commonly misused words   **195**

References   **197**

A Note to Readers   **229**

Index   **231**

He moves in darkness as it seems to me.
Not of woods only and the shade of trees.
He will not go behind his father's saying.

—ROBERT FROST
"Mending Wall"

ACKNOWLEDGMENTS

What follows is not intended to be a parody of Academy Award night. There really are this many people to thank— so many, in fact, that I came close to omitting this section for fear it would dwarf the rest of the book. Besides, I've been haunted by that sensation you get just after setting out on a long trip: I just *know* I'm forgetting someone. To make matters worse, I suddenly realized I hadn't been keeping track of all the friends and friends of friends and friends of acquaintances of friends who for months have been helpfully suggesting bits of folk wisdom to be included in the book and then casually inquiring whether they will see their names on the acknowledgments page.

Sorry.

But here are some people who will. Wray Herbert enthusiastically published the article that got the whole project rolling. Larry Ashmead seduced me into the world of Lite Reference Books. He and John Michel make a swell editing team, and working with both of them has been a joy.

Then there are the specialists in various fields, each of whom read a section of the book and made some teensy little suggestions for improvement, along the lines of: "If accuracy is at all important to you, you may wish to consider inserting the word *not* at various points throughout the text." I really don't mind such quibbling; in fact, I'm enormously grateful for the comments of Gar Alperovitz (Hiroshima), Elliot Dick (colds), Jeffrey Goldstein (laughter), Muin Khoury (inbreeding), Frances Moore Lappé (hunger), Jeannie Oakes (ability grouping), Mary Brown Parlee (menstruation), David Warren (blindness), Peter Watson (knuckle cracking), and Cathy Spatz Widom (child abuse).

The implication, as will have become obvious to anyone who can subtract, is that a good number of sections were *not* reviewed by experts. This poses a real problem for me—namely, how to avoid taking responsibility for any errors that may have found their way into the rest of the book. Most of my data were culled from written material (read: read), which leaves me in the rather desperate position of having to blame the copy machines in the library for getting some of the words scrambled.

Fortunately, my reading was supplemented by conversations with quite a number of researchers, and so in a pinch I could always blame them. For the time being, though, I will simply say how grateful I am for their patience and generosity—as well as, in some cases, the patience of their secretaries and spouses. These people did their best to help me understand the intricacies of their respective fields, to separate what is known from what is believed, and to point me to still other people and other monographs.

Thank you, then, to John Alexander, Elizabeth Allgeier, Duane Alwin, Teresa Amabile, Daniel Anderson, Arthur Aron, Virginia Aronson, Jeanne Bamberger, Hugo Bedau, Walden Bellow, Billie Louise Bentzen, Lee Berk, Elaine Blechman, Jack Block, John Bolzan, June Bruce, Larry Bumpass, Tom Cash, Dennis Chitty, Ray Ciszek, John Clausen, Dorothy Cline, David Costill, Carolyn Cowan, Jim Coyne, Michael Cunningham, Elliot Currie, Sheldon Danziger, Elliot Dick, William Dietz, Marian Dunn, Nat Durlach, John Eisenberg, David Engle, Leonard Eron, Hester Fassel, Emerson Foulke, Millard Freeman, William Fry, James Fulton, Howard Gardner, Meg Gerrard, Tom Gilovich, Norval Glenn, Bernard Goldstein, Jeffrey Goldstein, John Gottman, Joel Gurin, Jack Gwaltney, James Halikas, John Hallett, Ruth Hanno, Elaine Hatfield, Cindy Hazan, Julia Heiman, Frederick Helm, Ravenna Helson, Mavis Hetherington, Maria Hordinsky, Janet Hyde, Kent Jennings, Thomas Juster, Daniel Kahneman, Frank Katch, Kathryn Kelley, Ivan Kelly, Myriam Khlat (France), Muin Khoury, Devra Kleiman, Nancy Knight, Melvin Kohn, Margie Lachman, Bill Langbauer, John Larivee, Charles Levy, Harris Lieberman, Michael Liebowitz, Colin Loftin, David McClelland, John Malatak, Howard Markman, Colin Martindale, you'd better be paying attention because all of these names are going to be on the quiz, Robert Millman, John Money, Donald Mosher, David Myers, Joe Nadeau, Edward Nalebuff, Richard Nisbet, James Nordlund, Jeannie Oakes, Daniel Offer, Michael O'Hara, Mary Brown Parlee, Glenn Pierce, Joseph Pleck, Patricia Pliner, Peter Pochi, Ernesto Pollitt, Robert Prentky, Louise Priest, Wendell Primus, David Quadagno, Susan Rosenholtz, Martin Rosenthal, Lee Ross, Paul Rozin, Jeffrey Rubin, Mel Rubin, Virginia Sadock, Margaret Sanik, William Schull, Alan Shalita, Phil Shaver, Harvey Silverglate, Dean Keith Simonton, Clement Sledge, Graham Spanier, Joey Sprague, Bonnie Spring, Frederick Stare, Hank Steadman, Julian Stein, Abe Tesser, Jan Trost (Sweden), Mark Uslan, David Warren, Fred Wasserman, Malcolm Watson, Peter Watson (Ireland), Michael Weitzman, Barbara Foley Wilson, Tony Winsor, Kurt Wolff, Diana Woodruff, Judith Wurtman, Bill Young, Francis Young, Morris Ziff, and Franklin Zimring. If you helped me but cannot find your name here, all I can say is that the quality of typesetting isn't what it used to be.

As I have done twice before, it is my pleasure to acknowledge the roles played by two other people: John Ware, my agent, and Bill Greene, who reads my manuscripts with such unerring critical instincts that I have come to see him as a gyroscope on legs.

YOU KNOW WHAT THEY SAY...

INTRODUCTION

These days I spend my time writing, but I used to teach and probably will do so again some day. Among my annoying habits as a teacher is to make a point of stopping any student who uses the indefinite pronoun when talking about a book. ("They say on page eighty-seven that . . .") It's not the grammatical error that bothers me, but the disappearance of the author into the "they." Authors are fallible and have distinctive points of view, I remind my classes. When we lose sight of the person behind the words, we forget that those words can be challenged.

The author of *this* book clearly has a point of view, and from it comes a particular distaste for the expression "You know what they say . . ." Unlike students pointing at a text, people who use this phrase normally don't know who is behind whatever it is that "they" have said. (I haven't the foggiest idea, for example, who coined the phrase "Great minds think alike.") But for that reason it is even more important that we question these beliefs. The fact that they are part of the folk wisdom doesn't tell us very much about their value; many of them are dead wrong, as will soon become evident, and even those that turn out to be true are worth invoking *because* they are true, not because other people have invoked them. Moreover, the process of finding out whether they are true is valuable in its own right, and so is the general habit of questioning things we've heard.

Even Americans, who have acquired a worldwide reputation for asking rude questions, are all too willing to accept things at face value, to swallow whole what they have been told by parents, public officials, preachers, and professionals of many stripes. One of my most discouraging moments came on a morning about ten years ago, when I walked into a classroom wearing a Question Authority button. So unfamiliar was this concept to one teenager that she instinctively assumed the phrase was a descriptive label rather than an exhortation. She asked who had appointed me the question authority.

At the risk of depressing myself further, I am forced to consider the possibility that you are wondering the same thing. If so, you may be relieved to learn that I didn't write this book out of any solemn sense of mission. I didn't set out to preach the gospel of critical thought—or even, for that matter, to systematically examine a variety of common beliefs. It happened this way: In the summer of 1987, I was looking through some studies that asked what makes for a satisfying marriage. One of the issues these researchers considered was whether a relationship has a better chance of succeeding if the mates are similar or dissimilar. In a fit of uncharacteristic whimsy, some scholar had begun referring to this controversy in terms of whether birds of a feather flock together or whether opposites attract.

This, it occurred to me, was not the only instance of two proverbs contradicting each other. With the help of some friends, I came up with a few more and hit on the idea of writing an article that used psychological research to adjudicate between these conflicting adages. Because there weren't enough pairs to fill 3,000 words, the idea was soon expanded: I would look at individual truisms, too, in an effort to determine whether they were really true. The resulting article was published in the April 1988 issue of *Psychology Today* and then reprinted three months later, in shockingly abridged form, in *Rdr's Dgst.*

There the story would have ended, a mildly amusing diversion from the other projects I was pursuing at the time, but for Larry Ashmead at HarperCollins, a man who can recognize a book concept in embryonic form, even when it is sandwiched between "My Most Unforgettable Character" and "Humor in Uniform." When I protested that there weren't all that many proverbs I could confirm or disconfirm, he said that the book he had in mind might look at other bits of conventional wisdom (to borrow the phrase donated to our language by John Kenneth Galbraith) in various fields. These might include beliefs that exert considerable impact on our lives and in some cases do real damage even if they aren't exactly proverbial. Thus was I sold on the idea. The rest, as they say, is sociology.

As I look back, it's fitting that it all started with the simple observation that for every maxim holding X, there is another one insisting not-X. For every aphorism urging caution (Look before you leap, Haste makes waste), there is one exhorting us to Strike while the iron is hot or reminding us that He who hesitates is lost. We are advised, on the one hand, that He travels fastest who travels alone and that Too many cooks spoil the broth. On the other hand, it seems that Many hands make light work and Two heads are better than one. There are clichés commending novelty (Variety is the spice of life) and clichés commending conservatism (Old shoes are easiest).

To some, these contradictions merely point out that different situations call for different advice. To others, they suggest that proverbs cancel each other out and are worth very little in the long run. Intrigued by the way we react to such conflicting counsel, British psychologist Karl Halvor

Teigen devised a clever experiment in 1986. He took twenty-four proverbs and transformed each one into its opposite. Thus, Fear is stronger than love was inverted to read Love is stronger than fear; Truth needs no colors became Truth needs colors; and so on. Teigen presented his students with lists that contained some authentic sayings and some that he had just made up. He asked them to rate the proverbs for originality and for truth value. The students ended up making no distinction between the wisdom of the ages and the newly devised *opposite* of what this wisdom held. "In hindsight," comments David Myers, author of *Social Psychology,* a superb textbook, "almost any finding—or its opposite—can seem like obvious common sense." This strikes me as a pretty powerful argument against relying exclusively on common sense.

Proverbs, however, represent but a small portion of the beliefs I examine in this book. While there are hundreds of crusty sayings in each culture that qualify for that label, the great majority don't lend themselves to empirical validation. After doing a bit of research, I can tell you whether actions really do speak louder than words. (Yes.) But most sayings aren't nearly straightforward enough to be put to some sort of test. After all, it's not as though one can triumphantly announce that, according to recent studies, a stitch in time actually saves eight—or a picture is really worth 1,189 words. Likewise, what are we to say about the adage that truth is stranger than fiction? Whose fiction? For that matter, whose truth? (It occurs to me that middle age might be said to have arrived when one comes to regard Kafka as a realist.)

To make matters worse, many proverbs—perhaps most—don't even have as their chief purpose the description of some truth about the human condition. At least as plentiful and familiar are those that *prescribe* behavior for us. Prescriptive proverbs, such as Look before you leap, cannot be called true or false at all.

The various beliefs I do examine here were not chosen according to any objective set of criteria. They are not the most important or the most controversial or the most commonly held in America. They are simply ones I found compelling and wanted to inspect more closely. This calls to mind all those college English courses with intimidating titles like "The Literature of Freedom and Alienation" or "Spiritual Triumph, Futile Rebellion, Urban Dissolution, and the Novel." Were they more truthful, instructors would simply call these courses by their right name: "Some Books I Like." And so it is with this project. I don't know how many people seriously believe, for example, that breakfast is the most important meal of the day, but I became curious about what the evidence shows and so I decided to include this bit of popular wisdom.

If anything, the beliefs selected for this book are skewed toward those that turn out to be false. The reason for this is simple: it's not terribly interesting to show that a widely shared assumption is correct. "They" say that smoking causes lung cancer, that violent crime is more common in large cities than in small towns, that we are more likely to agree with opinions offered by people we already respect. And "they" are absolutely right. Big deal. It's both more illuminating and more entertaining to learn about the common beliefs that are at least partly inaccurate.

On the other hand, if I really wanted to stack the deck, I would have included simple superstitions, ranging from black cats and broken mirrors to astrology and "healing" crystals. You won't find them debunked in the following pages because, frankly, I didn't think they were worth my time or yours. (People who take horoscopes seriously are probably not going to be convinced by proof that the whole thing is a lot of Taurus, so what's the point?) What I'm getting at, though, is that the sample of popular beliefs and sayings that follows is neither random nor objective, so you shouldn't look for any broad conclusions about the wisdom of folk wisdom. All that can be said is that "they" are wrong often enough to warrant a healthy dose of skepticism about what is generally taken on faith.

Actually, that's not *all* that can be said. It also can be said that most interesting issues are not clear-cut. If you had a nickel for every time I hedge about a finding in this book, you would be able to buy another copy for a friend. Articles in newspapers and popular magazines are not big on qualification: they incline toward simple declaratives such as "stress is bad for you" or "abused children grow up to become abusers" or "kids are ignorant because they watch too much TV." This is infinitely irritating to researchers, and for good reason. Most findings, particularly about human behavior, are properly offered with a bundle of qualifications attached and with a tone of tentativeness.

The tentativeness is appropriate because of how limited most studies are (in design and thus in conclusion) and also because of the limits of science itself. Anyone who is truly open-minded will ask hard questions about the scientific method—especially when it is brought to bear on human beings—just as he or she would resist a blind faith in any other system or institution.

If you're like the people I talked to about this book as I was researching and writing it, you'll pride yourself on having already guessed the truth about some entries, you'll be surprised by others, and a few findings you will simply refuse to accept. The last reaction suggests that when we're particularly attached to a belief, we may refuse to believe the data that challenge it. I have no right to be indignant about this because I can't think of any reason that my conclusions (and the evidence on which they are based) should be exempt from the sort of questioning I've been extolling here. That's why I've included a rather lengthy reference section at the back of the book: if you are interested or skeptical enough, you can look up the original sources and judge for yourself. I hope you will, and I hope these sources will lead you to others, which will, in turn, suggest new questions.

After all, you know what they say: If you don't ask, you won't learn.

Don't swim for an hour after eating

Every child learns that going swimming right after lunch is about as smart as accepting candy from strangers. Summer camp schedules are arranged so as to avoid this appalling possibility. Some parents even instruct their children to wait for food to digest before taking a *shower.*

Solemn believers of this bit of folk wisdom had better brace themselves because it's absolutely false. It got started half a century ago when the Red Cross published a booklet on water safety that claimed stomach cramps and possibly death awaited the foolhardy swimmer who went straight from table to pool. A gruesome illustration accompanied this warning and for years no one thought to question it.

But in 1961, an exercise physiologist named Arthur Steinhaus quietly observed that the emperor wasn't wearing any bathing suit, so to speak. The very idea of a "stomach cramp" was questionable, he said, and "many athletes report swimming long distances regularly in training almost directly after eating." Writing in the *Journal of Health, Physical Education, [and] Recreation,* Steinhaus quoted a prominent physical educator (whose affiliation with the Red Cross apparently led him to request anonymity) as follows: "I have never seen a case of so-called stomach cramps . . . although I have observed hundreds of thousands of persons, among them participants in Red Cross summer institutes, engaged in recreational and instructional swimming immediately after eating."

Today, Louise Priest echoes that testimony. As executive director of the Council for National Cooperation in Aquatics—an umbrella organization whose members include the Red Cross, the YMCA, and the Boy Scouts of America—Priest has seen plenty of cramps of the calf, the foot, and even the hand. "But I've been in aquatics for thirty years and I've never seen a stomach cramp. I don't believe they exist—and if they do, they certainly have nothing to do with eating." Even assuming that someone might have suffered such a cramp without Priest's having learned about it, she surely would have heard about a drowning. No such word has reached her.

Nor has it reached John Malatak, the current officer for health and safety for the American Red Cross, who notes that the group's current brochure offers "no objection to people participating in aquatic activities immediately upon completing a meal." Nor has it reached Millard Freeman, national YMCA aquatic director, who says flatly that the belief has been "disproven."

It is true, Freeman concedes, that "if you're going to do any strenuous swimming, you'll feel uncomfortable when you've stuffed your body." In fact, doing *any* sort of vigorous exercise right after eating might not be a good idea: you won't be at your best and you might become nauseated. Even this is debatable. Steinhaus pointed out that "laborers and farmers customarily work hard immediately after meals." But there isn't any debate about the fact that no one ever drowned as a result of swimming on a full stomach.

Women want sex for intimacy; men want sex for pleasure

Maybe you've heard it put this way: Women use sex to get love while men use love to get sex. It's the sort of catchy, catch-all pronouncement that sets heads to nodding—particularly the heads of women who are less than thrilled with what they take to be the baser motives of men. Women, it would seem, tend to regard sex as an opportunity to "make love" and often prefer to use this phrase even when referring to a sexual encounter devoid of commitment. For their part, men snicker along with Woody Allen's remark that "sex without love is an empty experience, but as empty experiences go, it's one of the best."

A group of research psychologists phrased it a little differently in an academic journal not long ago. They declared that women develop a "person-centered" orientation to sexuality, which means that "the goal of sex is to express affection to another person in a committed relationship." Men, on the other hand, "are more likely to develop a 'body-centered' or recreational orientation toward sex, which means that the goal of sex is physical gratification."

In 1985, Janet Shibley Hyde, a researcher who specializes in gender differences, worked with two students to survey 249 undergraduates. Of those who said they had at some point found themselves "wanting and/or needing" sex, 58 percent of the women but only 19 percent of the men cited emotional reasons. Asked if an emotional involvement was a prerequisite for intercourse, 85 percent of the women said this was always or usually true—as compared to only 40 percent of the men. Nearly half of the men, meanwhile, declared that they never missed an opportunity to have sex; not a single woman said this.

The pattern this describes is that women want to feel something in their hearts while men (to paraphrase a very old joke) don't aim quite so high. Another study seems to confirm this disparity, this one conducted by Elizabeth All-geier and her colleagues at Bowling Green State University. Students there were given a list of fifty-four possible factors and asked to pick the ten most important to consider in deciding whether to become sexually intimate with someone. Four of the ten (physical attraction, sexual attraction, partner's sexual assertiveness, and passion) were endorsed only by men. Another four (expression of love, partner's emotional relationship commitment, partner's emotional attentiveness and responsiveness, and partner's stable emotional feelings) showed up only on the women's lists.

An open and shut case, you say? Well, before we shrug and concede that men and women really do see sex differently, let's look a little more closely. To begin with, only a superficial observer would take a man's bluster about "scoring" with women at face value and assume that the quest for intimacy plays no part in male psychology.

Even all those research findings aren't quite as decisive as they first appear. The researchers who claimed that women are person-centered while men are body-centered later conceded that "men and women are really not so different in the amount of caring and closeness they desire in the sexual relationship." Allgeier, too, found that men and women agreed on six of the ten sexual motives, including intimacy, mutual emotional feelings, expression of love, and desire for marriage. And nearly two-thirds of the men in Hyde's survey checked off "feeling loved/needed" when asked for the most important part of sexual behavior.

Some of the discrepancy may be cleared up by distinguishing between how we behave and how we think we ought to behave. Our sex lives are shaped by the messages we hear as children. Movies and books teach that real men are just out to get laid (intimacy is for wimps) and women aren't supposed to enjoy sex for its own sake (it's unfeminine to feel pure lust). But at least one recent study, conducted by Joey Sprague at the University of Kansas and David Quadagno at Florida State University, has shown that while questions about one's *usual* motive for having sex may produce a gender gap, that gap narrows to nothing in response to questions about *ideal* motive. When asked to name the most important thing that they could get from a sexual experience, some people chose closeness and some chose physical pleasure, but there was no consistent tendency for women to pick one and men the other.

But now comes the most significant challenge of all to the simplistic men-want-pleasure, women-want-intimacy view. Sprague and Quadagno's study also revealed a possibility so shocking that it apparently never occurred to any other researchers. Are you sitting down?

Not everyone thinks like a college student.

Perhaps because they've grown so accustomed to using their students as subjects, psychologists never bothered to check whether these attitudes about sex persist as people get older. Not until 1989 did anyone think to ask a wider population about their motives for sex. That's when these researchers distributed questionnaires to 179 people whose ages ranged from twenty-two to fifty-seven.

Older women were more likely to report a physical motive for having sex than younger women were—and they were also less likely to say they were doing it for love. With men, the stereotypical pattern also reverses, with the physical motive falling off after age forty and the love motive rising after thirty-five.

This study was small—particularly with respect to the number of older people surveyed—and limited to one midwestern city. But when Quadagno handed out questionnaires to another 250 people in Florida, he got comparable results. "Young women and older men have similar motivations for having sexual intercourse (emotional motivations), while older women and younger men are more similar in their motives (physical motivations)," he wrote.

Nor is age the only factor overlooked in previous research and in popular opinion. Just as it isn't safe to assume everyone is (or thinks like) an undergraduate, so should we question the premise that everyone is (or thinks like) a heterosexual.

Or, for that matter, a middle-class American. In a recent book called *Love and Sex in Twelve Cultures*, psychoanalyst Robert Endleman reviewed the work of anthropologists and came up with some surprising findings. Our expectation that sex should be embedded in a romantic attachment is virtually unheard of in many nonliterate societies, he reported. "At the very minimum, we have to reject the idea that 'love' in our Western sense is a universal of human experience." Furthermore, said Endleman, in tribes like the Mohave Indians of Arizona and the Mangaians of Polynesia, women are "just as likely to pursue, or at least accept, sex without caring as are the men."

Collect all these caveats—social training, sexual preference, culture, and especially age—and those casual generalizations about how men and women speak two different sexual languages begin to seem rather silly. The relation between sex and love is too tangled and too different from one individual to the next to be captured in any neat aphorism, regardless of whether it rings true at first hearing.

Chocolate causes acne

This myth was laid to rest back in 1969 by James Fulton, a dermatologist, and his colleagues. Every day for four weeks, he fed sixty-five acne-prone teenagers and young adults either a megachocolate bar (containing ten times the chocolate of an ordinary candy bar) or a dummy bar that looked and tasted like chocolate without containing any of the real thing. Then they switched to the other bar. None of the subjects knew what they were eating. But could their skin tell the difference? Nope. For most of the young men and women, there was very little change in complexion regardless of whether or not they were eating real chocolate. Nor was there any difference in the amount or type of oily secretion that their glands were churning out.

Two decades later, Fulton, a research scientist at the Acne Research Institute in Newport Beach, California, hasn't seen anything to change his mind. He's not willing to state flatly that diet, including sugar consumption, is totally unrelated to complexion, but chocolate is still off the hook—at least for the great majority of people. Peter Pochi, professor of dermatology at Boston University's medical school, agrees. "I've seen bona fide cases of people who break out from chocolate, but I can count the number of cases on the fingers of one hand. Chocolate isn't a major contributor to acne."

There are those, of course, who insist that the very word *Hershey's* is enough to ruin their skin, but this may be a textbook case of confusing correlation with causality. As every student of logic knows, the fact that two things occur together doesn't mean one must cause the other. It's possible that both are caused by something else, and, in this case, the something else may be stress. Apparently, stress can affect one's complexion *and* can lead some people to head for the candy store in search of sweet solace. To the casual observer, it might appear that the chocolate was responsible for the acne, but in reality the skin may be reacting more to how one feels than to what one eats.

Let's linger a moment on this idea of gobbling candy bars or truffles during times of stress. It is sometimes said that chocolate contains a chemical that makes us feel as if we're in love—or at least that it has uniquely pleasant effects on our mood. True or false?

Chocolate contains small amounts of caffeine, which is a stimulant. It also contains fat, which has a slight dulling effect on the senses, and sugar, which, like any other carbohydrate, generally has a calming effect. (Some people find that their mood improves after eating carbohydrates, while others just get sleepy.) The sugar-fat combination is what makes chocolate taste so good, and it makes sense that during times of stress we might turn to things that are pleasurable.

All of this is unremarkable and unmysterious. The special reputation chocolate has acquired is a result of articles in some popular magazines a few years back concerning an ingredient called phenylethylamine (PEA), which is chemically similar to amphetamines. However, such claims "weren't ever taken seriously by scientists," says Harris Lieberman, a research scientist at the Massachusetts Institute of Technology. "I haven't seen a single piece of evidence to support the idea that PEA is psychoactive in the dose it's found in chocolate."

A check with three other experts in the fields of nutrition, brain chemistry, and behavior yielded the same conclusion. First, other foods, too, contain PEA but are not particularly popular. Second, our body is extraordinarily efficient at breaking down such chemicals, with the result that they never make it to the brain. "The body is really protected from PEA," according to Michael Liebowitz, associate professor of clinical psychiatry at Columbia University, whose speculations helped to get people excited about chocolate in the first place. More generally, there are no data to support beliefs about the distinctive effects (or appeal) of chocolate—either for people who crave it or for the general population. "It's all speculation," Liebowitz says.

People become more conservative as they get older

Suppose that today's paper reports a new survey showing that older people are more conservative than younger people. (In fact, studies usually do show this.) You nod your head knowingly, remembering old Uncle Millard's right-wing ramblings at Thanksgiving last year. But hold on: This doesn't prove that the *process of aging* makes people more conservative. Such a finding might just be telling us what it was like to be born, say, in 1920 and raised in that era—rather than in 1960. Maybe the younger group happens to be better educated than the older group, a fact that would be relevant because education can affect attitudes.

So we abandon the idea of interviewing a cross-section of the population and decide instead to follow one group of people over many years, asking them about their attitudes every so often to see if they'll end up swinging to the right. Does this solve the problem? No. Political shifts in our subjects might simply mirror the shifts of the whole culture. Maybe Americans in general were growing more conservative during that period; maybe they'll turn liberal during the next. Once again, we can't be sure we've learned anything about the effects of getting older.

These are the sorts of problems that drive political scientists and sociologists straight up the wall, and the difficulty of agreeing on what is meant by *conservative* (and how to measure it) makes things even worse. But by combining different survey approaches and using a variety of statistical techniques far too boring to describe here, some specialists think they have a reasonably accurate picture of the effects of aging. The answer is that there is no general tendency to become more conservative with age. But there is a tendency to become less flexible about one's political preferences, whatever they happen to be, after early adulthood.

One of the most interesting studies was begun in the late 1930s, when graduating students from Bennington College in Vermont were asked about their political leanings. In 1960, they were surveyed again, and it seemed that very little had changed: Most were fairly liberal by the time they left college and most remained liberal into mid-life. A soon-to-be published follow-up report shows that when some of these same women were tracked down in 1984, the pattern continued. There was no sudden swing to the right as the subjects hit old age: Something like two-thirds were still on the left side of the fence.

Of course, it's possible that this was an unusual group of people—more stable in their attitudes, more liberal than most, and, in any case, all women. But other research has confirmed that people generally do their shifting in early adulthood and then tend to stick with those attitudes. Two researchers, for example, studied a large group of high-school seniors in 1965 and went back to them in 1973 and again in 1982. "Party identification remains fairly supple into the late 20s," they reported, "but hardens considerably soon thereafter."

One political scientist, David Sears, looked at changes in people's racial prejudices during an especially volatile period in recent American history—1972–1976. Attitudes were increasingly stable from age twenty-one to sixty but for some reason were *more* flexible among those older than sixty. This surprising softening in later life hasn't turned up in other research, however. In a newly published study, one batch of people was interviewed during the elections of 1956, 1958, and 1960 and another batch during the elections of 1972, 1974, and 1976. Attitude stability neither increased (as many of us would have assumed) nor decreased (as Sears found) for older people; it was about the same for folks in their seventies as for those in their mid-thirties.

There is one important qualification to this, though. Basic ideological measures—for example, political party preference—do tend to be fairly stable across most of the life span. But Duane Alwin, a researcher at the University of Michigan's Institute for Social Research, has found no relation between stability and age on various attitudes about public policy or on measures of racial and religious tolerance. That means that with richer measures of liberalism and conservatism, getting older not only doesn't mean moving to the right—it doesn't even guarantee becoming rigid in one's beliefs.

Overall, writes University of Texas sociologist Norval Glenn, "there is little credible evidence that aging beyond young adulthood tends to produce conservative attitudes or identification with the Republican party."

Lemmings commit mass suicide

They are funny little rodents, no doubt about that. If you show up in the Arctic regions where they hang out, you might have trouble spotting a single lemming. Then again, you might see thousands of them; it all depends on when you show up. The lemming population rises and falls so dramatically that people in the sixteenth century explained their sudden appearance by saying they fell from the skies. Conversely, their sudden *dis*appearance was thought to be due to the fact that lemmings throw themselves into the sea en masse. The idea has stuck, and today even people who wouldn't know a lemming if it fell on them still take this belief on faith.

All those animals plunging recklessly into the waves makes for a rather stunning image, to be sure, not to mention a useful figure of speech. Every time some group of people puts itself at risk, we trot out the lemming reference. Philip Howard, writing in a language journal called *Verbatim,* asserted that "the only animal that regularly commits mass suicide is Homo sapiens. But evidently we have a need for some vivid metaphor from Nature to illustrate the human propensity to self-destruction."

So what do the scientists say? It is true that lemmings migrate in large numbers, probably in search of food or a place to breed. Many of them don't survive the journey, particularly the part that takes them across bodies of water. Moreover, lots of lemmings obviously die as part of this population cycle. But this, experts agree, is unlikely to be due to suicide. "Biologically, it just doesn't make any sense," says Dennis Chitty, professor emeritus of zoology at the University of British Columbia and one of the leading authorities on the subject. After all, lemmings with a hypothetical death wish would never have a chance to pass this feature on to their descendants. Others without such an instinct would continue to reproduce and it would quickly disappear.

So what *does* happen to all the little critters? Disease? Predators? Weather? Rapidly shifting patterns of natural selection? The topic still starts arguments at scientific gatherings. After more than half a century, rodent specialists still don't know why. "We hope that some day we'll clear up the mystery," sighs Chitty.

Capital punishment is a good way to keep the murder rate down

The nineteenth-century French criminologist Gabriel Tarde was a champion of the death penalty until he took a look at the evidence: Once he realized that Parisian statistics showed virtually no relation between the severity of the punishment and the crime rate, he changed his mind about the guillotine.

Would most Americans do the same if it were proved to them that killing criminals doesn't make the streets any safer? It's hard to say. Many support capital punishment for other reasons; some argue in effect that we should electrocute, poison, or shoot people to death for failing to understand the sacredness of human life. The United States is nearly alone in this among Western nations, by the way: Most of these countries have by now come to regard the moral status of the death penalty as akin to that of slavery.

Opponents of capital punishment have some other arguments on their side, such as the very real possibility of executing someone who turns out to be innocent and the fact that race (of both the criminal and the victim) plays a big role in deciding who actually gets executed. But let's just look at the effects on crime. The relevant question here is not whether capital punishment has ever deterred anyone from taking a life. Rather, we want to ask whether it is consistently a better deterrent than life imprisonment. The answer, says one of the leading scholars in the field, Tufts University's Hugo Bedau, is that "so far as we know, the two penalties are equally effective or ineffective."

At first glance it seems only common sense that the threat of losing their own lives would keep would-be criminals in line. But a closer look reveals that most murders are actually committed (1) during a moment of rage, (2) under the influence of drugs or alcohol, or (3) unexpectedly, in the course of committing another crime, such as a robbery. In any of these cases, the killer doesn't sit down and rationally weigh the consequences of what will happen when he is apprehended, so the death penalty isn't going to stop him.* Most people who *do* kill in premeditated fashion probably think they'll never get caught, so they, too, are not terribly concerned about the penalty.

Thus it may not be as surprising as it first appears that social scientists have consistently found no crime-reducing

---

*Careful thought about why people break the law not only leads us to question the usefulness of capital punishment but also challenges the idea that throwing more people in jail for longer periods of time is a sensible response to crime in general. Elliott Currie, a criminologist at the University of California at Berkeley, writes that "virtually all the serious research evidence available to us . . . suggest[s] that very large increases in incarceration might result in small decreases in serious crime. . . . [The premise] that the level of crime was rising primarily because the 'costs' of crime in America were too low . . . was simply wrong." Despite the fact that the United States is "already one of the most prison-happy societies in the advanced industrial world," he goes on to point out that crime rates are far higher here than in most other countries. It may be time to ask whether more of the same is really a rational solution.

advantage for capital punishment. The single, celebrated exception came in the mid-1970s when an economist named Isaac Ehrlich performed a series of statistical manipulations on rates of murder and execution over four decades and announced that each additional execution would have prevented eight homicides. Almost immediately this study was exposed as thoroughly flawed. Ehrlich's case hinged on the fact that more murders were committed during the 1960s, when fewer executions were taking place. Besides the fact that he ignored regional differences in the murder rate and other possible explanations for the increase in homicides (the growing availability of guns, for one), it turns out that *other* crimes of violence—the kind that had never been punishable by death—increased even more rapidly than homicides. In any case, other researchers have looked for and failed to find the effect that Ehrlich got. That makes sense because his results contradicted almost every study done before then.

For many scholars, the final word on the subject was the report issued in 1978 by the prestigious National Academy of Sciences. The academy rejected the statistical technique Ehrlich had used (known as regression analysis) and concluded that "the available studies provide no useful evidence on the deterrent effect of capital punishment." In other words, we don't know. And surely a practice as drastic as killing people ought to be considered only if we *do* know that it makes our lives markedly safer.

But two leading criminologists at Northeastern University, William J. Bowers and Glenn L. Pierce, decided that just in case regression analyses did make sense, it was worth giving them another shot. They studied homicides and executions in New York State for every month from 1907 to 1963 and found that the death penalty not only failed to reduce the murder rate but actually seemed to increase it. On average, two additional murders occurred during the month following each execution. The death penalty had what they called a "brutalizing effect" that was probably due to criminals taking their cue from the state and imitating its use of violence.

"The lesson of the execution, then, may be to devalue life [and to teach] that it is correct and appropriate to kill those who have gravely offended us," Bowers and Pierce wrote. Another writer put it a little differently in an article in the *Journal of Criminal Law and Criminology:* "Use of the death penalty by the state, despite an intention to convey the message that killing is unacceptable, may convey the opposite message to the general public. 'Do as we do' may thus overpower 'do as we say.' " (See "Actions speak louder than words," pp. 78–79.)

Of course, the statistical method on which Bowers and Pierce based their claim is just as debatable as it was when Ehrlich used it. But even if one concludes that the death penalty really doesn't encourage people to kill, it certainly doesn't reliably prevent people from killing. In fact, there has never been a case where homicides went up after a state abolished capital punishment. The states with the highest murder rates, moreover, tend to be those where the death penalty *is* used. Dane Archer, a sociologist, and his colleagues found that the same thing was true worldwide. They dug out old crime records to see what had happened in twelve countries that had abolished capital punishment between 1890 (Italy) and 1968 (Austria). It turned out that "abolition was followed more often than not by absolute decreases in homicide rates." In fact, murder was down even when compared to other crimes—hardly what we would expect if the death penalty were responsible for stopping killers.

Anyone seriously interested in making our cities safer would do better to look into the real causes of crime. As Richard McGahey of New York University says, "The consensus among most scholars who have studied the issue is that capital punishment is not a deterrent to murder."

Beauty is only skin deep (or You can't judge a book by its cover)

In 1972, Karen Dion, Ellen Berscheid, and Elaine Walster showed that we confer various positive attributes on good-looking people. Their study, titled "What Is Beautiful Is Good," virtually launched a movement within social psychology, and scores of researchers since then have uncovered a major self-fulfilling prophecy: Because attractive people are treated as if they have more to offer, they live up to our expectations. Sadly, the reverse is true for those less pleasing to look at.

Dion and her colleagues asked sixty students to describe people solely on the basis of their photographs. Those whom the experimenters took to be most attractive were rated as more socially desirable and were expected to have more prestigious jobs and happier marriages.

But surely that's just the prejudice of the raters, right? It wouldn't be fair if good-looking people really had other things going for them, too. Well, get ready for another lesson in injustice. Researchers have secretly judged the attractiveness of their subjects,* measured them on a range of personality variables, and then looked for a relationship between the two. They have rarely been disappointed. Attractive people have turned out to have higher self-esteem, to be happier, less neurotic, and more resistant to peer pressure, than less attractive people. They also have more influence on others; are more valued as friends, colleagues,

*The extent to which they are able to agree on these ratings is startling. See "Beauty is in the eye of the beholders," pp. 112–113.

and lovers; get higher salaries; are dealt with less harshly in court; and are thought by their students to be superior teachers. While not all of these effects have been found consistently for males and females, the overall pattern for both sexes is that beauty is definitely subcutaneous.

Even more unsettling: Attractiveness is related to the perception—and perhaps even the reality—of serious mental disorders. Warren H. Jones and his colleagues at the University of Tulsa discovered that students assumed ugly people were more likely than others to be psychologically disturbed. Jones then made a point of telling another group of students that attractiveness was unrelated to disturbance; he explicitly asked them to disregard this factor. Even so, they, too, rated unattractive people as more troubled. Another researcher stopped people on the street and asked them to fill out a questionnaire assessing the likelihood that they, themselves, would eventually develop psychological disorders. He discovered that "increasing attractiveness was related to a decreasing perceived risk of mental illness."

The trouble is these predictions may be right. A study of female psychiatric patients in Connecticut showed that they were relatively unattractive compared to other women. It wasn't just that their troubles had spoiled their looks: Even before they were judged to be mentally ill, the less-appealing women had had more troubled relationships. And among the patient population, those who were viewed as particularly unattractive were also the ones who had been in the hospital longer and had received a more serious diagnosis. A later study of a similar group of patients found them less attractive than their peers even back in high school, based on yearbook photographs.

All of this may happen because appearance affects how we interact with people from the very beginning. Adults are more likely to look at, touch, and hold infants who are regarded as cute, and this preference for beauty persists.

"The way we treat attractive versus unattractive people shapes the way they think about themselves," says University of Hawaii psychologist Elaine Hatfield, "and, as a consequence, the kind of people they become."

Catherine the Great died from horsing around

You've probably heard the rumor: The curtain fell on Catherine the Great's life during the last, unnatural act. The woman who ruled Russia from 1762 to 1796 was said to have had a sexual appetite so voracious that mere humans couldn't satisfy her; she wanted a *real* stud. Thus she met her end when a horse fell on top of her.

The fact that most biographers and other Russian historians have not seen fit to address this tale is probably due neither to embarrassment nor to any desire to sanitize the czarina's life. Rather, the idea is so preposterous—Catherine II actually died of a stroke at the age of sixty-seven— that serious scholars haven't seen fit to dignify such salacious gossip with a refutation.

John Alexander, professor of history at the University of Kansas, was urged by his colleagues to follow suit. But the horse story "is so incredibly widespread," he says, that he decided to debunk it once and for all. This he has done in a 1989 book, *Catherine the Great: Life and Legend.*

Alexander points out that the story was circulated by Catherine's contemporaries; it was an attempt to undercut her "claims to greatness, by aggressively asserting that her primary motivation was unbridled [!] sex, the excesses of which resulted in monstrous death. . . . Notions of Catherine's sexual insatiability assumed virtually mythic proportions in Russia and abroad."

Whether Catherine had only a dozen lovers over the course of her life, as Alexander believes, or many more, there is no evidence that any of them had more than two legs. As for the circumstances of her death, she was found one morning on the floor of her living quarters, felled by what an autopsy subsequently confirmed was "a cerebral stroke, with hemorrhages in two places from burst blood vessels."

Lots of people are just tone-deaf

A lot of us tend to write ourselves off as being utterly devoid of a certain skill; we say we have "no sense of direction," "no artistic talent," "no mathematical ability," and so forth. What really turns out to be true in most such cases is that certain things just don't come as easily to us as to other people, or we can't reach the level of excellence associated with the very best in the field. That, of course, is a far cry from having an inborn or irremediable impairment.

Take music. With the exception of a handful of people suffering from a neurological disorder that prevents them from distinguishing among different pitches—most of whom appear to have found gainful employment as disc jockeys—no one with normal hearing is really "tone-deaf." You may not be able to *produce* a melody correctly, but surely you can recognize one. And even if you do have trouble telling one note from the other, the chances are good that you can be trained to do so.

In the early 1930s, two researchers scoured the elementary schools of Detroit and found seven children who not only couldn't sing but couldn't even distinguish a note from one an octave higher. Every day for three months these children were coached: They were taught the difference between pitch and volume and encouraged to form mental pictures of high and low notes. At first, the researchers reported, the "training required almost infinite patience." But eventually all seven learned to discriminate among tones along four octaves. They could recognize fifths, thirds, full-tones, and half-tones. They could even sing reasonably well.

Since then, other studies have reported comparable successes. With the benefit of simple behavioral techniques, thirteen of fifteen "tone-deaf" children rapidly learned to sing on key. One adult with no special musical gifts described in a technical journal how he taught himself absolute (perfect) pitch—the ability to identify by name any note that one hears or to sing a given note without hearing it first.

"If we are unable to burst into song," writes Frank Wilson in his book *Tone Deaf and All Thumbs?* "it is nonsense to criticize our genes; just as with the throwing arm, development of the voice takes practice." Wilson points out that we are able to recognize the subtle fluctuations in pitch that produce meaningful speech; these minute differences signaling anger or desire or doubt would pass unnoticed if we were truly tone-deaf. Alas, "for most children, a diagnosis of tone deafness becomes the basis of a lifelong conviction that music is out for them. And it is a great loss."

No two snowflakes are alike

A few years ago, Nancy Knight was flipping through some photographs of snowflakes she had just taken from a research plane high over Wisconsin. A visiting scientist at the National Center for Atmospheric Research, Knight was struck by the unusual structure of some of the crystals: They were thick, hollow columns with vaselike skeletons inside. She submitted a short article along with a few pictures to the *Bulletin of the American Meteorological Society,* only to have the editor point out that what was even more remarkable than the structure of the crystals was the fact that two of them were practically identical.

Two identical snowflakes! What next? The sun rising in the west?

Well, the number of possible snowflake shapes—which is to say, the number of possible arrangements for frozen water molecules—is indeed astronomical. According to John Hallett, professor of atmospheric physics at the University of Nevada, the shape of a flake is determined by the temperature when it formed, the amount of water vapor that was available, and the speed at which it fell. Thus, even though a snowstorm might be composed of trillions of flakes, the chance that any two—let alone two you happened to find—have exactly the same history is nearly nil. "Any two snowflakes picked at random most likely have followed quite different paths from where they started in the atmosphere," Hallett explains.

Still, he says, "You cannot absolutely make a statement that no two are alike. You can only say the *probability* of finding two crystals alike is less than something or other—

just as the probability of finding two virtually indistinguishable people who are not identical twins is pretty small." Even before Knight's lucky day, then, the adage that *no* two snowflakes are alike was something of an exaggeration. On the other hand, the flakes she discovered may well be the meteorological equivalent of identical twins: it seems likely that they formed while attached to the same larger crystal and, therefore, had a common history.

Rewards motivate people

Whether we know it or not, most of us act like Skinnerians. It was the Harvard psychologist B. F. Skinner who popularized the theory of positive reinforcement, which holds that presenting a reward after a desired behavior will make that behavior more likely to occur in the future. We apply this principle not only to training the family pet, but also to raising children, teaching students, and managing employees. If it's not a doggie biscuit we offer, then it's an extra dessert or an *A* on the report card or a performance bonus.

The problem is that this approach often backfires, particularly when we're trying to encourage people to be creative. In one study, fifth- and sixth-grade students were asked to teach a new game to a younger child. Those who were promised a free movie ticket for tutoring well turned out to be much *less* effective than the children who weren't promised anything: They took longer to communicate ideas, got frustrated more easily, and ended up with pupils who didn't understand the game. In another study, people who expected to receive a prize for making collages or telling stories proved to be less imaginative at both tasks than those who received nothing. And in a recent review of programs used by twenty-eight different companies to encourage seat belt use among employees, the worst results—especially over the long haul—came from the programs that used prizes to motivate people to buckle up.

Lots of other research shows the same thing: rewards can be counterproductive. The reason, it turns out, is connected to what psychologists call "intrinsic motivation"—a fancy term for enjoying what you do. The fact is that no artificial inducement to do a good job can motivate you as effectively as loving your work. (Just think about someone you know who is sensational at what he or she does. Now ask yourself whether that person enjoys doing it or is motivated by a paycheck.)

But not only are rewards less effective than intrinsic motivation—they actually *undermine* it. You started out doing something just because you found it fun. But once you were rewarded for doing it, you came to see yourself as working mostly to get the reward. Your fascination with the task mysteriously vanished along the way and now you can't be bothered to do it unless there's some reward at stake.

Sound familiar? Edward Deci and Richard Ryan, psychologists at the University of Rochester who have been studying these issues for many years, point out that people who think of themselves as working for a reward feel controlled by it—as if the reward were in charge of their behavior. "To the extent that one's experience of being self-determined is limited," says Ryan, "one's creativity will be reduced as well." Even praise can often feel controlling, and, to that extent, it can have the same destructive impact as tangible rewards.

Other researchers are concerned about the message given by the promise of a reward. The British educator A. S. Neill said it is "tantamount to declaring that the activity is not worth doing for its own sake." All we have to hear about a task is that we'll get a cookie or a bonus for completing it, and we tend to conclude that the task is probably unpleasant. That, we assume, must be why someone had to bribe us to do it.

In fact, anything that's presented as a means rather than an end will come to be seen as less enjoyable. Mark Lepper of Stanford University told some preschoolers that they couldn't draw with pastel crayons until they had spent some time drawing with felt-tip markers—or vice versa. When he checked back a week or two later, he discovered that the children no longer had much interest in whichever kind of drawing he had made a prerequisite for the other.

But rewards can be bad news for still another reason: They encourage us to focus narrowly on a task, to do it as quickly as possible and to take few risks. This approach is death to innovation and artistic exploration. "If they feel 'this is something I have to get through to get the prize,' they're going to be less creative," says Brandeis University's Teresa Amabile. The more emphasis that is placed on an artificial motivator, the more inclined someone will be to do the minimum necessary to obtain it.

If the question, then, is whether rewards motivate people, the answer is sure—they motivate people to get rewarded. Unfortunately, this is often at the expense of interest in, or excellence at, whatever it is they're doing. The result is that millions of well-meaning teachers and managers are at this very moment systematically destroying the very creativity and curiosity they're trying to promote.

Other researchers have found that rewards are just as deadly when it comes to encouraging good behavior. It's tempting to promise a child another hour of television or some ice cream if he or she does what you want. Indeed, positive reinforcement is seen by many parents as a progressive alternative to punishment. The trouble is that neither punishment nor bribes (which is really what rewards are) help a child to understand the *reason* for doing something, which means he or she is unlikely to keep doing it when there's no one around to dish out a goodie. Never mind that it's manipulative—rewarding is simply ineffective as a long-range strategy.

One study after another has found that the worst way to try to get people to be generous and caring is to reward or praise them for acting that way. Psychologists in Arizona showed in 1989 that the children of mothers who believed in using rewards as motivators were less altruistic than their peers. Another study found that adult blood donors who were reminded of altruistic reasons for giving blood said they were more willing to do so again than those who were reminded of the personal benefits of what they were about to do. Focusing attention on rewards actually reduced their motivation to go through with the donation.

Of all possible rewards, possibly the most destructive kind is victory in a contest. Even though most of us have been taught that competition is necessary for productivity, most research has shown just the reverse. Deci had a bunch of college students work on an interesting puzzle. Those who were told that it was a contest had less interest in doing the puzzle on their own time, while those who weren't asked to compete chose to keep at it. Amabile discovered that girls asked to make a "silly" collage turned in much less creative work (as judged by professional artists) when it was announced that a prize would go to the number one collage maker.

My own review of hundreds of similar studies on this subject has convinced me that not only is competition unnecessary for excellence but that its *absence* is usually necessary for excellence. We tend to confuse success with victory—being good with triumphing over others—even though research in the workplace and the classroom shows we're less productive when we're distracted by having to beat others. To some extent this is because competition promotes anxiety: If you're worried about someone else stepping on your face, you won't do your best work. Another factor is that we often work and learn better when we can share our talents and resources with each other—which a competitive environment pretty well rules out. But competition is also counterproductive simply because it is a reward, and like all rewards it makes us less excited about what we're doing and more concerned about what we're going to get for doing it.

Spicy food is bad for the stomach

Studies have shown that putting hot peppers—or capsaicin, their active ingredient—directly into the stomach by means of a tube can wreak havoc in there. But what about consuming spicy ingredients in the usual way? David Graham, a gastroenterologist at Baylor College of Medicine in Houston, was determined to get proof on videotape that eating fiery foods can damage the stomach lining. Using a video endoscope (a miniature camera that is actually swallowed), he and his colleagues fed healthy subjects either a bland meal, a bland meal with six tablets of aspirin, a pepperoni pizza, or a spicy Mexican dinner.

Here's what they found: The people who had taken aspirin developed small pits in the protective lining of their stomachs, but no one else did. Even munching enchiladas with jalapeño peppers for both lunch and dinner caused no damage at all.

Of course, Graham studied healthy people. Surely people suffering from duodenal ulcers would do better on a bland diet, right? Not necessarily. In 1984, some gastroenterologists in India sprinkled 3 grams of chili powder on the food of twenty-five ulcer patients every day. Another twenty-five went without this staple of Indian cuisine. After four weeks, the chili eaters' stomach linings were unaffected, and their ulcers had healed at the same rate as those condemned to a bland menu.* (However, what's true for Indians, who are accustomed to this sort of diet, might not apply to people whose idea of seasoning is a little salt and pepper.)

While we're at it, let's lay to rest another slander against spicy foods. Contrary to folk wisdom, they do not cause nightmares. "What did you eat before bed?" we ask knowingly when someone tells us about a particularly bizarre or unpleasant dream. But the psychiatrist Ernest Hartmann, a leading student of nightmares, says there is no evidence at all to substantiate what he calls the "pepperoni pizza" hypothesis. In fact, he personally questioned 100 frequent nightmare sufferers and wasn't able to find any association between spicy food and bad dreams.

Couples should beware The Seven-Year Itch

Is someone in a long-term relationship really more likely to show signs of dissatisfaction with his or her partner after seven years of being together rather than after, say, one year or five or ten? Systematic investigations of this question don't exist. One possible reason is that it's not easy to agree on what counts as evidence of an itch. Having an affair? *Thinking* about having an affair? Seeing a therapist? Taking separate vacations?

To find good data, we have to ask a more straightforward

---

*You may be interested to learn that milk does not qualify as bland. A 1982 study that investigated the stomach's response to nine different beverages found that milk produced more acid than any of the others—including tea, beer, three kinds of coffee, and three kinds of carbonated soft drinks. If gastric acid is related to ulcers, the researchers wrote, then "milk is not a rational therapeutic choice."

question, such as, When are married couples likely to get divorced? (We also have to ignore the fact that the third year of marriage may actually be the fifth year a couple has been together; demographers don't start the clock until the wedding bells ring.) Given these qualifications, though, the answer is clear: there is no such thing as a seven-year itch. About 2 percent of married couples divorce before the first year is over, 4 percent of those remaining split up during the next year, and roughly 5 percent of surviving marriages end in *each* of the next three years. After that, the divorce rate starts to drop off. Couples who make it past the fifth year have a good shot at staying together into old age. There is no sudden rash of itching in the seventh year.

It is true that the *median* length of American marriages is about seven years, which means that half of all divorcing couples will split up before that point and the other half after it. That's just a statistical abstraction, though; it doesn't mean there's anything special about year number seven for any given couple.

There are lots of ways to shake out the overall statistics on marriage, by the way. Those who view divorce as inherently bad may be cheered by the news that the average marriage will last almost twenty-five years. The other side of the coin is that about half of all married people will eventually divorce rather than wait to be parted by death. In fact, demographers at the University of Wisconsin recently argued that when separations (in addition to legal divorces) are taken into account, and when corrections are made for underreporting of divorces, about two-thirds of all married couples will ultimately split up if current trends continue.

The rich get richer and the poor get poorer

If this is true, it reflects not some law of nature, but simply the way particular economic systems operate. And as far as our economic system is concerned, at least over the last few decades, the saying is all too accurate.

We have to be careful here. This is just the sort of issue that skeptics have in mind when they talk about being able to prove *anything* with statistics. That's why it's important to define one's terms—to decide what is meant by *rich* or *poor* (what percent of the population is included in each category), what measure we are using (income, assets, or net worth), whom we are measuring (families, households, or individuals), and what two years we are comparing to spot a trend. No matter how one juggles the numbers, however, there is no getting around the fact that a huge share of the national wealth is in the hands of a relatively small number of Americans. At best, the extent of this maldistribution has stayed about the same; by many measures, it has been getting worse.

Let's consider income. In 1987, the wealthiest one-fifth of the population earned 24 percent more than they did in 1973. But the income of people in the *bottom* fifth dropped 11 percent during the same period. (These figures, reported by the U.S. House Ways and Means Committee, are adjusted for inflation and family size. But even when the numbers are sliced differently, the rich still got richer and the poor poorer.)

The wealthy clearly profited at the expense of the needy during the 1980s—precisely at the time that many government benefits to the poor were being cut back. Still, it would be inaccurate to blame the fundamental inequity of our economic system on one administration. A glance at the U.S. Census Bureau's *Current Population Reports* makes it clear that things have actually gotten slightly worse for the bottom fifth and better for the top fifth since 1947, the first year for which figures are given. While one group of Americans, representing 20 percent of the population, earned only 4.6 percent of the country's total income in 1987, another, equal-size group earned almost *ten times* that much—44 percent of the total income.

After comparing figures for two other years, Sheldon Danziger of the University of Michigan and Peter Gottschalk of Boston College summed it up this way: "Real median family income in 1985 was at about the same level as in 1969, poverty as officially measured was higher, and the income share of the bottom 40 percent was lower than at any time in the postwar era."

But even these figures don't tell the whole story because they deal only with income. When we look at what people own rather than what they earn, we find that the top 10 percent of the U.S. population were in possession of 65 percent of this country's wealth in 1962. By 1983, that share had climbed to 69 percent. Most families don't own very much, relatively speaking, and most of what they do own are things like a car or equity in a house. These are not easily cashed in when someone gets fired or becomes sick, so a better measure of one's wealth is financial assets— bank accounts, stocks, bonds, and other means for earning money while you sleep, as one writer put it. Amazingly, while most of us slave away to make ends meet, or are reduced to throwing away money in state lotteries in the desperate and futile hope of striking it rich, one-tenth of the U.S. population owned *86 percent* of the country's total financial assets as of 1984, and a mere 2 percent of the richest folks owned more than half of them.

All of these figures remind us that a country's gross national product or total wealth is not by itself a terribly useful number to know. It doesn't just matter whether there is enough to go around, but whether it *is* going around—that is, whether a country's productivity is enjoyed by all its citizens or only by a select few.

The eminent economist John Kenneth Galbraith likes to point out that U.S. policymakers seem to believe that the promise of financial reward will make rich people work harder (or invest more) but will make poor people lazy. This is why we give tax breaks to the people who are already affluent while cutting food stamps for those who are already miserable. An analogous "surrender of thought to doctrine allowed the old communist leaders in Europe to ignore the emerging reality that has now destroyed them," Galbraith observed dryly at the end of 1989. Our leaders (and the economic system to which they all pledge their allegiance) are in no immediate danger of being overthrown, he conceded, but "even here, people will suffer in silence only so long."

Familiarity breeds contempt

While it's true that you can see a person's flaws better from up close, familiarity by itself is more likely to breed comfort than contempt, all things being equal. That's an English translation of the original psychologese (used here by Robert Zajonc): "Repeated exposure is a sufficient condition of attitude enhancement."

Zajonc gave experimental subjects a set of seven-letter Turkish words and, in a similar study, a set of Chinese characters. His subjects had no idea what the words meant, but they consistently said a word meant something "better" if they had seen it more often. Likewise, after being shown yearbook photographs of male strangers, people said they liked the men whose photos had already been shown to them.

More than 200 similar experiments have been conducted since Zajonc published his classic paper in the late 1960s. After sifting through their findings, Robert F. Bornstein of Gettysburg College concluded in a 1989 article that Zajonc was right. However, if the same stimulus is presented too often or for too long a time on each occasion, familiarity may breed boredom. This is especially likely to happen with younger subjects: Children tend to prefer new words or pictures to those they have seen before.

Even for adults, of course, more encounters with someone or something you find distasteful aren't going to change your mind or warm your heart. But where you have no aversion to begin with, it seems to be true—as advertisers know only too well—that we like things more as we get used to them.

Women's moods change at "That Time of the Month"

Most women report that they not only feel some physical pain or discomfort during their menstrual periods but that their emotions are also affected. Typically, the question is not *whether* they will experience tension, irritability, depression, or mood swings, but rather how severe these symptoms will be. Not surprisingly, then, when researchers ask women to describe their periods, such complaints show up regularly.

Because no one is in a better position than you to know what you are feeling, it might seem that this would end the discussion. The trouble is that what we *assume* is true can affect what we notice and remember even about our own moods. A number of researchers over the last two decades have tried to get a reading of women's emotional lives without tapping stereotypical beliefs about menstruation. Over and over again, these researchers—the vast majority of whom are women, incidentally—have found little or no evidence of emotional changes that correspond to the menstrual cycle.

One experimental approach is to measure the moods of a number of women on one particular day and then to determine where they were in their cycles. Two researchers did that with 158 high-school girls in 1981. Those who were in the premenstrual and menstrual phases were not, on average, any more anxious or depressed than the other girls.

An even better technique is to ask women to keep a regular diary of their emotional states for a month or longer without arousing their suspicions that this request has anything to do with the menstrual cycle. The subjects fill out questionnaires every day about how they're feeling; only later do the researchers compare this information to each woman's cycle. Paula Englander-Golden and her colleagues did this with forty-six college students in 1978. When the women were later asked explicitly about their periods, they ticked off the usual emotional effects. On their daily questionnaires, however, there was no connection between mood and cycle. Pauline Slade, an English psychologist, got similar results in 1984: Daily reports reflected the fact that women experienced more pain and water retention during and just before their periods, but there were *no* psychological effects. In 1989, Cathy McFarland and her associates used two different samples of women, ninety subjects in all, and found that physical symptoms varied with the time of the month, but emotional symptoms didn't. However, the more a woman *believed* menstruation had a negative effect on her moods, the more negatively she described her symptoms in retrospect—even though her actual self-reports showed no such effects.

These are only a few of the studies that have produced such surprising results. After reviewing the evidence carefully, two psychologists, Diane N. Ruble and Jeanne Brooks-Gunn, wrote, "The data do not seem sufficient to support the commonly held assumptions that psychological fluctuations related to the menstrual cycle do exist for most women [or] that such fluctuations [where they do exist] are tied to underlying hormonal fluctuations."

So why do these assumptions persist? One theory is that when a woman happens to feel cranky or sad around the time of her period, she may automatically blame it on the menstrual cycle. By contrast, her feelings of crankiness or sadness at other times of the month will be attributed to various other things having to do with herself or her environment. Thus beliefs about menstrual effects are never challenged. One consequence of this, as McFarland and her colleagues observed, is that the true sources of distress in women's lives are less likely to be examined so long as hormones are held responsible.

Mary Brown Parlee, a psychologist at the City University of New York who has been writing on this subject since the early 1970s, is not persuaded that all anecdotal reports of period-related emotional changes can simply be dismissed. Too many women insist that their feelings *are* different at certain times, that their occasional tearfulness just before getting their period has a different feel to it than tearfulness at other times. "The hard scientific evidence is that the effects are zip," Parlee says, "but this may reflect the lack of sensitivity of the measurement." Specifically, almost all the studies have used the same Menstrual Distress Questionnaire, developed in the 1960s, which lists various emotions and asks women how much of each they experienced. If the form misses certain mood effects, then the research findings would have to be reevaluated.

Still, it seems undeniable that widely held assumptions about premenstrual or menstrual effects on emotions are, at the very least, greatly exaggerated. A 1989 report in the *American Journal of Psychiatry* offers a conservative estimate: 40–50 percent of women who say they are afflicted with what has come to be known as premenstrual syndrome (PMS) actually "do not show symptoms in a predictable relationship to the menstrual cycle when studied prospectively."

Even if one's period *is* accompanied by emotional changes, we should note, it might be a mistake to interpret this as meaning that moods are caused by hormonal changes. "Physiological states and changes of the menstrual cycle are influenced by social and psychological processes as well as the reverse," Parlee wrote. In other words, what's going on in a woman's life and how she feels about it can affect what happens to her body. Indeed, scientists have been finding other examples where behavior transforms biology just as surely as biology transforms behavior.

Related to the matter of mood is the question of whether women's performance at various tasks is affected by the menstrual cycle. An embarrassing number of men have questioned the fitness of women for important jobs or have written off things that women say or do on the grounds that it's "that time of the month." This attitude got a big boost in late 1988 when the front page of both the *New York Times* and the *Los Angeles Times* carried reports of a series of experiments by Canadian psychologist Doreen Kimura and a graduate student. These studies purported to show that women's performance on an assortment of tasks varied depending on their estrogen levels. The clear implication was that gender differences in performance can also be explained biologically.

Unfortunately, this research was fatally flawed in several ways. First, no measures of hormone levels appeared to have been taken in the study, which means that one subject's low estrogen level might have been higher than another's high level, undermining any conclusions about the relation of hormone to performance. Second, the subjects apparently knew the study's purpose—a serious problem in light of widespread beliefs about the effects of the menstrual cycle. Third, the measures of performance were laughably trivial: *Verbal skills* referred to the speed with which subjects could repeat "a box of mixed biscuits in a biscuit mixer" five times. Finally, too few women were tested to support front-page headlines about the significance of hormones.

When we look at good research on skills relevant to the real world, we find a very different pattern. The performance of undergraduate women on class exams, for example—and on tests of critical thinking—is absolutely unrelated to their cycles. One study showed that even menstruating women who were in physical discomfort while taking a test did not score more poorly as a result. "The preponderance of evidence indicates that cognitive performance or mental ability is not significantly affected by menstrual cycle variables," concluded psychologist Barbara Sommer—a conclusion far less likely than Kimura's study to make the front page of your newspaper.

Speaking of blaming the hormones, let's take just a moment to look at menopause. Contrary to popular belief, surveys have suggested that only a minority of menopausal women say they experience "hot flashes" and other symptoms widely associated with the "change of life." Moreover, there is no evidence that menopause per se causes depression. "The old idea of a change-of-life emotional crisis in women is a myth," Robert O. Pasnau, a psychiatrist at UCLA, told *The New York Times* in early 1990. "Women going through menopause are no more likely to suffer depression than are women of other ages, nor than men, for that matter." (Being treated as though one is over the hill and undesirable by virtue of being middle-aged, however, might well have an effect on one's mood.)

A review of cross-cultural data in 1986 notes that "response to menopause is conditioned by the cultural context which shapes the pattern of a woman's roles." The writer, a medical anthropologist, cites reports from Islamic and African cultures to show that women there "experience few, if any, of the physiological or psychological symptoms of which Western women commonly complain in connection with menopause." Interviews with Mayan women in Mexico, as well as with their doctors and other healers in the community, indicate that these women, too, experienced neither physical discomfort nor behavioral changes when they stopped menstruating.

When college teams win, the bucks roll in

The relationship between universities and their athletic departments, particularly at the big state schools, seems to prove that the tail can sometimes wag the dog. Maybe we can laugh away the college administrator who was quoted as saying he wanted a university the football team could be proud of, but there is no denying that learning sometimes is upstaged by winning.

A favorite justification for this emphasis on athletics— and the roughly $1 *billion* a year that colleges spend on sports—is that the entire academic community benefits from teams that win: It is said that alumni reach for their checkbooks if and only if their alma mater triumphs over the visiting team. This assumption is dubious from the start because sports-happy grads may well earmark these contributions for the athletic programs, just as TV earnings and ticket sales from successful football teams are typically plowed right back into sports. At best, then, athletics would be less of a financial drain on the institution, but they wouldn't subsidize faculty salaries or students on financial aid.

In any case, the premise here, that alumni contributions vary with the teams' performance, has pretty well been debunked. In 1979, two researchers scrutinized the donation records of nearly 100 schools over fourteen academic years. The win-loss records of the football and basketball teams were completely unrelated to alumni giving. Even when they allowed for a one-year lag—comparing last year's sports results to this year's contributions—or when they looked at *improvement* in athletic records instead of the absolute number of victories, they came up with nothing.

Two years later, another pair of researchers tried again with fifty-eight schools, this time breaking them down by size and type to see if any associations appeared. They found a few, but it wasn't clear whether, given the number of variables they were juggling, these might have occurred by chance. So a third study was undertaken in 1984, this one including schools from Dartmouth to San Diego State but focusing on those with NCAA Division 1A (i.e., big-time) sports programs. The conclusion: "There is no apparent connection between a university's performance in major sports and the propensity toward generosity on the part of its donors."

Absence makes the heart grow fonder vs. Out of sight, out of mind

You couldn't hope for a clearer case of dueling proverbs than this pair, where opposite predictions are offered for the effects of absence. So which is it? Do we get more or less attached to someone who's away? In a nutshell, the effect of absence depends on how you felt to begin with about the person or thing that's gone. Assuming you aren't distracted by someone new, separation is likely to intensify whatever you felt before you were torn apart. If you felt positively, absence will allow you to idealize your beloved, to cling to an exaggerated version of that person that can't be disconfirmed by real-life imperfections.

That's the conclusion of Abraham Tesser, a psychologist at the University of Georgia, and it's based on more than a decade of work with attitudes toward everything from people to paintings. "Absence has the *potential* for making the heart grow fonder," he says, "because absence reduces the reality constraints on self-generated changes in beliefs and, therefore, feelings." But "given both an initially negative feeling and thought, rather than increasing fondness, absence will make the heart grow colder."

Phillip Shaver and his associates at the University of Denver arrived at a similar conclusion. They surveyed 400 college freshmen to see what had happened to their feelings about the people they left back home. It turned out that their relationships with family members had improved. On the other hand, high-school romances tended to disintegrate with distance. As Shaver's colleague Cindy Hazan puts it, "Whether your heart grows fonder or you forget about a person depends on whether that person is a primary attachment figure or not."

Salt raises your blood pressure

This claim remains controversial in the medical community, but as researchers continue to assault us with evidence, it becomes more and more difficult to justify. In fact, a 1988 editorial in the *British Medical Journal,* after reviewing several new studies, concluded that "the evidence that salt is [an] important [contributor to high blood pressure] is weak . . . [and] the more complex the analysis the weaker the relation."

This subject has been studied in three basic ways. The first searches for a connection between salt consumption and hypertension (high blood pressure) within a given society. Such research has often come up empty-handed. In one of the largest such investigations, which tested more than 7,000 residents of Scotland, it turned out that weight and age were much more reliable predictors of hypertension than salt consumption was. "The true association between sodium and blood pressure is extremely weak," the researchers wrote.

The second approach is to look at many different countries to see whether the places where hypertension is common are also the places where people eat a lot of salt. The results are finally in from an enormous study of more than 10,000 subjects at fifty-two testing centers around the world. Indeed, there was a real worldwide association between sodium in the urine and systolic blood pressure. But on closer examination, the link turned out to be far less impressive. Once adjustments were made for the subjects' age, weight, and alcohol consumption, the relation was statistically significant in only eight of the fifty-two centers. And when the results from four nonindustrialized societies (where salt consumption was extremely low) were set aside, the overall relation vanished.

Of course, even if eating lots of salt and having high blood pressure *did* go hand in hand, that wouldn't prove that one was responsible for the other. Something else could be at work here—a third factor that might be associated with certain eating habits and also with hypertension. That would help to explain the rather striking exceptions such as Japan, where salt consumption is high but blood pressure is not.

In the last type of study, researchers ask people to eat less salt and then watch to see what happens to their blood pressure. A 1986 review of twelve such studies found that sodium restriction *was* a useful strategy for older patients with hypertension. But there wasn't much reason to think that using less salt would lower the blood pressure of people who were not hypertensive to begin with. Moreover, such studies have nothing to say about whether salt *caused* the hypertension—a hypothesis that seems increasingly doubtful.

The full moon makes people crazy

By now you may have heard that *lunacy* comes from *lunar*, suggesting that human behavior can be affected by the phase of the moon. Before taking this on faith, however, we ought to remind ourselves that etymological connections are sometimes misleading: Just ask someone who is "hysterical" but doesn't have a defective uterus—or any left-handed person who is neither "gauche" nor "sinister."

In 1972, an article in the *American Journal of Psychiatry* breathed new life into the age-old belief that people act funny when the moon shines bright. The murder rate in Dade County, Florida, seemed to be at its highest during the full moon and, for some reason, two days after the new moon. Of course, the popular press paid less attention to the rest of the study, which acknowledged that the murder pattern in Ohio's Cuyahoga County didn't match Dade's and didn't show any significant relation to the lunar phase. Also unreported was a follow-up paper in the same journal that looked at homicides in Harris County, Texas, for the same period of time and found nothing in common with either the moon or the other two counties. In fact, critics have suggested that there is less even to the Dade data than meets the eye: The authors seem to have played with dozens of different ways of measuring moon periods (two days before the full moon, one or two days after, three days before *and* after, and so on) before finally finding one that worked.

Next time your TV set is on the fritz, spend a day in the library flipping through journals like *Psychological Reports* and *Perceptual and Motor Skills.* You'll find numerous attempts to charge the moon with murder (or suicide) and you'll soon realize that it's a bum rap. Most studies, particularly the recent ones, find no significant relationship whatever. Those that do turn up something don't agree with one another on the key period: Report A finds that phone calls to a suicide hot line were highest during the new moon and the first quarter, while report B announces that admissions to certain mental hospitals increased during the third quarter. When someone gets all excited about an apparent full-moon effect on homicides or suicides, other researchers come along and point out that he or she forgot to take into account that more murders occur on Friday and Saturday nights and the full moon happened to overlap with weekends during the period under review. One set of researchers had to eat crow in public in 1983: They reanalyzed their own data more carefully and found that all the moon effects had vanished.

Some writers have been very imaginative in trying to find something—anything—about human behavior that the moon affects. They've looked at the number of injured people showing up at hospital emergency rooms, at assassinations and railroad disasters, and even at the number of penalties for roughness in hockey games. The results: nothing, nothing, and nothing. In a systematic review of thirty-seven studies, James Rotton and Ivan Kelly, two tireless debunkers of lunatic claims, couldn't find evidence of a moon effect on any behavioral measure. The only meaningful correlation they came up with was between *belief* in a moon effect and belief in things like reincarnation.

That may be a tad unfair. Lots of unflaky police officers and mental health workers will swear the moon makes mischief. But this would appear to be just one more example of selective perception. As Kelly, a psychologist at the University of Saskatchewan, puts it, "There's a built-in bias. If a person already believes that there's more activity during the full moon, he or she will be more vigilant and notice what happens then. But when do you ever hear someone say, 'Look at that accident—and it's the third quarter!' or 'What a quiet night—and it's a full moon!'?"

One belief that persists among even the most sensible and discerning people (i.e., my friends) is that the birthrate soars during the full moon. Once again, a couple of studies fuel the fire and attract the attention but most research finds no effect. Three analyses, one of 500,000 births in New York City over three years, one of all births in an Ohio hospital over three years, and one of 12,000 births in a busy Los Angeles hospital over four years, couldn't find anything labor intensive about a full moon. Likewise, a review of twenty-one American and European studies concluded in 1988 that the moon apparently doesn't affect birth any more than it affects death.

The squeaky wheel gets the grease

Obviously we don't get everything we ask for, but many people have had the experience of receiving better treatment just by demanding it. If we quietly submit to poor working conditions, inadequate repair jobs, and other frustrations, those in a position to make our lives better may simply leave us to suffer these indignities silently.

Salaries might be a case in point, speculated Brenda Major and her colleagues at the State University of New York at Buffalo. They asked students at a management school, most of them with real-world work experience under their belts, to play the role of a personnel supervisor at a department store. Folders from mock-applicants indicated what salary levels were expected—some of them below, some at, and some above the range advertised.

The result? Pay expectations didn't affect who was offered a job. But of the applicants hired by the students, those who squeaked louder got more grease. "Although applicants did not receive exactly what they asked for, the more pay an applicant requested, the more pay he or she was offered," the experimenters wrote.

On the other hand, there is such a thing as squeaking too loudly (or too often), in which case one may find oneself released rather than greased. This is true in negotiations, too. While one review of the research concludes that "bargainers attain higher and more satisfactory outcomes when they begin their interaction with extreme rather than more moderate demands," others who specialize in conflict resolution caution that this approach often backfires. Extreme demands can undermine one's credibility and even scotch the whole deal. Roger Fisher and William Ury, authors of *Getting to Yes,* suggest that everyone ultimately benefits from viewing negotiations as mutual problem-solving rather than as an adversarial exercise in which each person just tries to get as much as possible for himself.

Abused children grow up to abuse their own children

Are victims of child abuse more likely than other people to turn into abusive parents? Yes. Will all of these victims, or even most of them, wind up abusing their children? No.

A good number of the relevant studies are so poorly designed that one sometimes despairs of finding the truth about this subject. Most of them don't include a control group of children, matched for family income and education, who were not abused. Many of them classify people as abused on the basis of subjective definitions and unreliable memories. A lot of them work backward, trying to figure out how many current abusers were themselves abused, rather than following young victims forward in time to see how many complete the cycle. Still, careful reviews of the existing research, together with some meticulous work over the last few years, suggests that it is simplistic to say that violence necessarily begets violence—even if the adage does have a grain of truth to it.

There is little question that, as a group, abused (and also neglected) children tend to be more aggressive than their peers. When they grow up, they are more likely than other people to get into trouble with the law. At Indiana University, Cathy Spatz Widom, a leading researcher on this topic, collected thousands of juvenile court cases from the late 1960s and early 1970s, tracking these children—along with a control group—into adulthood. Of those who were abused or neglected, she reported in 1989, 28.6 percent had a criminal record by the time they were in their twenties. That compares with 21.1 percent of those who were not abused or neglected but who had the same age, sex, race, and socioeconomic background. On the one hand, the difference is statistically significant; on the other hand, the majority of abused children apparently do not commit crimes.

What about abusing their own kids? After casting a critical eye on the available research, Joan Kaufman and Edward Zigler of Yale University estimated in 1987 that between a quarter and a third of abuse victims will become abusive parents. Once again, this news may be viewed as either depressing or hopeful. A 30 percent rate of abuse is about six times higher than that for the general population—an enormous disparity. But the idea that abuse is inevitably passed along from one generation to the next is simply false. In fact, not only do most people who were abused manage to avoid doing the same to their own children, but most parents who *are* abusive were not abused when they grew up.

Why do some battered children break the cycle while others perpetuate it? A variety of factors seem to play a role: It matters how severe the abuse was and how early it occurred, how smart the child was, and how he or she perceived the episode. Likewise, it's important to look at the life circumstances of the grown children—how much social support they receive, how they feel about having kids, how openly they've confronted the facts of their own abuse, and so on. In the final analysis, though, no amount of information about someone's history will ever allow us to know for sure who will turn out to be a healthy, loving parent and who will strike fear and rage into his or her children.

Of course, we shouldn't understate the effects of having been abused. Even if only a minority wind up abusing their own children or turning to crime, it isn't clear how many other victims carry their pain with them in the form of depression, self-destructive behavior, or warped relationships. However, it is just as important that we avoid repeating folk wisdom about the cycle of abuse lest we *turn* this belief into truth. As Kaufman and Zigler put it, "Adults who were maltreated have been told so many times that they will abuse their children that for some it has become a self-fulfilling prophecy."

Time flies when you're having fun

Experimental psychologists really earn their pay when they come up with findings that challenge common sense. For some examples of these, see "Rewards motivate people" (pp. 31–35), "There's safety in numbers" (pp. 178–179), and "Expressing hostility gets it out of your system" (pp. 113–117). At other times, though, researchers spend time proving and reproving things that everyone already knew to be true.

By way of illustration, consider the umpteen experiments showing that time really does seem to go faster when you're doing something you enjoy than when you're bored silly. Time perception, in fact, was one of the first subjects to be examined by psychologists. Back in 1904, it was found that a given interval of time seems shorter when you're active than when you're just sitting around. And a 1933 Harvard study concluded that when someone is "bored or feels despair time seems long; when he is interested or eager, time seems short."

One of the best ways to make time slow to a crawl is to read all of the studies that support this thoroughly predictable conclusion. But it should be said in the researchers' defense that a few other findings about time have turned up along the way that are a bit more interesting. Among them:

- Your time estimates were a lot less reliable before you reached the age of eight.
- If asked several times to estimate a given interval, your guesses are more likely to be too long the first few times you try it.
- You're more apt to overestimate a very brief time period and underestimate a longer one.
- Your body temperature may affect your ability to judge time.
- Not only does time fly when you're having fun, but you'll think you had fun if you believe that time flew. In a 1986 study, students filling out questionnaires who were artificially led to think that time was going by quickly—because they were given caffeine or were sitting next to a fast-ticking metronome—were more likely than others to say they enjoyed the task. (Of course, the caffeine may have affected their mood for reasons having nothing to do with perception of time.)
- Finally, you'll probably overestimate the passage of time—that is, time will seem to go slower—if you're waiting for something to happen. This is why the days before Christmas creep by at a maddening pace for children. But the anticipated event doesn't have to be particularly exciting; it can be as mundane as the heating up of a container of water. Here the folk

wisdom triumphs again, because, according to two experiments published in 1980, watched pots really do seem to take longer to boil. People who were asked to summon an experimenter from the next room when the water in a coffeepot started to bubble were more likely to overestimate the time it took than those who simply waited during the same four-minute period without being told to watch the water. In one of the studies, time went slower for subjects asked beforehand to estimate how long the boiling would take than it did for subjects who were asked after the fact.

If the Atomic Bomb had not been dropped on Hiroshima, the war would have continued and even more lives would have been lost

Many nations have tested nuclear weapons, but only one has ever used them. That nation, of course, is the United States; the bombs it dropped on Hiroshima and Nagasaki in August of 1945 incinerated more than 100,000 residents of those cities and left perhaps twice that number dying slowly from radiation poisoning. But, as President Harry Truman and countless other Americans have maintained, there was a compelling justification for these acts: Short of using the A-bomb, only a full-scale invasion of Japan would have convinced its leaders to surrender, and that would have resulted in an even higher death toll.

How many lives actually would have been lost in such an invasion is not clear. While Truman threw around figures such as 500,000 and even 1 million Americans dead, the historian Barton Bernstein writes that military planners at the time put the number between 20,000 and 46,000. But far more disturbing than this discrepancy is the strong possibility that neither an invasion nor a nuclear attack was actually necessary to get Japan to surrender.

By June 1945, U.S. firebombing had already wiped out substantial portions of Japan's six largest cities and the people who lived there. As many as 1 million residents of Tokyo were left homeless from such bombing in March. No oil shipments were getting into the country, which was utterly dependent on imported fuel, and, by early August, 90 percent of Japanese merchant shipping had been destroyed.

It is true that the Japanese were famous for fighting to the death; indeed, there were some elements in the country's military who resisted the idea of surrender even *after* Hiroshima and Nagasaki. But there is good reason to believe that the men in charge were on the verge of calling it quits before the bombs were dropped. The only thing holding up a surrender, which almost surely would have come before an invasion, was the Japanese concern that their emperor retain his title. This condition, of course, the United States ultimately accepted.

In 1944, the War Department* set up a study group called the Strategic Bombing Survey to investigate the effects of aerial attacks. A report issued from that office in 1946 contains the following conclusion:

> The Hiroshima and Nagasaki atomic bombs did not defeat Japan, nor by the testimony of the enemy leaders who ended the war did they persuade Japan to accept unconditional surrender. The Emperor, the Lord Privy Seal, the Prime Minister, the Foreign Min-

*The name was subsequently changed to the Department of Defense to imply that American military actions are, by definition, never offensive.

ister, and the Navy Minister had decided as early as May of 1945 that the war should be ended even if it meant acceptance of defeat on allied terms. . . . Based on a detailed investigation of all the facts and supported by the testimony of the surviving Japanese leaders involved, it is the Survey's opinion that certainly prior to 31 December 1945, and in all probability prior to 1 November 1945, Japan would have surrendered even if the atomic bombs had not been dropped, even if Russia had not entered the war, and even if no invasion had been planned or completed.

Recently, another 1946 document was discovered in the National Archives. This one, a secret intelligence study by the army's top planning and operations group, came to essentially the same conclusion: An invasion "would not have been necessary" and the A-bomb was not decisive in ending the war. The Japanese surrender had more to do with the possibility that our ally, the Soviet Union, was about to get involved in the Pacific war.

This view was echoed by key U.S. military leaders. "The Japanese were already defeated and ready to surrender. . . . In being the first to use [the atomic bomb] we had adopted an ethical standard common to the barbarians of the Dark Ages," said Admiral William D. Leahy, who was the president's Chief of Staff and the nation's senior military officer. Much the same opinion was offered by General Dwight D. Eisenhower ("Japan was already thoroughly beaten [by late July]. . . . It wasn't necessary to hit them with that awful thing") and by Winston Churchill.

One might object that these assessments were merely speculative. The fact is, however, that *U.S. policymakers knew beforehand that Japan was ready to surrender.* In July, American intelligence had intercepted a cable from Japanese Foreign Minister Shigenori Togo to his ambassador in Moscow that referred to "His Majesty's strong desire to secure a termination of the war. . . . Unconditional surrender is the only obstacle to peace."*

Even to the extent that any doubt remains about whether the Japanese would have given up, the most damning evidence against Truman may be the way he approached the decision. The fearsome new weapon was not treated as an option of last resort. It would be easier to accept the argument that he had no choice but to drop the bomb if other possibilities—such as demonstrating its power to Japanese leaders on an unpopulated island and demanding surrender—had been carefully considered. They were not. There was never a serious attempt to find a strategy short of obliterating the population of Hiroshima and Nagasaki. As Yale sociologist Kai Erikson put it, using nuclear weapons was not, "by any stretch of the imagination, a product of mature consideration. . . . We have it on the authority of virtually all the principal players that no one in a position to do anything about it ever really considered alternatives" to dropping the bomb on Japan.

This leaves us to agonize over one of the most important questions of the century: Why? A review of the historical record suggests two reasons. First, so much money had been sunk into the development of the bomb that many policymakers came to feel its use was inevitable. We had managed to invent a weapon of unprecedented destructive power and we were determined to try it out—it was that simple. The fact that we wiped out a second city after having made our deadly point at Hiroshima lends credence to this idea: The second bomb was made of plutonium instead of uranium, and it has been suggested that the people of Nagasaki died in what was, in effect, a grotesque scientific experiment.

Second, the bombs were dropped as the United States

*"Unconditional surrender" refers to the issue of the emperor being allowed to remain in place.

was busy preparing to take political and economic control of much of the postwar world. Thus the intended audience of what we did to Hiroshima and Nagasaki may have been the Soviets rather than the Japanese; August 6, 1945 could be seen as the opening salvo of the Cold War.

This theory, along with detailed documentation for it, has been offered by Gar Alperovitz in his book *Atomic Diplomacy*. He points, for example, to the fact that the powerful Secretary of State James Byrnes did not suggest to Truman that the bomb was necessary to win the war; he emphasized instead that it "might well put us in a position to dictate our own terms at the end of the war." In fact, Alperovitz argues, the bomb also gave U.S. policymakers "sufficient confidence" to consciously and unilaterally breach "specific understandings Roosevelt had reached with the Soviet leadership" with respect to the future of Europe. This, needless to say, is not the version of the Cold War taught in high-school history classes (although it is being given more credence these days by mainstream historians).

In sum, by the middle of 1945, most remaining Japanese soldiers were fighting chiefly to preserve their emperor. But Truman had by that time agreed to accept a surrender that left the emperor in place, which means, in Alperovitz's words, that "at the time he permitted the Hiroshima and Nagasaki bombings he was aware—on the best advice available—that the war could in all likelihood be ended on terms which he had already deemed acceptable." The idea that the A-bomb had to be used to save lives would, therefore, seem to be a fiction—and the shocking but unavoidable implication is that its use must be numbered among the most horrific crimes in human history.

Boys are better at math than girls

Girls are full of sugar and spice, while boys are naturally better at calculating the ratios of these ingredients. You think so? Think again.

Janet Shibley Hyde and her colleagues at the University of Wisconsin sorted through all the available evidence on this question—an even 100 studies that tested a total of 4 million subjects—and published the findings in 1990. It seems that *girls* actually have the edge in math during the elementary- and middle-school years, although that edge is slight. The advantage shifts to boys only in high school, which happens to be the time when students are given some latitude in selecting their courses. (Interestingly, another psychologist has shown that when we measure math performance with grades instead of with standardized test scores, girls come out ahead even in high school.) While groups of mathematically "gifted" children typically contain more boys than girls, there are practically no differences in tests of the general population. Finally, the researchers found that the more recent the study was, the smaller the gender difference tended to be.

This last bit of evidence is a particularly powerful refutation of the idea that differences are biologically based. What's more, differences have been narrowing over the years in areas other than math. Alan Feingold at Yale University reports that high-school girls scored higher on Differential Aptitude Tests of spelling and language back when the tests were first given in 1947. As of 1980, however, "boys had completely closed the gap."

Girls, Feingold continues, now do just as well as boys on

tests of verbal reasoning, abstract reasoning, and numerical ability; they have cut in half the differences on mechanical reasoning and space relations. Hyde and a colleague conducted a rigorous review of 165 studies in 1988 and found the evidence even more decisive: "The magnitude of the gender difference in verbal ability is currently so small that it can effectively be considered to be zero," they wrote.

The problem is that these facts aren't generally known. In a large cross-cultural study published in 1990, boys and girls in elementary school scored about the same overall on reading tests. But many of these kids' *mothers,* when questioned, said they thought girls were better in reading than boys were. Such false beliefs about gender differences "may have strong effects on the ways boys and girls direct their effort," the researchers warned.

Laughter is the best medicine

In 1964, a California psychiatrist named William Fry conducted a pilot study to determine whether it was feasible to measure the physiological effects of laughter. He decided such research did make sense and, despite being unable to attract funding for it, proceeded to use Stanford University's facilities to prove that laughing stimulates the body in much the same way that exercise does—raising the heart and respiration rate and then causing them to drop briefly below their original level.

Something else happened in 1964 that was widely seen as even more significant with respect to the healing effects of humor. A magazine editor named Norman Cousins came down with ankylosing spondylitis, a degenerative disease that attacks the body's connective tissue. He survived, due to some combination of luck, positive attitude, huge doses of vitamin C, and self-administered humor therapy (consisting mostly of watching episodes of *Candid Camera*). It was the last of these factors that attracted the most attention, particularly when Cousins wrote in the *New England Journal of Medicine* in 1976 (and in a subsequent book) that "ten minutes of genuine belly laughter had an anesthetic effect and would give me at least two hours of pain-free sleep."

Such reports gave rise to a widespread assumption that laughter is literally the best medicine—to the point that Cousins himself, although still intrigued by the possibility of howling one's way to health, was moved to write in 1989 that he was "disturbed by the impression these accounts created that I thought laughter was a substitute for authentic medical care."

Laughter feels good and gives the body a good workout, but does it really have an effect on disease? Here we need large, well-controlled studies—a single case history like Cousins's does not really prove very much—and here, as the psychologist David McClelland says, "The publicity given to this field has gotten way ahead of the facts." Those large, well-controlled studies don't yet exist; all we have are some intriguing findings that are both indirect and inconclusive.

Kathleen Dillon and her colleagues, for example, showed that the concentration of immunoglobulin A in the saliva (S-IgA) went up when people watched a Richard Pryor movie but not when they watched a boring instructional film. Other research has found that S-IgA defends against respiratory infections, but Dillon and her associates had to admit that their study did not directly demonstrate "what these changes in immunity mean in terms of disease resistance." This qualification is particularly important because S-IgA levels went right back down after a few minutes, and also because only nine subjects were tested in their study.

Lee Berk and other researchers at Loma Linda University Medical Center, meanwhile, have been looking at two other chemical substances in the body, cortisol and epinephrine. In a 1989 study, watching a funny video caused the level of these substances to decline, which is good because they can interfere with the body's ability to defend itself from illness. Again, though, the connection to health is rather round-about: Laughter may lead to lower cortisol levels, which may lead to increased production of interleukin, which may help the immune system to resist disease.

Also, not only was this study very small, with only ten subjects altogether, but the subjects may have been different from each other in any number of ways, meaning that we don't know for sure that it was their laughter that had an effect.* Finally, a close reading shows that Berk and his colleagues actually got mixed results: Cortisol levels dropped for the viewers of both tapes, not just the funny one. (There was no difference between the two groups, incidentally, in the amount of the famous "feel-good" chemical, beta-endorphin, that was produced.)

Other evidence is also interesting but less than overwhelming. Laughing at Bill Cosby or Lily Tomlin tapes had the same effect on undergraduates in one study as putting them into a relaxed state—namely, it allowed them to cope with more pain. In 1989, the *Journal of the American Medical Association* published two letters to the editor reporting on humor therapy. In one, a Swedish doctor found that "general well-being" increased for six depressed women with painful illnesses (which, of course, doesn't mean they got well); in the other, a Tennessee doctor found that listening

*The same is true for a later study by Dillon and a colleague. Mothers who said they used humor as a coping device had higher levels of S-IgA (and babies who were less likely to have respiratory infections) than those who didn't. But there was no attempt to check the women's education level, diet, or various differences in personality to see if such differences between the two groups might have been more important than their use of humor.

to Jack Benny tapes during surgery with a local anesthetic made absolutely no difference in feelings of pain or anxiety.

Finally, three sets of studies have looked into the consequences "When bad things happen to funny people"—that is, whether someone with a good sense of humor is less likely to get depressed when unpleasant things occur. In 1982, two Illinois psychologists said No: Their survey of 161 college students found that "humor, at least by itself, does not moderate the effects of life stress." The next year, two Canadian psychologists said Yes: The relation between negative life events and depression was less pronounced for students who said they had a good sense of humor or who could be funny on demand. In 1987, an Ohio psychologist said Sort of: Higher humor scores meant less depression in general but no advantage in coping with stressful events—and no effect on physical illness.

So what does all this mean? As far as William Fry is concerned, "We're at the cutting edge of a significant development in medical science." After all, it's only recently that many physicians have grudgingly admitted that *any* psychological and social factor can affect the immune system, and some of those connections now seem pretty hard to deny. The fact that there's little research to prove a therapeutic effect of laughter may say more about the state of medical research than it does about laughter.

But Jeffrey Goldstein, a Temple University psychologist who has specialized in the study of humor, is more concerned about how claims concerning the healing power of laughter are resting precariously on a very slim body of data. He points out that laughing at a videotape is not the same thing as having a lifelong sense of humor, that appreciating funny things is not the same thing as being funny, and that humor is not the same thing as a positive attitude toward life. Researchers haven't yet been attentive to these distinctions.

Besides, Goldstein says, "We're always looking for external agents, something to point to as a cause or cure. It's almost a way of saying, 'If you have the right sense of humor you don't need my compassion or concern because you'll get better all by yourself—and if you don't, it's your own fault.'

"It's not clear that humor affects our health more than other things do," he adds. "I don't want to denigrate humor because it probably helps people to get through life with a little less stress. But neither do I want to attribute to it powers it doesn't have."

Reading in the dark will ruin your eyes

Tell your mother she was wrong. As a pamphlet prepared by the American Academy of Ophthalmology puts it, "Reading in dim light can no more harm the eyes than taking a photograph in dim light can harm the camera."

Another myth is that wearing glasses that are too strong will make you nearsighted. You might get a headache after a while, but looking through "something hung in front of the eyes . . . cannot cause harm" to the eyes themselves, according to the ophthalmologists.

Humans are naturally aggressive

In 1986, scientists from a dozen nations gathered in Spain to draft what has come to be called the Seville Statement on Violence. "It is scientifically incorrect," they declared, to say that violence is "genetically programmed into our human nature" or that "humans have a 'violent brain' " or that war "is caused by 'instinct.' " They concluded that "violence is neither in our evolutionary legacy nor in our genes."

The people who signed their names to these words are not fuzzy-headed utopians. They are some of the world's leading experts on behavior and the brain. A decade earlier, another specialist in the field, psychologist Robert A. Baron, had concluded that violence cannot be blamed on something called "human nature." After citing more than 300 studies, including two dozen of his own, he emphasized that aggression is "*not* essentially innate. Rather, it seems to be a learned form of social behavior."

Once we exclude the act of killing in order to eat, even animals are much less aggressive than many of us assume. (Even if they were very aggressive, of course, this would not tell us very much about our own behavior.) Organized group aggression is extremely rare in other species, and the aggression that does occur is typically a function of the environment in which animals find themselves. Scientists have discovered that altering that environment, or the way an animal has been reared, can have a profound impact on the level of aggression found in virtually all species. Furthermore, animals cooperate, both within and among species, far more than many of us believe on the basis of watching all those exciting nature documentaries on TV.

But back to humans. The aggression-is-natural view finds itself in trouble almost immediately because there are so many people who are not aggressive at all—unless, of course, we stretch the word so that it includes acting assertively or getting angry. It's not clear what we are supposed to make of these peaceful people, given that they are obviously no less human than their violent neighbors.

More striking are entire societies that are nonaggressive. We Americans happen to live in one of the most violent and warlike countries on the planet, as reflected in both our murder rate and the number of times we have intervened militarily in the affairs of other nations. It's easy to assume that what's true in our society must be true everywhere. But the fact is that some cultures are apparently devoid of any traces of aggression or war. These are hunter-gatherer cultures, which some of us snidely refer to as "primitive." (Perhaps we should just call them "non-VCR cultures.") It is rather interesting, though, as the late psychoanalyst Erich Fromm once pointed out, that "the most primitive men are the least warlike and that warlikeness grows in proportion to civilization. If destructiveness were innate in man, the trend would have to be the opposite."

It is true that the presence of some hormones or the stimulation of certain sections of the brain have been experimentally linked with aggression. But after describing these mechanisms in some detail, the physiologist K. E. Moyer emphasized that "aggressive behavior is stimulus-bound. That is, even though the neural system specific to a particular kind of aggression is well-activated, the behavior does not occur unless an appropriate target is available . . . [and even then] it can be inhibited."

Those last words are particularly important. Regardless of the evolutionary or neurological factors said to underlie aggression, "biological" simply does not mean "unavoidable." The fact that people voluntarily fast or remain celibate shows that even hunger and sex drives can be overridden. In the case of aggression, where the existence of such a drive is dubious to begin with, our ability to choose our behavior is even clearer.

Partly because popular magazines and TV programs keep emphasizing biological factors—the Seville Statement, for example, received virtually no coverage from major news organizations in the United States—the real causes of aggression are often ignored. There are piles of studies pointing to the role played by parenting practices (for example, see "Spare the rod and spoil the child," pp. 135–138), violent entertainment, competitive sports, political propaganda, dehumanizing conditions, and so forth. We are aggressive, according to the bulk of the evidence, because we are raised that way—not because we are born that way.

All of this concerns the matter of violence in general. The idea that war in particular is biologically determined—a proposition with which about 60 percent of Americans agree, according to several surveys—is even more farfetched. "When one country attacks another country, this doesn't happen because people in the country feel aggressive toward those in the other," explains Harvard University biologist Richard Lewontin. "If it were true, we wouldn't need propaganda or a draft: All those aggressive people would sign up right away. State 'aggression' is a matter of political policy, not a matter of feeling."

The point was put well by Jean-Jacques Rousseau more than two centuries ago: "War is not a relation between man and man, but between State and State, and individuals are enemies accidentally." That states must "psych up" men to fight makes it even more difficult to argue for a connection between our natures and the fact of war. In the case of the nuclear arms race, this connection is still more tenuous. Says Dr. Bernard Lown, cochair of International Physicians for the Prevention of Nuclear War, which received the

Nobel Peace Prize in 1985, "The individual's behavior, whether he's aggressive or permissive or passive, is not the factor that makes up his outlook toward genocide. Even the person who's aggressive won't readily accept extinction."

The bottom line, then, is that pessimism is not necessarily realism. Or, as the scientists who signed the Seville Statement put it, "The same species [that] invented war is capable of inventing peace."

Watch out for subliminal advertising

Trivia buffs may know that actor Cliff Robertson made his debut in a movie called *Picnic*, which also starred Kim Novak and William Holden. But that film made entertainment history in another way, too. At one showing in 1957, an audience in Fort Lee, New Jersey, just across the river from New York, got more than the *Picnic* they had come for. Unbeknownst to them, they were part of a marketing experiment. Over and over during the movie, the words *Drink Coca-Cola* and *Eat popcorn* were flashed on the screen—each time for a mere three-thousandth of a second.

The people responsible for these sneaky microcommercials claimed that Coke and popcorn sold more briskly than usual that evening, which led to an outpouring of outrage as editorial writers and politicians conjured up images of millions of consumer zombies spending their life savings on junk without knowing why they were doing so.

Skip forward now to the early 1970s, when a book called *Subliminal Seduction* was published by Wilson Bryan Key. Erotic images and words, he warned readers, are hidden in magazine ads, making us want the advertised products even though we don't realize what we find so appealing about them. The book became a best-seller, and *subliminal* became a household word.

Since then, the premise that our attitudes and behavior can be affected by stimuli we're not consciously aware of has popped up elsewhere. Hucksters have sold tapes that promise to teach us French or help us lose weight while we sleep. Fundamentalist ministers have warned that rock music contains satanic messages recorded backward—which implies that these alleged sounds will somehow have an impact even if listeners don't notice or understand them.

Should we take such claims seriously, or are they, to speak satanically for a moment, a parc fo tol? You may be surprised to learn that studies on subliminal perception have been conducted since the 1930s or even earlier, and they do provide some evidence that we can be affected by things we don't notice. In certain experiments, for example, subjects were more likely to express a preference for a word if they had earlier been exposed to it subliminally.

But it's a long trip from such findings to the idea that Madison Avenue can effectively brainwash us into buying things without knowing why. The more extravagant claims on subliminal perception have never been scientifically confirmed. Take the Fort Lee movie theater experiment: there was no control group to provide a true comparison of refreshment purchases, the findings were never documented or published in a reputable journal, and the study was never replicated. (Also, an exposure of one three-thousandth of a second is a lot shorter than that used in most laboratory studies, so experts are even more doubtful that such flashes could have had any effect.) As for Key's sex-in-the-liquor-ads claims, it's not easy to find a researcher who places any stock in these speculations. The headline for a 1985 article in *Marketing News* pretty much sums up the response: "Subliminal Ad Tactics: Experts Still Laughing."

Lots of psychologists have been unable to get any effect

at all when they investigate subliminal exposure. Subjects in one study weren't any more likely to remember vacation-type slides with the word "sex" embedded in them than those with no hidden message. In another study, quick flashes of *Hershey's Chocolate* over slides didn't affect subjects' purchases of candy during the following ten days.

Timothy E. Moore, a Toronto psychologist, points out that we are not passive pieces of putty that can be molded by messages—least of all by messages that wouldn't have much effect if we were consciously aware of them. There's something fascinating about the idea that clever advertisers can circumvent our critical faculties and reach a part of our brain that will automatically do their bidding. But there's simply no good evidence to support this idea.

Even if subliminal influences can affect our attitude, Moore goes on to point out, the size of that effect is likely to be tiny compared to the effects of what we *do* notice. "If you do not actively search for hidden extras, what you see is what you get. . . . The fine print near the bottom of an ad is likely to be far more important than any concealed genitalia could be." Moreover, changing our mood is a far cry from motivating us to buy. And finally, some people are more perceptive than others, which means that flashed messages would have to be brief enough to escape detection by everyone, and this further reduces the probability of their having an effect.

Moore conducted a comprehensive review of the research in 1982 and concluded that while "subliminal perception is a bona fide phenomenon, the effects obtained are typically subtle" and the whole enterprise has "no apparent relevance to the goals of advertising."

Breakfast is the most important meal of the day

If you want to get technical about it, no study has even come close to proving that breakfast is literally more important than any other meal. The more reasonable and interesting claim is that we may suffer some adverse consequences from rushing off to work or school in the morning without eating. Surprisingly, though, there is reason to doubt even this common assumption. In 1982, after reviewing all the studies they could find, N. H. Dickie and A. E. Bender, both nutritionists at the University of London, concluded that there was "little evidence to support the contention that omission of breakfast is detrimental in terms of measured performance . . . [let alone] to support what has become the nutritionists' dictum that 'breakfast is the most important meal of the day.'"

The idea that something dreadful will befall us unless we eat in the morning owes much of its popularity to the frequently cited (but rarely read) Iowa Studies, most of which were published in the late 1940s and early 1950s. Blow the dust off them and you'll get a good lesson in how not to conduct research. First, the major measure of performance, referred to as "maximum work rate," was how hard people pedaled a bicycle—not a terribly relevant skill in most workplaces and classrooms. Second, each study was conducted with only six to ten subjects. Third, all of the experiments were funded by the Cereal Institute, a group that just possibly could have benefited from positive findings.

Anyone who looks at the actual data soon realizes that they were inconclusive, but this fact is less than clear from reading the better-known summary paper, written anonymously and published in 1962 . . . by the Cereal Institute. With characteristically dry British understatement, Dickie and Bender observe that this report "drew general conclusions somewhat at variance with the actual findings."

So far as I can tell, not a single reputable study since then has shown that adults who make a habit of not eating until noon are at any sort of disadvantage. A 1965 survey of almost 7,000 Californians found that breakfast eaters reported that their health was slightly better than nonbreakfast eaters, but they also were more likely to be nonsmokers; no proof was offered that breakfast by itself was associated with any benefit. At least one study has shown that adults' mental performance is highest when they follow their normal morning routine, regardless of whether that means eating or not eating.

Most researchers have looked at the effects of breakfast on children, and the results of their work are mixed at best. After a full year of eating a hot breakfast, several hundred low-income Los Angeles elementary school students were absolutely indistinguishable from their peers on reading scores, math scores, psychological tests, and all other measures.

That was in 1976. Thirteen years later, another set of researchers compared children in Lawrence, Massachusetts, who participated in a school breakfast program with those who didn't. This time, achievement test scores did show a difference. Unfortunately, it's hard to know whether this means anything for several reasons. First, the students were not randomly assigned to the breakfast or nonbreakfast group; those who chose to eat may also have been more motivated to learn. Second, the breakfast group could have benefited from an overall improvement in their diet; the fact that it was due to a nourishing *breakfast* might well be irrelevant. Third, the breakfast-program children missed school less often than the others, which means they might have had a chance to learn more. "That's one possible interpretation of our findings," concedes Michael Weitzman, a Boston pediatrician who was one of the study's authors. "Maybe they did better because they came more and they came more because they got food."

Let me be clear that these objections are not arguments against school breakfast programs. Using food to lure children to school may be perfectly sensible. Likewise, one can hardly imagine a better use of public funds than providing children with what may be their best, or even only, meal of the day. But any benefit they derive from this meal doesn't tell us very much about the importance of *when* one eats, which is our concern here.

There have been other studies. Some have found that children who eat breakfast are slightly better at solving problems; others find no differences; many find an advantage on one or two measures but not on the rest. Skipping breakfast didn't affect children's memory in one British study; in a 1981 U.S. experiment, it actually seemed to *improve* children's memory, while having no effect on problem-solving abilities.

Unfortunately, many researchers have neglected to ask the children in their studies whether they are accustomed to having breakfast. It may turn out that whatever decline in performance does result from fasting is found only with those students who usually have something to eat in the morning. Another possible factor is how well nourished a child is to begin with. Ernesto Pollitt, a leading researcher in the field who teaches at the University of California at Davis, doubts that this matters much. "I don't have any biochemical evidence that fasting for eighteen hours is going to affect an undernourished child differently from the way it affects a well-nourished child," he says.

But several Jamaican studies, conducted by Sally Grantham-McGregor and her colleagues, are hard to dismiss. In one, published in the *American Journal of Clinical Nutrition* in 1989, children classified as severely malnourished or undernourished did indeed do better on some (not all) academic tests when they had eaten a full breakfast than when they had had only tea. But well-nourished children did not improve on any measure of performance; in fact, they did better, on average, at problem-solving and arithmetic when they had skipped breakfast. Several years earlier, another study had led Grantham-McGregor and her associates to speculate that "school-feeding programmes might have a greater effect" in areas where children's diets are substandard.

In any case, the overall conclusion from studies to date is that there is little cause for alarm as regards children—and certainly adults—who eat well-balanced meals starting with lunch.

Actions speak louder than words

What plays a larger role in shaping our impressions of people: what they say about themselves or how they act? Common sense suggests the latter, but Brandeis University psychologist Teresa Amabile wanted to see for herself. She and a student videotaped women who, following a script, described themselves as either introverted or extraverted. These women were also taped conversing with other people while they *acted* either introverted or extraverted.

After watching some of the monologues and conversations, 160 students were asked to give their impressions of the women they had seen, evaluating how outgoing, friendly, shy, or withdrawn they were. Both sorts of evidence affected these ratings, but when self-descriptions and actual behavior conflicted, the latter influenced the raters more decisively. On a combined index of eleven adjectives related to introversion and extraversion, how the women acted was about twenty times more influential than what they said about themselves in determining the students' judgments.

Other research, meanwhile, has shown that adults who want to encourage children to be generous will be more effective by setting a good example than by preaching. James H. Bryan and Nancy Hodges Walbek awarded gift certificates to fourth graders for playing a miniature bowling game and then allowed them to put some of their winnings in a box "for the poor children," if they chose. The children were exposed to adults who either donated or didn't and praised either generosity or selfishness.

Again, the real test came when the models' actions didn't match their words. And again, what they actually did had a more powerful effect on the children's decision to be charitable. "Behavioral example is a stronger influencer than verbal exhortations in affecting altruistic behavior," the researchers concluded. Or, as the philosopher David Hume wrote 250 years ago, "Actions are, indeed, better indications of a character than words."

After the baby comes the blues

Are new mothers susceptible to depression? Depending on whose estimate you believe, anywhere from one-quarter to three-quarters of women experience a brief bout of tearfulness a few days after giving birth. Unfortunately, these figures are meaningless without a point of reference. In 1987, Valerie Levy, who teaches midwives in England, had the bright idea of comparing the frequency of the postnatal blues to that of the post-*surgical* blues. It turned out that, if anything, slightly more women who were in the hospital for other reasons had episodes of weepiness; apparently, there is nothing unique to having a baby that makes most women sad. The only difference Levy found was that new mothers were most likely to break into tears for no apparent reason on the third day after delivery—one day later than women having some kind of operation. (Giving birth also produces a certain amount of euphoria, another researcher later speculated, which might briefly postpone the usual sadness that follows the trauma of surgery.)

As for the sort of depression that is more serious and shows up later, it appears that the average mother is not any more vulnerable than other people. Previous research had sounded a more pessimistic note, but it tended to be based on very small samples and also failed to point out that lots of women who were depressed after giving birth were also depressed *before* giving birth.

Now, as the studies get better, the whole idea of postpartum depression is being called into question. A Canadian study of almost 300 women published in 1989 discovered that between 20 and 25 percent reported some feelings of depression both during pregnancy and during the postpartum period. When more careful diagnoses were made, the researchers decided that 10 percent could be called clinically depressed a few weeks before giving birth; a month or so afterward, the figure was 7 percent. Neither figure is dramatically different from that for the general population.

While this study measured women's levels of depression just a few weeks after their babies were born, a large British study checked in at three months, and again at six months, following birth. Between 8 and 9 percent were seriously depressed—just about the same as the proportion of a matched group of women who had not been pregnant. A brand-new study by researchers at the University of Iowa comes to the same general conclusion: Rates of postpartum depression aren't higher than those of prepartum depression or of depression for other women.

Finally, while estrogen and progesterone levels drop in the week following delivery, researchers haven't been able to find any differences in hormone levels between women who do and don't get depressed after giving birth. If some women's moods *are* negatively affected by having a child, the most likely explanation has less to do with biology than with an absence of social support or the presence of other stress factors in their lives.

Competition builds character

From Little League fields to Rotary Club meetings this phrase is repeated—an all-purpose justification for pitting people against each other at work and at play. If competition is America's state religion, then the reference to building character is the benediction we repeat during our ritual contests.

What soon becomes obvious is that people who talk about how "character" is enhanced by participating in sports (or other activities that sort people into winners and losers) almost never specify how they are using the word. But regardless of how it is interpreted, the idea turns out to be nearly impossible to support. Having researched this question for more than seven years, I have been unable to find a single study that supports the idea that competition builds character. In fact, the available research points unmistakably in the other direction.

"The traditional assumption that competitive sport builds character is still with us today in spite of overwhelming contrary evidence," writes psychologist Dorcas Susan Butt. Some of that evidence comes from Bruce Ogilvie and

Thomas Tutko, both at San Jose State College. After testing some 15,000 athletes in an effort to identify sports-specific personality traits, these researchers reported that they could find "no empirical support for the tradition that sport builds character. Indeed, there is evidence that athletic competition limits growth in some areas." Among the consequences of competing they found were depression, extreme stress, and relatively shallow relationships. They also found that many players "with immense character strengths" *avoid* competitive sports. Those with such strengths who do participate are not improved by competition; whatever positive qualities they display were theirs to begin with.

Let's look at the word *character* a little more closely. If we use it to mean something like tenacity or discipline, then there is no need to engage in an activity where one person (or team) can become successful only at the expense of another. One can try hard to improve oneself without trying to beat other people. To the extent it is useful to learn that one can't always reach one's goals—and there is reason to think that the psychological benefits of failure are actually overrated—competition is, once again, unnecessary at best and positively destructive at worst. You don't have to lose in order to fail—any more than you have to win in order to succeed.

If *character* refers to confidence or faith in oneself, then competitive activities would seem be a particularly dumb way to try to develop this. In fact, you might say that competition is to self-esteem as sugar is to teeth. Ideally, people should believe that they are basically good even when they screw up or do something foolish. But competition makes acceptance of oneself dependent on how many people he or she has beaten at how many activities. Losing, which is always possible in a competition, typically feels terrible. But even winning doesn't provide a lasting sense of security. One needs more and more victories to get that same sense of exhilaration—exactly like building up a tolerance to a drug.

The research bears this out. A 1981 study of more than 800 high-school students found that the self-concept of competitive teenagers was unusually dependent on how well they performed at certain tasks and on what others thought of them. Other studies have shown that competitive people—or people placed in competitive environments—are less likely than their peers to think that they can control the events that affect their lives.

Consider the consequences of different approaches to education. Children tend to have higher self-esteem when they can cooperate to help each other learn than when they must compete to become number one in the class. In 1989, David and Roger Johnson at the University of Minnesota reviewed 154 studies on this subject. Nearly half found no significant effect one way or the other between competition and cooperation, but of those that did find a difference in self-esteem, the score was eighty-one to one in favor of the cooperative classrooms.

Finally, if *character* refers to how we deal with other people, then it is even clearer that competition is more a destroyer than a builder. Over and over, studies find that competition produces people who are less generous and empathic, less trusting and sensitive to the needs of others, less likely to see things from someone else's point of view, and less likely to use higher level moral reasoning than those who are not competing (or are not personally competitive). As one health educator puts it, "In a sense, competition *does* build character. It just builds the wrong kind."

An elephant never forgets

Never? Well, hardly ever. The fact is that elephants do have rather impressive memories, although not necessarily the best in the animal kingdom. The classic monograph on the subject was published back in 1957 by a German zoologist who conducted some interesting research with our pachyderm pals. Professor B. Rensch heard wondrous tales in India of how these animals could memorize dozens of commands. Back in his laboratory, he taught an elephant to "prefer" one visual pattern over another and then repeated this for thirteen pairs of cards, each with a different design. A full year later, in over 500 trials, the beast remembered most of what he had learned—and also proved a quick study at learning and remembering differences in musical pitches. In all, Rensch wrote, "This was a truly impressive scientific demonstration of the adage that 'elephants never forget.' "

This faculty comes in handy when elephants pack their trunks for long trips: They have to remember a route they haven't taken for years and then find their way back. In fact, says Bill Langbauer, a Cornell University researcher who has spent time in west Africa studying elephants, they often travel more than 30 miles in search of water. "The most likely explanation for their being able to find these sources of water is that they remember where they are," he says.

Another bit of folk wisdom, however, has less validity: Elephants are not afraid of mice. Like any other plant-eating animal, they "get disturbed when there are sounds that they can't identify, but that has nothing to do with mice," says John Eisenberg, a wildlife expert at the University of Florida and coauthor of a book on mammalian behavior.

And speaking of mice, the common assumption that they are especially fond of cheese isn't really true either. Sure, they'll eat it—along with anything else that isn't nailed down. If farmers were more likely to leave cheese in the pantry than other foods, the fact that mice helped themselves to it might have led to the belief that a mouse loves nothing more than a properly aged Gorgonzola. But "mice also love peanut butter, oatmeal, and chocolate," says Joe Nadeau, a staff scientist at Jackson Laboratory in Maine, where thousands of mice are raised and sold for research. "In fact, you can catch mice with virtually anything."

Great minds think alike

Normally people invoke this saying both to congratulate and to mock themselves—such as when two friends independently come up with the same nonearth-shaking idea (for example, where to have dinner tonight). But what about the truly great minds? Do they really solve problems in a distinctive fashion that separates them from ordinary folks?

The psychologist and philosopher William James thought so, and in 1880 he described the "highest order of minds" as working this way:

Instead of thoughts of concrete things patiently following one another in a beaten track of habitual suggestion, we have the most abrupt cross-cuts and transitions from one idea to another . . . the most unheard of combinations of elements, the subtlest associations of analogy; in a word, we seem suddenly introduced into a seething cauldron of ideas, where everything is fizzling and bobbling about in a state of bewildering activity.

A century later, the creativity researcher Dean Keith Simonton, a psychology professor at the University of California at Davis, argued that James was on the right track. In his 1988 book *Scientific Genius,* Simonton reviewed the careers of some of science's leading lights. He concluded that they all seem to have the capacity to "generate remote associations to various ideas." They are naturally curious and likely to notice "unusual stimuli on the fringe of focused attention"—stuff that other people might dismiss as irrelevant or silly. Then highly creative people play with these stimuli and with their own reactions to them, often coming up with unpredictable, even bizarre connections. Their thinking is impulsive and flexible. They take intellectual risks, apparently unafraid to make mistakes or produce nonsense along the way. They seem driven, disciplined, and full of energy that allows them to *do* something with all these new ideas.

So does this mean that supercreative people think alike? Yes and no. "There's a contradiction there," says Simonton. "What's distinctive about their thinking is how unpredictable and dissimilar it is." On the one hand, "the similarities will loom larger than the contrasts"—even if one compares geniuses from different fields. (Galileo the scientist had more in common with Michelangelo the artist than either shared with the plodders in his own field, Simonton maintains.) On the other hand, what makes them similar is precisely that neither worked according to any set pattern. What they share is uniqueness.

Other psychologists aren't so sure, though. Ravenna Helson, who has been studying creativity since the late 1950s, suggests that highly creative people never give up—

but she admits that ordinary investigators can be just as tenacious. As for personal style, "one creative person finds inspiration in thick smoke, late hours and liquor, while another prefers the pure life and the early morning dew."

Boston University psychologist Robert Prentky adds a few more wrinkles. "We've had very brilliant minds that have produced little in the way of what we'd consider greatness," he says. Plus, some creative people work by drawing on enormous quantities of information to see where it all leads, while others push away everything except the question itself. Some need stimulation while others prefer solitude. And he agrees with Helson that "there's an enormous portion of the world that's obsessive and persistent but not terribly creative."

The implication here is that the search for characteristics that define great minds—and only great minds—may be a wild-goose chase. Howard Gardner, whose books include *Art, Mind, and Brain* and *Frames of Mind,* adds his voice to this skepticism. From a distance, exceptional scientists and artists may seem to share some features, but "the closer you get the more you become impressed by the differences," he says. In some respects, Darwin and Einstein might exhibit some similarities, but in other respects their cognitive styles had nothing in common.

"I don't think *any* two people think alike," Gardner says. "And great people probably think less alike than any other two people. The more a person is a genius, the more almost by definition he's not going to be like other people."

Carrots are good for your eyes

Carrots contain carotene, which your body turns into vitamin A. A complete deprivation of this vitamin, which is needed by the cells in your retina, would cause night blindness. But the human body has immense reserves of carotene stored in the liver, which are replenished from any number of foods. There is no real danger of running low, at least for people in the developed world. Ingesting vitamin A above the minimum you need doesn't do your eyes a bit of good. Practically speaking, then, there is no vision-related benefit to eating carrots.

Plead insanity and you can get away with murder

The plea of not guilty by reason of insanity is based on the idea that people should not be punished if they are not responsible for their actions. Consider someone who believes he received a command from space creatures (talking to him through his TV set) to kill his neighbor. Can such a person have what lawyers call *mens rea*—a "guilty mind"—and be held accountable for his actions in the way that you and I are? As long as his delusions persist, it may be necessary to keep him in a place where he can't do any harm. But should he be *punished*? For at least 150 years American and British law has suggested that the answer may be no.

People's resistance to the idea of an insanity plea rises in proportion to the ease and frequency with which it is thought to be invoked. When John Hinckley tried to assassinate Ronald Reagan in 1981, his lawyers successfully made use of this plea—eliciting massive public outrage and widespread calls for abolition (or at least restriction) of the defense.

The problem is that one celebrated case often leads us to assume that a given practice is widespread. The people who are reluctant to fly after hearing about a plane crash are not inclined to think about the thousands of planes that land safely every day or to compare the actual risk of dying in a plane to, say, the risk of dying in a car. Thus the question here is How many murderers actually get off on the grounds that they're crazy?

A comprehensive study of forensic referrals in Alaska from 1977 to 1981 turned up 150 cases in which at least one mental health expert doubted the sanity of a defendant. Forty-five defendants were found guilty anyway, and most of the rest were either found not guilty by reason of insanity (twenty-nine) or, usually for nonviolent crimes, had the charges dropped (sixty-seven). Even if we count both of the latter two categories, we are still talking about *one-tenth of 1 percent* of all criminal cases in the state during the period studied.

Other investigators, meanwhile, were scrutinizing the system in Oregon. They found, first, that only one out of eight defendants pleading insanity had been charged with murder or attempted murder; the defense was usually used, in other words, for less-serious crimes. Second, the plea was rejected in four out of every five cases. Third, the proportion of felonies that ended in a finding of "not guilty by reason of insanity" was about one-half of 1 percent.

In Massachusetts, the same pattern appeared: For the years 1978, 1980, and 1982, less than 1 percent of defendants who received a sentence were found not guilty by reason of insanity, and of that tiny group only one out of twenty had committed murder.

Supplementing these figures is the first large-scale, multistate study of the insanity defense, which is now underway. While it has not yet been published, there are already enough data to refute the idea that people routinely escape punishment by claiming they're insane. After five years of collecting statistics from eight states, the researchers, funded by the National Institute of Mental Health, have found that insanity pleas are only *offered* in 2 or 3 percent of felony cases, and most of those pleas don't get anywhere. To be successful, it is almost always necessary that the defendant be diagnosed as schizophrenic—which does not mean, incidentally, that most schizophrenics are dangerous—and already have spent time in psychiatric hospitals. Just doing something horrendous or saying you were out of your mind is not enough.

Henry J. Steadman, adjunct professor of sociology at the State University of New York at Albany, is heading up the study. "It's relatively rare to raise an insanity plea even in a homicide case," he concludes, "and simply raising it doesn't at all ensure success." Moreover, defendants who are found insane are typically incarcerated for just about the same length of time that they would have spent in prison—and they are *less* likely than convicted felons to commit another crime when they are finally released.

Ultimately, people will make up their minds about the virtues of the insanity plea based on their beliefs about the nature of responsibility and the proper role of punishment. But if opposition to it is based on the frequency with which criminals actually use this plea, it's useful to see just how rarely it keeps killers out of prison.

Another common belief is that criminals regularly escape conviction on a "technicality": a smart lawyer need only point out that the arresting officer made some trivial error and—presto—the murderer or rapist is back out on the street.

Once again, these cases make good newspaper copy but are relatively rare. The General Accounting Office looked at nearly 3,000 cases in federal courts around the country and found that a motion to suppress evidence based on improper search or seizure of evidence was granted in only about one case in a hundred. Data from California prosecutors, meanwhile, suggest that things aren't all that different in state courts. There, about 2 percent of felony convictions were rejected by prosecutors or thrown out by judges because Constitutional protections were ignored by the police. For crimes of violence, the rate was even lower. A 1983 review of this and several other studies in the *American Bar Foundation Research Journal* concluded that the effect of the so-called exclusionary rule on criminal prosecutions is "marginal at best."

Playing hard to get makes one more attractive

Trying to appear less attracted to a potential love interest than one actually is—in the hopes of fanning the other's passion—amounts to nothing more than deception. It is gamesmanship, posturing, and as such would seem a poor foundation on which to build a relationship.

That said, we turn to the question of whether it is likely to work. A careful reading of four sets of studies offers a reminder that simple ideas, too, can be hard to "get"—or at least hard to nail down in social psychology experiments. How do you distinguish between selectivity and rejection—which could have very different effects on a would-be suitor—or between someone who doesn't like you and someone who simply doesn't want to date you? Even if we could tease these apart, it's not immediately clear which provides the best test of the folk wisdom.

Of course, some people are not playing—they really *are* hard to get because of external obstacles—such as disapproving parents. The so-called Romeo and Juliet effect received limited confirmation from a 1972 study of both dating and married couples that found a significant correlation between expressions of romantic love and reports of parental interference. However, this interference was also associated with less trust and more criticism between partners, leading the researchers to predict that if parents continued to make things difficult, their efforts eventually would be "likely to undermine the overall quality of the [children's] relationship."

In any case, we usually use the expression "hard to get" to indicate that someone is pretending not to be interested or is otherwise regarded as unattainable. Already convinced that such people are more attractive, Elaine Walster and her colleagues asked college men why this was so. They explained that if a woman can afford to be selective, she must have something going for her; besides, trying to win her heart presents an intriguing challenge. An easy-to-get woman, by contrast, must be desperate and might even (one shudders at the thought) demand a commitment from the man. "We then conducted five experiments designed to demonstrate that an individual values a hard-to-get date more highly than an easy-to-get date," the researchers reported. "All five experiments failed."

In the first two studies, teenagers were shown photos and biographies of a couple and were told how romantically interested one was in the other. It turned out that the teens rated that person as more socially desirable if he or she had expressed a *higher* level of interest in the other. In the next two experiments, men used a computer dating service to meet women, some of whom had been instructed either to pause before accepting an invitation for a second date or to decline and then change their minds. The men, however, didn't like these women any more than those who said yes right away. Finally, when prostitutes (who, in yet another example of professionalism in social psychology, had been asked to work with the researchers) told clients that their schedules would henceforth allow them to see only their favorite johns, these men were slightly *less* likely to call again.

Walster and company went back to their male college informants, this time demanding to know why a hard-to-get woman might *not* be attractive. Always eager to please, the guys now explained that such a woman might be cold, inflexible, or likely to humiliate them. This led to experiment number six, in which it turned out that male students loved the sort of woman who would seem fussy about most people . . . but interested in them. They wanted, in other words, someone who would pick them out of a crowd.

There's reason to doubt that this last study succeeds in resurrecting the hard-to-get hypothesis: The men may have simply felt flattered. In fact, Karen A. Matthews and her colleagues showed several years later that even this sort of selectivity might not be appealing to everyone. Both male and female college students were shown how someone of the opposite sex had allegedly rated a bunch of people, including themselves. These subjects tended to prefer undiscriminating raters—and they didn't seem to like someone any more just because he or she had expressed approval only for them. Of course, there was no promise of an actual date here, but the point is that selectivity itself wasn't seen as a plus.

In 1986, Rex A. Wright, having already published a paper arguing that any goal is less attractive if it's too easy or too difficult to attain, joined with a colleague in taking one more shot at the question. Sure enough, they found that moderately selective individuals were judged by college students as being more desirable than either those who would "go 'steady' with almost anyone" *or* those who hadn't yet met a single person they "liked enough to go 'steady' with." It being the eighties and all, these students may have simply been confused by the use of this quaint slang, but several other experiments confirmed that people of the opposite sex seem most appealing when they're a little bit discriminating.

That undergraduates have their doubts about someone who's hot for anything on two legs, however, hardly constitutes an endorsement for pretending that you're bored by someone who likes you. Taken collectively, the research on the subject raises more doubts than it allays about the wisdom of playing hard to get.

You can catch cold from being chilled—and cure it with chicken soup

More people come down with colds during the winter than during the summer, but that doesn't mean lower temperatures are responsible. It could be that the cold weather brings us closer together for longer periods where we can infect each other. The only way to catch a cold is to be exposed to one of the relevant viruses, most of which are called rhinoviruses. You can sit on an ice floe in Antarctica until the penguins come home and not catch cold if there's no one around to give you the virus. In fact, it's possible to have the virus and still not develop any cold symptoms.

Of course, it's conceivable that walking around without a coat can lower your resistance and thus reduce your chances of fighting off the virus once you've been exposed to it. But the limited research on this question suggests that temperature really doesn't seem to matter. Back in 1958, more than 400 subjects were exposed to colds and also to temperatures of either 10 degrees (in heavy coats), 60 degrees (in their underwear) or 80 degrees Fahrenheit. They all got sick at about the same rate.

Ten years later, three Texas researchers repeated the experiment, but with important improvements. They dropped the actual rhinovirus into their subjects' noses, making infection all but certain. (Earlier experiments couldn't do that because the first strain of rhinovirus wasn't discovered until 1956 and made available for laboratory use after that.) Then they exposed the subjects—forty-nine men borrowed from the local prison—to low temperatures, and they made a point of doing so at different times, ranging from initial infection to recovery. Some of the men sat around in their underwear for a couple of hours in forty degree weather or were submerged in water just cool enough to bring down their body temperatures. It turned out that neither the frequency nor the severity of their colds was greater than that of the men who were not exposed to lower temperatures. For at least this one rhinovirus, then— and remember that when we talk about "the common cold," we are actually using an umbrella term that refers to quite a few different varieties—it seems that we neither catch colds nor make them worse by being exposed to cold weather.

This, however, doesn't tell us how we *do* catch cold—that is, how the rhinovirus is passed from one person to the next in real life. You'd think this would be known by now, but the answer keeps changing. At first all the experts thought the virus was spread through the air. ("Cover your mouth when you cough!") Then Jack M. Gwaltney, Jr. and his colleagues at the University of Virginia announced that that theory should be discarded: The primary route of transmission is actually from A's nose to A's fingers (sometimes to an object) to B's fingers to B's nose. ("Wash your hands if you're sick!")

In what has to be one of the most unappetizing experiments ever conducted, Gwaltney asked several infected subjects to blow their noses into their hands and then stroke the fingers of fifteen other people who, in turn, had to touch their own noses. No information is reported about the number who lost their lunch, but eleven of the fifteen caught the virus and nine of them actually came down with colds. On the other hand, when twenty-two subjects were coughed at, sneezed at, or breathed on for a while by infected people, only one got sick. At least one previous study had shown that colds are rarely spread through coughing. With his 1978 experiment, Gwaltney seemed to clinch the case against airborne transmission.

But wait. Three years earlier, British researcher Sylvia Reed had found that while the rhinovirus could survive for three days on various objects—in this case, spoons, pens, and plastic tabletops—and while it could be transferred to someone's fingers *from* those objects, it wasn't easy getting the virus *to* the objects just by having a sick person touch them. So how do people who don't blow their noses into their hands make each other sick?

In 1987, Elliot C. Dick and his colleagues at the University of Wisconsin tried to figure out once and for all whether we're more likely to catch a cold from breathing or touching. He infected several students with the rhinovirus and had them play a marathon twelve-hour poker game with other people, which involved handling cards and chips that were literally gummy with infected mucus. A few of these students wore plastic collars or arm restraints that prevented them from touching their noses, meaning that they could be infected only through the air. And indeed they did become infected—at the same rates as those who breathed *and* touched the virus. Then Dick set up a barrier between some of the players so they exchanged germ-laden cards but had clean air. No one in this group caught cold.

In a later experiment, the Wisconsin researchers used a

sophisticated mechanism for recovering and measuring the cold virus on fingers, noses, chips, and cards. They concluded that while sick people may be covered with germs, few make it to the objects they touch, and not many of those that do will ever reach the other person's nose. So, as a 1988 editorial in *The Lancet* concluded, "For the moment it looks as though coughs and sneezes *do* spread these diseases more often than sticky fingers."

Why didn't Gwaltney's sneezed-on subjects get sick, then? Apparently they weren't exposed long enough. "It takes a lot more than forty-five minutes to get transmission," Dick says. The surprising finding that emerges from all this research is that it's harder to get sick than most of us think. It takes a lot of time to become infected by air, and the only other way to contract the virus is by directly touching someone else's wet mucus and then immediately bringing your fingers to your nostrils, which is probably not the sort of thing you're likely to do for fun. (If it is, kindly keep the details to yourself.) In fact, as Dick and his coworkers showed in a 1984 experiment, even *kissing* someone who's sick is probably safe: Of sixteen people who smooched for at least a full minute with an infected individual, only one caught a cold. (The mouth is, as subsequent tests showed, a far less efficient route of transmission than the nose.)

In sum, hanging around a coughing, sneezing cold sufferer for several hours and touching his or her personal property probably won't make you sick. Even if you *live* with someone who has a cold, the chances are still only fifty-fifty that you'll be missing work by the end of the week.

This contradicts what is common knowledge on the subject, but maybe it shouldn't be surprising that pop epidemiology is so untrustworthy. After all, when was the last time you came down with a cold or the flu and someone *didn't* say, "Oh, yeah—something's going around now"? And maybe it shouldn't be surprising that folk wisdom is just as worthless when it comes to finding cures. Feed a cold?

Starve a cold? It doesn't make much difference, says Gwaltney. He invokes a somewhat more recent, and more accurate, adage: "Treat a cold and it'll go away in seven days; don't treat it and it'll take a week."

But surely chicken soup will help, no? Maimonides, the twelfth-century philosopher and physician, recommended it for everything from asthma to leprosy to sexual dysfunction. (Not for nothing is he a major figure in Jewish thought.) In 1978, everyone was talking about a study conducted by researchers in Miami Beach (where else?) that seemed to revive this fowl remedy.

However, the entertaining news coverage about the experiment didn't emphasize that all fifteen subjects were healthy. Marvin A. Sackner and his colleagues weren't interested in rhinoviruses, only in "nasal mucus velocity"—measured by an elaborate apparatus which is, alas, unavailable for holiday gift-giving—on the theory that the faster the mucus travels, the faster it'll take the germs out of your system. Sipping about 6 ounces of chicken broth did get the fluids moving faster, but so did sipping plain old secular hot water. All the fuss about the study came from the fact that drinking soup through a straw also had a slight effect, while drinking hot water through a straw did not. In any case, the effect from all of these treatments lasted less than half an hour, suggesting that no self-respecting rhinovirus will lose sleep over the fact that you plan to drink chicken soup next time you have a cold.

Picking up babies every time they cry will only spoil them

Here is a familiar scenario, as Jean Liedloff describes it in her unforgettable book, *The Continuum Concept:* The loving mother, having been taught that infants must sleep in a separate room and learn to be independent, kisses her baby's cheek tenderly and heads for the door. As she closes it behind her, he starts to shriek. He sounds like he is being tortured—and, in fact, he is. Human beings are not *meant* to be alone during the first half-year of life, Liedloff argues. Any number of psychological problems that plague older children and adults can be traced back to their having been deprived of body contact and warmth when they most needed it.

Many of us assume that responding to children whenever they cry or ask to be held will only make them dependent on us. In fact, Liedloff and others reply, exactly the opposite is true. Infants who are reassured by the constant presence of a parent in early life have their emotional needs fulfilled and can become more *independent* as a result; confident that the world is a safe place, they can venture forth happily to explore it. By contrast, those who are left to cry themselves to sleep—or who, in general, learn they cannot count on a loving adult to soothe them when they need it—may spend their lives searching for the love, affection, and simple physical contact that was denied them during their earliest days.

Taking this view seriously raises a host of practical questions and objections, at least for parents in industrialized cultures where each family is pretty much on its own and where both parents often must work. But if there is even a small chance that Liedloff is right, then the implications are mind-boggling and the urgency of rethinking how we raise our children—and, by implication, how we organize our society—cannot be overstated.

Let me be clear that I am talking about comforting babies when they need it, not buying children every toy or granting them every privilege they demand. There is a huge difference between being responsive to a child's needs, which is motivated by love, and being afraid to say no, which is motivated by the parent's fear of losing the child's love. The latter isn't recommended, but the more tragic problem is that many parents are so afraid of spoiling their children (or of being accused of this by relatives and friends) that they ignore desperate cries for care and attention. This may be the ultimate example of throwing out the baby with the bathwater, and it may create exactly the sort of dependence and neediness from which these parents want to free their children.

Every parent, grandparent, pediatrician, and psychotherapist has an opinion on this general question, but controlled studies are hard to find. The one classic piece of research that does address how one should deal with a crying baby supports Liedloff's view and challenges the folk wisdom. Silvia Bell and Mary Ainsworth, then at Johns Hopkins University, followed twenty-six mothers and their infants for a full year, observing them every few weeks and taking note of how often (and how long) the babies cried and what their moms did about it.

The results, published in 1972, are striking. Bell and Ainsworth divided the year into quarters and matched the mother's behavior in one three-month segment with the baby's behavior in the next. They found that the more a mother tended to ignore a cry (or the longer she took to respond to it), the more likely the baby was to cry in the following quarter. In fact, a mother who didn't respond set a vicious circle into motion: Ignoring the newborn's cries led to more crying as the baby grew, which further discouraged the mother from responding promptly, which made the baby even more irritable, and so on.

Bell and Ainsworth's conclusion should ring in the ears of every parent:

> [Some mothers] are deliberately unresponsive, in the belief that to respond will make a baby demanding, dependent, and "spoiled." Our data suggest the contrary—that those infants who are conspicuous for fussing and crying after the first few months of life, and who fit the stereotype of the "spoiled child," are those whose mothers have ignored their cries or have delayed long in responding to them. . . . [By contrast,] infants whose mothers have given them relatively much tender and affectionate holding in the earliest months of life are content with surprisingly little physical contact by the end of the first year; although they enjoy being held, when put down they are happy to move off into independent exploratory play. . . . [They] have less occasion to cry—not only in the first months but throughout infancy.

Power corrupts

The interesting question here is whether a position of power has a corrupting effect or whether people who are already corrupt gravitate to positions of power. More broadly, social scientists have spent decades debating which is more important: who we are or what kind of situation we find ourselves in.

This dispute is far too complicated to be resolved in a few paragraphs. Even the specific question about power isn't easy. But we can hardly help noticing how many of us, at least in this culture, are inclined to attribute human behavior to individual character and to overlook the structures in which we live. If people commit crimes, we say they are evil; if people are on welfare, we say they are lazy; if children fail to learn, we say they aren't studying hard enough. We treat each instance of criminal behavior, poverty, or poor learning as if it had never happened before and as if the individual in question was acting out of sheer perversity.

The problem isn't just that this approach is oversimplified, although it surely is. It's that we ignore the historical, political, and economic structures that help to shape the kind of people we are—probably because it's easier to blame someone in distress than to figure out what deeper forces might have played a role in making him or her that way. Once we acknowledge the importance of these forces, we might have to do something to change them.

Perhaps the most famous experiment regarding the effects of power was conducted by Philip Zimbardo and his colleagues at Stanford University. They set out to test what happens to people when they're imprisoned by choosing twenty-one male college students to take on the roles of guards and inmates in a very realistic "jail" created in the basement of the psychology building. The twenty-one subjects were selected from a group of seventy-five volunteers precisely on the basis of their normality: They were stable and scored in the middle range of a personality profile. Equally important, they were randomly assigned to the role of prisoner or guard.

Almost immediately, the subjects began to take on the pathological characteristics of their respective roles. The guards delighted in devising arbitrary tasks and absurd rules for the inmates, demanding absolute obedience and forcing them to humiliate each other. The prisoners became passive and obedient, taking their frustration out on each other and otherwise assuming the role of victim. As the guards became more abusive, the prisoners became more helpless and dependent. The patterns became so pronounced that Zimbardo grew alarmed and ended what was to have been a two-week experiment after only six days.

Given the design of this study, what happened cannot be explained in terms of the individuals involved. The researchers, like the subjects, had been inclined to "focus on personality traits as internal dispositions for individuals to respond in particular ways," said Zimbardo, thus "underestimat[ing] the subtle power of situational forces to control and reshape their behavior." Specifically, it seemed to be the power given to the young men by virtue of their role as guard that "corrupted" them.

Zimbardo argued that most of us make the same error, which leads us to try to solve problems by "changing the people, by motivating them, isolating them . . . and so on." In fact, he concluded, "to change behavior we must discover the institutional supports which maintain the existing undesirable behavior and then design programs to alter these environments." Individuals' personalities matter, but so, too, do the situations in which those personalities develop and interact.

Boston drivers are the worst

"Ingrained collective insanity"—that's how a social psychologist I know described driving in the Boston area soon after he came to town. Indeed, the Boston Driver has become legendary across the United States for viewing lanes as mere suggestions, for reading STOP as SLOW DOWN A LITTLE, and for improving on the concept of "right turn on red" by expanding it to include "left turn on red" and "straight ahead on red." Put it this way: If a Boston Driver were having dinner with you, he wouldn't reach across you for the rolls, he'd simply take one off your plate—while shouting an obscenity at you. By the time tourists return home from Boston, they can no longer remember Walden Pond, the Old North Church, or Harvard; what lingers is the experience of having been cut off by cars turning left from the right-hand lane in a traffic rotary.

Those who travel abroad insist that even Boston seems serene compared to certain cities in other parts of the world. But are Boston roads really the most likely places to be driven crazy in the United States? As a Bostonian, my own sanity is at stake here, so I wanted to be absolutely sure. Several years ago, I collected statistics on collision claims received by auto insurance companies in selected American cities; then I adjusted the figures to correct for population disparities. Based on 1983 data, Boston was miles ahead of the competition, with an astounding twenty collision claims for every hundred drivers that year. New

York City and Chicago drivers reported accidents at a rate of just over twelve per hundred. By the time you got to Phoenix, the rate was below seven.

The trouble with my little survey, as someone subsequently pointed out to me, was that a lot of drivers don't bother to carry collision coverage. Thus these claims may not accurately reflect what goes on in the streets. I tried again more recently with another measure: requests for compensation under the category of liability protection—a form of coverage that is nearly universal. Data were unavailable for Dallas, Houston, and Detroit because of unusual record-keeping procedures, but here are the rates in other large cities, based on statistics for either 1987 or mid-1987 through mid-1988. Again, the figures represent the number of claims per 100 drivers.

Newark	10.8
Boston	10.6
Baltimore	7.0
Los Angeles	5.8
Washington, D.C.	5.7
San Francisco	5.5
New Orleans	5.3
Chicago	5.2
Cleveland	4.9
Miami	4.6
Seattle	4.3
Philadelphia	4.2
San Diego	4.2
Atlanta	4.1
Jacksonville	4.1
New York City (Manhattan)	3.7

This is not the last word on the subject: Just as I had neglected to request the figures for Newark on my first pass, so I might have left out some other dangerous city this time around. Moreover, 1987 might have been atypical for some reason; we can have only limited confidence in a ranking based on data for a single year. Finally, there may be a better measure of bad driving than the number of liability claims filed. For the time being, though, visitors to Boston might want to check on the availability of rental tanks.

You're never too old to learn vs. You can't teach an old dog new tricks

Many cultures have long assumed that age brings wisdom, tolerance, and understanding. Indeed, it may be true that as people turn gray, they are less inclined to see everything in blacks and whites. But as a rule, older adults seem to have more difficulties with intellectual functioning than younger adults do. Several studies have shown that elderly people construct fewer categories in organizing information. Other research suggests that they not only have more trouble remembering things they have read or heard, but they also are less likely to distinguish between more- and less-important ideas in a text.

How do we know that what is true of older people is really due to the process of aging, though? As we saw with tracking political beliefs ("People become more conservative as they get older," pp. 17–19), the difference might be a function of some characteristic of the particular group of people born in the early part of the century, such as the fact that they received less formal schooling than people born later. That's why Warner Schaie and Christopher Hertzog at The Pennsylvania State University began following a group of 162 people in 1956 to see how intelligence changes over time. They found, using a number of different measures, that there was indeed a decline in ability that became evident after age sixty. (Of course, the fact that this is true as a general rule doesn't exclude the possibility that *some* seventy year olds may experience little or no decline—and may be a good deal sharper than some thirty year olds. But that, as two researchers reminded their fellow psychologists several years ago, shouldn't prevent us from acknowledging the existence of a general pattern.)

In any case, the interesting question is whether these older people can be taught new tricks that will compensate for or reverse this decline. Here we find room for qualified optimism: Training sessions often do improve the memories of people over sixty. It helps, for example, to be shown how to keep rehearsing all the items on a list rather than just the most recent one. On the other hand, studies suggest that (1) the effects of such strategies don't always last very long, (2) the skills learned on one task aren't always transferred effectively to other situations, and (3) memory rarely can be brought all the way back to the level of younger adults.

Two studies published in 1986 indicate that more meaningful sorts of intellectual functioning (as opposed to simple memory) also can be enhanced artificially—again with certain caveats. Paul Baltes and his colleagues at the Max Planck Institute in Berlin put more than 200 seniors through a training program that helped them to identify rules and concepts that would allow them to solve problems better on intelligence tests. The subjects' scores did improve. Although they had begun to fall back six months later, they were still ahead of where they were before the training began.

The other study was conducted by Schaie and Sherry L. Willis. A group of subjects (average age: seventy-three) went through five one-hour training sessions that included work on reasoning and spatial skills. They were then tested and compared to their own levels of fourteen years earlier. The training brought 40 percent of them back to their previous mark and helped many others to a less dramatic extent.

For a "substantial proportion" of older people, Schaie and Willis concluded, "observed cognitive decline is not irreversible, is likely to be attributable to disuse, and can be subjected to environmental manipulations involving relatively simple and inexpensive educational training techniques."

Similarly reassuring is the news that older people, contrary to the conventional wisdom, are not any more depressed than those who haven't lived as long. Polls in the 1940s and 1950s did show a moderate negative relation between age and happiness, but that association subsequently disappeared. In 1985, Marjorie Chary Feinson reviewed the results of twenty-seven studies on the question. In six, older adults reported more distress than younger adults (although in only three of them was it clear that the differences were greater than could have been expected by chance); in another three, the findings were mixed. The rest of the studies—eighteen of twenty-seven—found either that age was unrelated to distress or that older people were *less* unhappy than younger folks. The idea that growing old means growing depressed is a myth, Feinson concludes.

Don't marry your cousin

It is commonly believed that relatives who marry and have children, a practice known as inbreeding or consanguineous reproduction, are flirting with disaster. Never mind incest—even first-cousin marriages are against the law in many places because they are assumed to produce children who are deformed, diseased, or likely to die young. Do epidemiological studies support these fears?

Most of our inherited features—even eye color—are actually the result of an interaction among several genes. But some diseases are caused by just one. Usually these diseases are recessive, meaning that only if both parents are carrying that particular gene is it possible (though not certain) that their children will be born with the disease. And parents who are related to each other share more genes than two people picked at random: First cousins, for example, have about one-eighth of their genes in common. Thus the probability of having a child with an inherited, recessive, single-gene disease is somewhat higher for consanguineous couples.

How much higher? A number of studies, most of them conducted in Japan, India, and Brazil, have attempted to quantify the risk. Unfortunately, much of the early research didn't take into account the fact that poor, rural, and uneducated people are more likely than others to marry relatives—and also more likely, for various other reasons, to have children who die young. Thus simply figuring out the rate of child mortality (death) or morbidity (illness) among consanguineous couples doesn't prove that the inbreeding itself is responsible. This is particularly true since single-gene diseases are not a leading cause of death.

What has to be done, then, is to compare the children of consanguineous and nonconsanguineous couples who are at the same social and economic levels. Newer research along these lines has found that marrying your first cousin is much less chancy than people used to think—but not entirely safe. The risk, in the words of Muin J. Khoury, a medical epidemiologist at the Centers for Disease Control, is "small but measurable." William Schull, whose 1965 study of inbreeding in Japan is one of the classics in the field, estimates that the offspring of first-cousin parents are twice as likely as other infants to have the sort of severe congenital defect that can be recognized right at birth, but this means a risk of only about 2 to 4 percent instead of 1 to 2 percent. A 1976 study concludes even more optimistically that the risk of first-cousin parents having a child with a recessively inherited disease is less than 1 percent.

Even these small numbers may overstate the risk because they represent an average for all parents, including those from groups that have high rates of certain single-gene diseases. If genetic counseling suggests that neither of two related parents is at special risk, then there is no reason to think their children will be different from anyone else's.

In most of the world, and particularly in Europe and North America, this whole discussion is fairly academic because inbreeding has declined markedly over the last century. There are pockets where it remains, however, such as Beirut, where very recent research suggests that one out of four marriages is between relatives, and there is no sign that this practice is on the way out. But even if consanguineous reproduction were thriving around the world, researchers agree that it still would not be a significant contributor to premature death. If the practice were eliminated tomorrow, childhood mortality would drop by only a few percentage points at best. All told, the idea that kissing cousins are sure to produce a diseased or disabled child represents a much exaggerated version of a simple genetic truth.

Female praying mantises eat their mates

She doesn't bother to ask whether it was good for him, too, because she's already bitten off his head just before copulating. If you still believe this is always true of sex between praying mantises, you must have missed the August 1984 issue of *Animal Behaviour.* * That's when Eckehard Liske and W. Jackson Davis confessed to making insect porno movies: videotapes of thirty pairs of praying mantises going all the way. For centuries it was thought not only that the female decapitates the male prior to mating, but that this was somehow necessary for reproduction to take place (which lends new meaning to the idea of wanting someone only for his body). Liske and Davis recorded an elaborate sequence of body posturing on the part of both partners, but not a single male lost his head over a mantis mistress.

A little time in the library revealed to these researchers that other scientists, too, had observed nonlethal matings of the bugs. They speculate that when females *do* decapitate their mates, this is "an artifact of captivity." Specifically, earlier investigators may have distracted the mantises, which led to an unusual display of aggressive behavior, or else they simply failed to feed them enough in

*Either that or you were too busy reading the article "Why Does the Herring Gull Lay Three Eggs?" in the same issue.

the laboratory. However unsettling it may seem to us, a handsome male may appear to a hungry mate as lunch first and lover second.

Beauty is in the eye of the beholder

Attractive people are regularly seen as possessing a variety of desirable features (see "Beauty is only skin deep," pp. 25–27); what is beautiful becomes good. But Alan E. Gross and Christine Crofton of the University of Missouri wondered in the mid-1970s whether it is also true that what is good becomes beautiful. In other words, do our judgments of someone's appearance rest partly on perceptions of what kind of person he or she is?

Gross and Crofton sorted photos of people by their attractiveness and then made up personality descriptions for each of them. Some were presented as good students, friendly, energetic, and so on; others as average; and a third group as losers. Subjects were asked to say how attractive they found these students, and it turned out that the more favorably described they were, the better looking they were judged to be. (Other researchers, trying to replicate this effect, found that only women were said to be more attractive as a result of the descriptions about their character.)

This seems to make sense. After all, you may well grow to find someone good-looking after becoming fond of him or her for other reasons. To take another sort of example, children are more likely to be seen as cute when rated by their own parents than when judged by strangers. And other factors, too—not merely knowing an individual—can affect the perception of beauty: James Pennebaker and his associates at the University of Virginia found that as the evening wore on, men sitting in bars rated the women around them as increasingly good-looking—likewise for the women's judgment of the men—thus confirming a country-and-western song lyric that "the girls all get prettier at closing time." The more general conclusion is that the eye of the beholder does define beauty: There are no absolute benchmarks where esthetics are concerned.

On the other hand, one of the most intriguing things about all the studies showing that we ascribe superior qualities to attractive people is that the researchers who conduct these experiments never seem to have any trouble deciding how attractive their subjects are. They don't call attention to this fact, but it dawns on you after reading a bunch of these reports: When several experimenters or subjects must independently sort photographs or rank people on the basis of appearance—the first step toward measuring judgments about these people—the level of agreement between their ratings is exceptionally high. Perhaps our culture is the "beholder" and most of us share a sense of what it means to be good-looking.

Expressing hostility gets it out of your system

Get out that number two pencil and let's take a little quiz. I'll describe a few experiments; you guess the results. Ready?

1. A group of third-, fourth-, and fifth-grade boys watch a short boxing video, while others either watch gymnastics or just sit quietly. For the next few minutes, the experimenters keep an eye on all the boys to see how they act. It turns out that those

who saw the heavyweight championship (a) are less likely to shove or hit someone who makes them mad (because watching the boxing has purged them of aggressiveness). (b) are just as aggressive as anyone else. (c) are more aggressive than the others.

2. One day, a bunch of engineers and technicians, already disgruntled at the way they've been treated by the California aerospace firm they work for, are told they are being laid off. Psychologists come in to interview these employees, and they encourage some of them to express their hostility toward the company. Afterward, all the workers fill out a questionnaire designed to measure aggression. Those who had just finished verbally blasting their employer are now (a) less hostile toward the company (because they've had a chance to blow off some steam). (b) no different from the other employees. (c) more hostile than everyone else.

3. Male college students are given electric shocks by someone who is (unbeknownst to them) in cahoots with the researcher. This gets them plenty irritated. Next, each student is asked to teach a maze task to the very guy who had just angered him, and some are told to use electric shocks as a teaching aid. This means they get to zap the fellow who had just zapped them. Finally, the subjects are asked to teach the same person another task, but this time are given a choice as to how strong a shock to deliver. What happens? The guys who already had been given a chance to retaliate (a) go easy on the juice (because they had vented their anger the first time around). (b) choose the same voltage as the subjects who hadn't had a chance to zap their persecutors earlier. (c) are even more aggressive than the other subjects.

The answers are (c), (c), and (c). See?

These and dozens of other studies were designed to investigate the popular idea that anger or aggression builds up inside us like steam in a boiler. If we don't periodically vent this pressure, it is said that we will explode into violence. If we *do* vent it (by watching or participating in aggression or simply by expressing anger), we will calm down.

This is an appealing model because it's so easy to visualize. It is also false. Not only is aggression more a function of external stimulation than a spontaneous force (see "Humans are naturally aggressive," pp. 69–72), but researchers also have shown that over the long haul expressing hostility is likely to make us *more* aggressive or angry than when we started.

This doesn't mean that the whole idea of "catharsis," which comes from Aristotle's idea that we can be purged of unpleasant emotions by watching tragic dramas, is worthless. James Pennebaker, having moved beyond research on perceived attractiveness in bars (see p. 112), devised a series of interesting experiments to show that talking about your problems, describing traumatic experiences, and expressing grief can (at least to a point) relieve stress and help you to be less preoccupied with what's been bothering you. In this sense, it's true that "keeping everything inside" isn't a great idea.

But anger and aggression—that's a different story. Most studies have discovered that athletes and sports spectators are more likely to find their aggression increasing rather than decreasing, both in the short-term and over longer periods. The same is true for watching violent movies, shooting guns, delivering electric shocks, and expressing verbal hostility. These activities don't "get it out of your system"; they tend to lower your inhibitions against violence so you are more apt to respond that way again. They direct your attention to the object of your anger and teach you to respond aggressively.

A few researchers have found that under very specific circumstances, reacting violently to a person who has angered you may indeed calm you down right afterward. But other psychologists suspect that something other than real catharsis is going on here: It may be guilt over having hurt someone that reduces your anger. It may be a primitive sense of justice that is satisfied by aggressing against an aggressor.

Or it may be that *any* response that has proven effective at dealing with someone else's aggression can quiet you down. This last theory has two important implications. First, it means that there is nothing about "human nature" to suggest that violence is the only (or even the best) response to violence. If I've learned that my anger toward others usually evaporates, say, when I punish myself or when I crack a joke, then either of these strategies would become just as cathartic as screaming or punching.

Second, the theory means that while hurting you may "vent" my rage today, this result will only reinforce the anger for tomorrow. "Every instance in which aggression alleviates anger increases the probability that aggression will occur in future cases of anger inducement"—and it may take less and less anger to trigger that aggression, according to Vladimir J. Konečni, a leading student of the catharsis effect. In other words, I get in the habit of lashing out to make myself feel better and I become a more aggressive person.

Keep in mind that these are reflections on the few studies to have found that acting violently seems to "drain" some people's aggression. But the majority of experiments show just the opposite. In addition to those I've already mentioned, consider the fact that yelling at each other and hitting each other are behaviors that often go together in married couples, according to a study by Murray Straus.

Similarly, combative sports and a tendency to make war often go together, according to a study of twenty cultures by Richard G. Sipes. Both findings suggest that supposedly harmless ways of expressing aggression (yelling or playing rough games) do not reduce the chances of taking part in harmful aggression as the catharsis theory would predict.

All of this raises some serious questions about approaches to psychotherapy that encourage individuals to "work out" or "discharge" their hostility—say, by screaming or swinging foam rubber bats—or that encourage couples to vent their rage at each other. "My clients do not need to learn how to express anger," says psychotherapist Bernie Zilbergeld. "They need to learn how to shut up."

This may be a bit of an overstatement. Shutting up doesn't solve problems, after all, but neither does simple ventilation of anger. What people really need to do is to understand what's making them angry—and then figure out what they can do about it. After quoting Zilbergeld's remarks, psychologist Carol Tavris summarizes the available research by saying that regardless of how someone came to be angry,

> frequent talking about it, expressing it, acting on it, and otherwise "releasing" it have cumulatively unhealthy effects: Such repeated anger expression tends to solidify a hostile attitude, emphasize the emotion of anger to the exclusion of other, simultaneous emotions; . . . create an angry habit; rile up one's opposition; and, in many cases, make people angrier instead of less angry.

In a book called *Anger,* Tavris puts it more succinctly: "Letting off steam can make the atmosphere very hot and humid."

Fright can turn your hair white overnight

Such reports have been around for a long time, but typically they "sound more like fairy tales than scientific observations," as a German doctor wrote back in 1866. Authenticated cases of sudden whitening of the hair are awfully hard to come by. The most recent article on the subject I could find in an English-language medical journal was published more than two decades ago. It described a forty-five-year-old man who had developed a disease that caused most of his brown hair to fall out, leaving only the white hair. This gave the impression that his hair had *turned* white.

Something similar probably accounts for most, if not all, tales of sudden whitening, according to the six specialists I checked with. Presumably a disease—usually one called alopecia areata—selectively attacks the dark hairs. An expert on pigment, James J. Nordlund, says the idea that "white hair and black hair would have different responses to stimuli makes perfect sense, although we don't understand the phenomenon." (For that matter, it's not even fully understood why our hair normally turns gray or white as we age.)

In theory, there are two other possible explanations. One is that each dark hair that falls out is replaced by a white hair. Another, more controversial, view is that a stress-induced illness can screw up the relation between the cell that makes hair and the cell that makes pigment. The hair above the scalp doesn't have any blood supply or nerves—it's essentially inert matter—but the part below the surface is very much alive and it could cause changes all the way to the tip.

The problem with these two explanations is that both processes would take a very long time—probably months. Nothing short of a visit to a beauty parlor can actually cause the hair to change color overnight. So if cases really exist of people whose hair seems to go white very quickly, we're back to our original theory: These folks had had some white hair mixed in with the dark all along, and only the latter fell out.

While we're brushing off false beliefs, here's another: The more you cut your hair, the faster it will grow. That's what they say, but it's not true—regardless of whether we're talking about scalp, face, or body hair. When the hairs start to grow back, they may feel *coarser* because they're short and all of the same length, but the speed of growth doesn't vary.

Nearsighted people are smarter

What's the quickest way a TV director can signal that a character is supposed to be an intellectual? Hint: Remember the kid in elementary school everyone called "Four eyes"? Well, here's one where the folk wisdom pans out . . . sort of. Data on more than 150,000 Israeli soldiers showed that myopia (nearsightedness) was positively related both to number of years spent in school and to scores on intelligence tests. The study, published in 1987, found that only 8 percent of the young men with the lowest test scores were myopes—as compared with more than 27 percent of those with the highest scores. A study of Danish draftees was published the next year in another journal:

Once again, the higher the intelligence, the worse the eyesight, on average.

Still not convinced? A U.S. Public Health Service survey in the late 1960s found that only one out of five teenagers scoring in the bottom 10 percent on a reading test was nearsighted—versus nearly half of those scoring in the top 10 percent. And a look at kids who got very high scores on Scholastic Aptitude Tests (SATs) before they had even turned thirteen revealed that more than *half* of these extremely precocious tykes were myopes.

Even someone with thick glasses can see that something is going on here. The interesting question is: What causes what?

Consider three possible explanations. (1) Children become nearsighted for genetic reasons and, as a result, have trouble with activities that rely on distance vision, such as sports. They take up reading instead, which makes them seem smart. (2) Myopia and intelligence are both at least partly inherited and the two features, like eye color and hair color, are genetically related. (3) Kids who read a lot, particularly at an early age, *become* nearsighted from all that focusing on close objects—that is, books.

The question of whether any good evidence exists to show that intelligence is inherited, a premise of the second theory, has long been a hot topic of debate and is too messy to get into here. Let me simply note that many of the studies used to support that claim have been severely criticized. Moreover, the very idea that IQ tests measure a single, fixed thing called "intelligence" has been largely discredited.

Both the first and second ideas share the assumption that nearsightedness is inherited, and this, too, has been called into question. By some accounts, the prevalence of myopia in the United States has doubled from the 1930s to the 1970s, a fact hard to reconcile with genetic explanations. These explanations also become shakier, at least in the minds of some specialists, given that the age at which people first become myopic is extremely variable.

The first theory, that nearsighted kids turn to books because they can't do much else, is especially dubious. Most children get fitted for glasses very soon after it becomes obvious that they need them; after this, they are hardly confined to the library. Indeed, a British study showed that while myopes were twice as likely as their peers to read books for fun, they were just as likely as anyone else to play outdoor games and sports. That same study, as well as an earlier one, reported something even more telling: Myopic teenagers, who scored higher than their peers on achievement tests, were already scoring higher at age seven or eight—*before* they were found to be nearsighted. If the smarts came before the glasses, it's hard to see how the myopia caused the smarts.

This leaves us with the idea that lots of reading ruins distance vision, which is called the "use-abuse" theory. At least three sorts of evidence support it. First, Francis Young at Washington State University, who has been working on these issues since the mid-1940s, has found just such an effect in his primate laboratory. When monkeys are placed in an environment where they can see only things that are close to them, they eventually become nearsighted.

Second, the results of a natural change in the lifestyle of Alaskan Eskimos offers strong reason to think that what is true of monkeys is true of humans. When several hundred Eskimos had their vision checked back in the 1960s, only 1 or 2 percent of those over age forty-one were nearsighted, as compared with more than half the teenagers and young adults. The older generation, it turns out, had grown up as illiterate nomads, while the younger folks had spent their childhoods in the city with formal schooling. It's impossible to prove that reading made the difference, but it seems a reasonable guess. Also, virtually no relation was found between the myopia of parents and their children, which led Young to conclude that nearsightedness "has nothing to do with genetics and everything to do with environment."

The third argument for the use-abuse position comes from a closer reading of those intelligence studies mentioned above. Toward the end of the paper describing that huge Israeli study, the authors admit that their tests included a verbal component and thus that the advantage enjoyed by myopes might be due to reading-related skills "rather than [to] any innate intellectual superiority." Several years earlier, William R. Baldwin, an optometrist at the University of Houston, made exactly this point. Myopes aren't more intelligent than people with good vision—they're just "superior in scholastic performance and in achievement tests associated with reading skills," he wrote.

At least two studies, one American and one British, have shown this directly. Standard tests showed an advantage for nearsighted children, but when the researchers looked at measures of nonverbal intelligence, or when they set aside the paper-and-pencil section of the test and concentrated on the results of an oral question-and-answer session, those who needed glasses suddenly lost their advantage.

These results challenge the idea that nearsighted people are really "smarter" than others. They also seem to support the idea that early reading may have affected their vision. Indeed, even specialists who think heredity is important recognize the existence of "school myopia." Says Melvin Rubin, chair of the ophthalmology department at the University of Florida, "A lot of kids are nearsighted when they leave school in the spring, but when they come back to school in the fall, they're much less so." Nevertheless, Rubin and others believe that this effect is neither severe nor permanent enough to support the use-abuse theory. Furthermore, even Young acknowledges that the statistical association between nearsightedness and time spent reading isn't overwhelming, even if it is significant.

The researchers who looked at the Danish soldiers have another idea. Maybe the "use" that causes myopia—or at least helps to explain it—takes place long before children pick up their first Dr. Seuss story. "Habitual visual exploration of the near environment" in infancy could be associated with both "higher intelligence levels and myopia later in life," they speculate.

Of course this is just a theory; to assume the answer is clear would be, well, shortsighted.

He who lives by the sword, dies by the sword

If the contemporary "sword" is a handgun, then this maxim seems to be true. A study of all gunshot deaths in the Seattle area from 1978 to 1983—there were 743 in all—found that the majority of these deaths occurred in the home where the gun was kept. Moreover, these guns were far more likely to kill a resident than an intruder. In only two cases was a stranger killed; the rest were accidental deaths, suicides, or homicides where the victim was a friend or family member. Another statistic drives the point home: In Detroit, more people died from handgun accidents in one year than were killed by home-invading robbers over the course of nearly five years.

No pain, no gain

American culture is distinguished by a peculiar blend of decadence on the one hand, in which having to watch TV without a remote control is seen as a dreadful ordeal, and self-punishment on the other, in which we feel vaguely uneasy if we're not suffering. This combination of laziness and drivenness produces such absurdities as people taking taxis to their health clubs. When we are not pampering ourselves, we are pushing ourselves, running in circles to the point of dehydration or paying to enter fitness centers so we can insinuate our bodies into devices that seem to come straight out of the Spanish Inquisition. If it doesn't hurt, we tell ourselves, it can't be doing us any good.

Nonsense. If our goal is really to be healthier, to have a stronger heart and better endurance, then this slogan of self-abuse is simply wrong. The latest in a long line of research on the topic was published in the *Journal of the American Medical Association* in November 1989. What was remarkable about this study of more than 13,000 white, affluent Texans was not that the 283 people who died over the course of the study had been in worse shape than those who remained alive. It was that the risk of dying went way down for those who got even a modicum of exercise. "A brisk walk of 30 to 60 minutes a day will be sufficient to produce the fitness standard" that was associated with a major reduction in the chances of dropping dead prematurely, according to the researchers. Plenty of gain without any pain at all.

But what if you're an athlete who wants something beyond basic fitness, who feels a compulsion to break records or triumph over competitors? These goals, it is true, will require some discomfort, a willingness to push yourself beyond what you thought you could do. Even here, though, the idea that pain is necessary has been oversold; in fact, it can actually interfere with effective conditioning. Specialists in the field like Bryant Stamford of the University of Louisville medical school are coming to see this. "Training with pain can be counterproductive," Stamford wrote in the journal *Physician and Sportsmedicine.* It can make it "more difficult to continue training . . . [and] increase your vulnerability to injury."

David Costill, director of the human performance laboratory at Ball State University, came to the same conclusion when he saw the results of an experiment with eighteen collegiate swimmers. After their training program was cut nearly in half (from 9,560 to 4,940 yards a day), the men not only experienced no decline in endurance but actually swam faster in competition than they ever had before.

"It's true that you're going to have to stress yourself for the body to grow stronger," Costill says, "but that doesn't mean you have to fall down and throw up every time you work out. Most coaches and athletes think that the person who trains the hardest is most fit. The fact is you can beat yourself to a frazzle to the point where you literally get worse instead of better. Sometimes it's when you back off and rest up that you actually perform better."

Laugh and the whole world laughs with you; cry and you cry alone

Apart from whether it prevents illness (see "Laughter is the best medicine," pp. 64–68), laughter itself is indeed contagious. Back in 1940, a sociology journal reported that people laughed more often (and longer) at a play as the size of the audience increased. More recent studies have confirmed this and have also shown that children listening to funny stories and songs tend to laugh and smile a lot more when even one other person is listening to the same thing. That's why the recorded laugh track was invented: If you believe that an entire audience finds tonight's TV sitcom hilarious, maybe you, too, will find it funny.

The more interesting part of this proverb is the second half: the idea that people want nothing to do with folks who are depressed. This, too, would appear to be true more often than not. Psychologist James C. Coyne, among others, has discovered that while misery may love company (depressed people seek emotional support from others more than those who are not depressed do), company clearly does not love misery. In 1976, he had forty-five college students talk on the phone for twenty minutes with women, some of whom were depressed. Even though they were not told anything about the person on the other end, the students indicated they were much less interested in spending time with the depressed women. More recently, two psychologists found the same was true of rehabilitation nurses: They indicated they would rather spend time with a patient who was disabled than with one who seemed depressed.

Researchers at Vanderbilt University and at the University of Western Ontario have reported that students talking face-to-face with depressed people did less talking, offered fewer supportive statements, smiled less, and even spent less time making eye contact with them, as compared to their conversations with nondepressed individuals. These differences showed up almost immediately after their conversations began. In one of the studies, undergraduate women sat farther away from someone they had been told was depressed and lonely.

Such findings are particularly important because they suggest that depressed people cannot be faulted for inaccurate beliefs or perceptions. If they think others are viewing them negatively, they may well be right. Moreover, they may find themselves caught in a vicious circle: Unhappy people end up driving away those whose support and acceptance they need, thereby worsening their depression and their need for support.

Most homeless people are crazy

Although people on the streets who talk to themselves or give other evidence of psychological disorder are distressingly conspicuous, most experts say that only a minority of the homeless are actually mentally ill. A *New York Times* report said that estimates hover between 20 and 30 percent; an article in the *American Journal of Psychiatry,* summarizing various studies, put the figure somewhere between

25 and 50 percent. Several sociologists like to use one-third as a rough guide.

But David A. Snow and his colleagues at the University of Texas suspected that even these surprisingly low numbers may be exaggerations because they are based on diagnoses from a single brief encounter with each homeless person. In 1984–1985, these researchers spent twenty months in the field, getting to know 164 homeless people quite well and conducting shorter interviews with a random sample of another 767 people who used Salvation Army services in Austin. They concluded that only 15 percent of the combined sample could properly be diagnosed as mentally ill, and only 10 percent had ever been institutionalized.

Some of what seems bizarre behavior to the passerby "may instead be adaptive responses to the arduous nature of life on the streets," they suggested. Moreover, unusual behavior isn't necessarily pathological. Still another possibility is that their condition—the constant absence of security and comfort and dignity, the cold and hunger, the risk of being robbed or beaten—may be a *cause* of disorganized thinking and depression. This is rather different from blaming their condition on their insanity.

Snow's 15 percent estimate strikes some social scientists as too low, but even the highest figures make it clear that most homeless people are not psychotic. After lengthy interviews with 379 people on Los Angeles's skid row in 1988, researchers estimated that 28 percent were mentally ill; however, most of the people they talked to were single men and, therefore, were unrepresentative of the homeless as a group. In fact, all of these studies are based on examinations of adults even though a horrifying proportion of those with no place to go are children, and their situation can hardly be attributed to mental illness. Furthermore, the U.S. Conference of Mayors reports that about one in four homeless people works—the implication being that having a job in this country isn't enough to ensure that one can afford a place to live.

Jonathan Kozol, who has lived among the homeless and written extensively about his experiences, says the real cause of homelessness is simply "the lack of homes and of income with which to rent or acquire them." We may just find it more comfortable to assume that people lead unsafe, unsanitary lives on benches and heating grates because they are crazy. "The notion that the homeless are largely psychotics who belong in institutions, rather than victims of displacement at the hands of enterprising realtors, spares us from the need to offer realistic solutions to the deep and widening extremes of wealth and poverty in the United States."

Religious people are more altruistic

In a society that teaches us to associate morality with religion, it is easy to assume that a strong relationship exists between piety and pity, between God and good. After all, the sacred texts of Judaism and Christianity, like those of most supernatural belief systems, contain reminders to be compassionate and charitable.

These familiar injunctions, however, have not been sufficient to prevent the commission of a range of horrors under the banner of one religion or another, from the Hebrews who "utterly destroy[ed] the men, women, and children, of every city" as they invaded Canaan (Deut. 3:6) to the barbaric Christian Crusaders to contemporary fanatics killing in Allah's name. Less dramatically, there also exists a "long parade of findings demonstrating that churchgoers are more intolerant of ethnic minorities than nonattenders," according to the late social psychologist Gordon Allport, although most of those findings are several decades old.

When we turn to the topic of altruism, we find that there is virtually no connection between religious affiliation or belief, on the one hand, and caring or helpful behavior, on the other. This conclusion has emerged with remarkable uniformity from many different types of research over many years. A careful study of about 2,000 Episcopalians in the 1950s turned up "no discernible relationship between involvement [in the Church] and charitable acts." In a questionnaire-based study of altruism involving several hundred male college students in 1960, there was only a slight correlation between altruism and belief in God, and none at all between altruism and attendance of religious services. In interviews with randomly selected adults in 1965, "the 'irreligious' . . . [were] nearly as frequently rated as being a good Samaritan, having love and compassion for their fellow man, and being humble as the most devout and religious of our group studied."

Two experiments with undergraduates during the 1970s found essentially the same thing: In one, students who believed in the Bible's accuracy were no more likely than others to come to the aid of someone in the next room who seemed to have fallen off a ladder. In the other study, students were classified as being "Jesus people" (born-again Christians), conventionally religious, nonreligious, or atheists. There was no statistically significant difference among these groups in their willingness to volunteer time with retarded children or to resist temptation to cheat on a test. (There was only one group in which a majority did not cheat: the atheists.)

In 1984, a researcher who surveyed more than 700 people from different neighborhoods in a medium-size city expected to find that religious people were especially sociable, helpful to their neighbors, and likely to participate in neighborhood organizations. Instead, she reported, religious involvement was virtually unrelated to these activities. Finally, an ambitious new study of people who risked their lives to rescue Jews from the Nazis found that "rescuers did not differ significantly from bystanders or all non-rescuers with respect to their religious identification, religious education, and their own religiosity or that of their parents."

Women reach their sexual peak after age thirty; men, in their teens

It is hard to imagine how any romantic pursuit could be as fraught with heartache and frustration as the attempt to find out whether this belief is really true. After an exhaustive search of the published literature and interviews with fourteen—count 'em, fourteen—experts, after a journey (by telephone and mail) that led from the Masters & Johnson Institute in St. Louis to the University of Uppsala in Sweden, I still have no definitive conclusion to report.* However, there seems to be more reason, on balance, to be skeptical than to take this bit of folk wisdom at face value.

The claim can be traced to the famous Kinsey surveys of half a century ago, which simply polled people on the frequency of various sexual behaviors. Based on the number of times those interviewed said they had masturbated or had intercourse or erotic dreams, Kinsey's crew figured that women reached their peaks in their mid- to late-thirties—long after men. (As one female comic put it more

*Maybe this is just one of those cases where nothing can take the place of good old-fashioned field research.

recently, just around the time she was starting to hit her sexual stride, her husband was beginning to discover he had a favorite chair.)

Sexual peak is an ambiguous term, though. The number of sexual experiences per year may be different from how much one enjoys them, and this, in turn, may be different from how often one thinks about sex or how much enjoyment one brings to one's partner. Which one of these is most relevant to the idea of a peak period?

Even if we decide to limit our discussion to frequency, the problem with using a simple Kinsey-style count is that it's unclear whether women are said to peak later in life for physiological, psychological, or social reasons. It is possible, according to Virginia Sadock, who directs the program in human sexuality at New York University Medical Center, that giving birth may help women to become more sexually responsive because they develop more capillaries in the genital area. But it isn't clear how significant that difference is, and Sadock points out that a crying baby in the next room may do far more to cool sexual desire than a few more blood vessels could do to inflame it. On the basis of considerable research and clinical experience, Patricia Shreiner-Engel at Mt. Sinai School of Medicine in New York has found that a good proportion of women who "develop a loss of desire report that they lost it after the birth of a child."

John Money, at Johns Hopkins University, is probably the best-known investigator of sex hormones and their effect on behavior. Nevertheless, he insists that how we are raised to think about sex is more relevant than how much estrogen or testosterone we secrete. "You need a certain amount of hormone to get the system going, but any additional hormone doesn't do anything," he says. If women have sex more, or simply enjoy it more, at forty than at twenty, this probably reflects the time required to shake off early lessons about sexual desire. "A great deal of what we think of as biological in women is hopelessly intertwined with these concepts of how girls are educated," says Money.

Elizabeth Allgeier, a professor of psychology at Bowling Green State University and author of a textbook on sexuality, agrees. "Women are told that if they're horny they must be sinful. These sorts of findings [may reflect the fact] that women have to get over some twenty years of socialization before they learn that sex can be fun." The case against a biological explanation for a late sexual peak is strengthened, she observes, by the fact that it would make no sense from an evolutionary point of view for women to become most interested in sex just as they were nearing the end of their childbearing years.

If the issue is socialization, then we would expect the gap between women's and men's peaks to narrow as sexual mores come to reflect less of a sexist double-standard. And, sure enough, Bernard Goldstein reported in the mid-1970s that studies since the Kinsey report have shown that "women are reaching high levels of arousal at earlier ages." Likewise, Kathryn Kelley, editor of a 1987 anthology titled *Females, Males, and Sexuality,* observes that "there seems to be more of a convergence between the sexes these days in terms of frequency and enjoyability" of sex. On the other hand, recent research still shows that women aren't likely to report a physical motive for having sex until they are in their late thirties (see "Women want sex for intimacy; men want sex for pleasure," pp. 11–14). What is really needed to corroborate these impressions is a large national survey of sexual attitudes and behaviors, but nervous politicians have resisted funding such a project.

There's another problem with the claim that women reach their sexual peak at thirty-five or forty or whenever: A peak suggests that something drops off *after* that year. In fact, says Schreiner-Engel, "With more sexual experience, women tend to develop a greater ease and frequency of orgasm. I've found no evidence of a decline after the so-called peak."

Physiological changes in men's sexuality as they age are somewhat more predictable than in women's: Most forty year olds ejaculate less often and take longer to become aroused than most fifteen year olds. However, the context in which that arousal takes place counts for a lot here. It's hard to talk meaningfully about someone's increasing or decreasing sexual excitement without knowing who, if anyone, is on the other side of the bed. A longitudinal study of men and women ranging in age from forty-six to seventy-one found that at all ages in between, "men reported higher levels of sexual interest and activity than women"— although this, again, might say more about the attitudes of women from these age groups than about some built-in characteristic of either gender.

Besides, the idea that men have passed their sexual peak before their twentieth birthday should raise the question of whether a state of constant sexual readiness means someone is at his "peak" in any real sense. The middle-aged tortoise may well win the race in terms of the sexual satisfaction he gives and receives. (In fact, a study of healthy middle-aged to elderly men published in 1990 indicates that while sexual arousal and activity were lower for older men, "sexual enjoyment and satisfaction did not show a decline with increasing age.") Moreover, as sociologist John Gagnon points out, "masturbation accounts for the huge surge in early life" that led Kinsey to talk about men reaching their sexual peak in late adolescence. "Is that the measure you're really interested in?" he asks.

This much is clear from survey data: Most men and women can enjoy sex at any point from puberty until death. "Some people don't reach their peaks until they're in their eighties," says Bill Young, deputy director of the Masters & Johnson Institute. It would appear that no evidence exists to suggest that biology takes precedence over social conditioning, psychological factors, and individual situations—which means there is no fixed prime that one can be past.

Spare the rod and spoil the child

Some Bible readers argue that this adage has been taken out of context—that it was not originally intended as an injunction to use physical punishment. Nevertheless, this is the way it is commonly understood, so it makes sense to investigate the saying on these terms. And even the most casual investigation of the relevant research suggests that no other bit of homey advice may have caused more harm than this one. Certainly one is hard pressed to think of any other proverb that grows out of so faulty an understanding of human development.

Does physical punishment "teach the kid a lesson"? Absolutely. It "teaches that the way to solve problems is to beat up others," says Leonard Eron, a research psychologist at the University of Illinois at Chicago. Now obviously not all "rods" are equivalent: There's a big difference between a light swat on a child's fanny and the sort of abuse that causes bruises. But the overwhelming majority of child development experts emphasize that slapping, spanking, or otherwise using violence on children is never necessary and always potentially harmful.

A spate of studies in the 1950s and early 1960s showed conclusively that corporal punishment produces children who are more, not less, aggressive than their peers. In 1960, Eron and his colleagues studied 875 eight year olds in rural New York and found a clear-cut relationship between the severity of the physical punishment they received and how aggressive their peers judged them to be. Twenty-two years later, the researchers tracked down some of these same subjects and found that many of the aggressive children had grown into aggressive adults. Even more disturbing, many of them were now using physical punishment on their own children.

As we have already seen ("Abused children grow up to abuse their own children," pp. 54–56), the experience of having been abused doesn't *guarantee* that one will eventually become an abuser. Nevertheless, even "acceptable" levels of physical punishment may perpetuate violence and unhappiness, as researchers keep finding.

- A large survey in 1976 by Murray Straus and his colleagues revealed that people who had been punished most severely as teenagers were four times more likely to beat their spouses than people whose parents had never hit them at all.
- In 1988 a St. Louis study found that alcoholics and people suffering from depression were much more likely than other individuals to have been beaten when they were children.
- A new Brandeis University study, still unpublished at this writing, found that three to five year olds who were spanked by their parents were more likely than other children to be aggressive while playing at a day-care center. (Whether they usually played with toy guns or watched violent TV programs also was related to aggression, but not as strongly as physical punishment was.)

Apart from the long-term damage it can cause, physical punishment is simply ineffective. It may suppress misbehavior—or whatever the parent arbitrarily defines as misbehavior—in the short run, but it ultimately promotes little more than a determination to avoid getting caught. The way to raise children who respect and care for others is to respect and care for them, to explain what they've done wrong and *why* it's wrong, and to work with them in devising ways to solve problems. This allows children to feel good about themselves and invites them to think of their parent as someone they can trust. Eventually, it will help them to *internalize* positive values, which means they'll keep behaving well even when there is no one around to punish them.

Not so for children raised on a diet of fear and violence. In fact, some data suggest that hitting children is also counterproductive when they are toddlers. In 1986, Thomas G. Power and M. Lynn Chapieski reported in the journal *Developmental Psychology* that "infants of physically punishing mothers showed the lowest levels of compliance and were most likely to manipulate breakable objects." An earlier study of more than 800 toddlers and their mothers in California also discovered that "the more frequent the punishment for the child"—especially physical punishment and especially as administered by the mother—"the more severe were all of the behavior problem syndromes studied in the child." (Even if the punishment didn't cause these behavior problems, it certainly didn't eliminate them either.)

Despite all of this research, polls indicate that an overwhelming majority of American parents still resort to physical punishment. In one survey, a plurality of parents (41 percent) even chose this as the preferred way of dealing with a child who deliberately hurts someone else. (Apparently they believe that the best way to teach that hurting is wrong is by hurting.) Why do these parents do it? Perhaps they think that harm is caused only by real child abuse—not by normal spanking. Perhaps they lack self-control or the skills to deal with their children more positively and productively. Perhaps they are afraid, as the proverb says, of "spoiling" their children—as if there were no way to be firm without using force.

Or perhaps, as the psychoanalyst Alice Miller suggests, some of these parents were themselves victims of physical discipline and, rather than confronting the implications of what was done to them at a tender age, prefer to treat their own children the same way. This keeps up the pretense that violence is appropriate and good for the child. Whatever the reason parents resort to the rod, though, they would clearly do better to throw it away.

Cracking your knuckles will give you arthritis

Pulling on your fingers or pressing them hard at the joints often leads to a sharp cracking sound that is inexplicably pleasurable to those who do it and inexplicably irritating to others in the vicinity. Where does the sound come from? The tension applied to the finger lowers the pressure of the fluid around the joint and creates a bubble of vapor. As fluid rushes in at high speeds, the bubble bursts, causing an audible release of energy.

Ask the next orthopedist (or rheumatologist or hand surgeon) you meet whether this causes arthritis and you'll probably get an answer somewhere between "Nah" and "No one knows." Most physicians doubt that there is any real harm to cracking your knuckles, but it soon becomes clear that this reassurance is offered without much more conviction—or evidence—than are the dire warnings from laypeople.

It's surprising, really, how little research has been done. As of 1987, this is all there was to read on the subject in English:

- Two articles describing what happens when a knuckle is cracked, one published in 1947 and the other in 1971, neither of them taking a stand on whether the practice is harmful.
- A report from the early 1970s on a grand total of two young adults who cracked their knuckles constantly and seemed to have some damaged cartilage or ligament—maybe as a result of their habit and maybe not. The author, a Dallas rheumatologist named Morris Ziff, added recently, "You have to be a compulsive knuckle cracker to develop osteoarthritis. Ordinary knuckle cracking is harmless."
- A 1975 study of twenty-eight residents of an old-age home (average age: seventy-eight) who answered with certainty when asked whether they had spent their lives cracking their knuckles. Of the fifteen who said yes, only one showed signs of degenerative joint disease; of the thirteen who said no, five had the disease. It's not clear how long or how often the fifteen had cracked, let alone why the noncrackers seemed to be in worse shape. But the researchers cheerfully concluded that "the chief morbid consequence of knuckle cracking would appear to be its annoying effect on the observer."

For obvious reasons, no one has ever conducted the ideal study, which would be to follow a large group of crackers and a large group of noncrackers for several decades to see who developed arthritis. Absent that, the scanty available evidence appears to be fairly reassuring to those who crack.

Or so it seemed until Peter Watson came along in 1988, waving his hands wildly and warning that the habit really is bad news after all. Watson, a bioengineer in Northern Ireland who, believe it or not, wrote his doctoral dissertation on this subject, has been working with Raymond Mollan, a respected orthopedic surgeon at Queen's University of

Belfast. Watson has built a knuckle-cracking machine that, judging from photographs published in an engineering journal in 1989, should be outlawed by the Geneva Convention. He has published a new case study of a compulsive cracker, age twenty-five, some of whose cartilage has calcified. He has applied an ultrasonic welder to chunks of frozen cartilage from cow knees in a fashion meant to suggest the effects, over time, of cracking living human fingers.

Watson's calculations and extrapolations from all of this work leave him shaking his head and frowning. "For us to be able to hear a cracking sound loudly," he says, "it must contain a fair amount of energy, and in a knuckle joint this energy is confined to a small space. Also, engineering dynamics tells us that shock waves, which is what a cracking sound is, are incredibly damaging. Both of these taken together point toward damage of some sort due to cracking."

No one, he quickly adds, knows why slight damage to cartilage isn't a problem for some people while in others it produces further breakdown, causing swelling, stiffness, and pain—in short, osteoarthritis. And no one, including Watson himself, has yet been able to show that this is indeed the fate of knuckle crackers. It may well require constant cracking over many years, he speculates, and even then may cause arthritis only for a subset of the population mysteriously susceptible to cartilage problems.

No one knows. You cracks your knuckles and you takes your chances.

Basketball players shoot in streaks

Sometimes it seems we'll do anything to deny the reality of randomness. We invent patterns and meanings, project them onto the external world, and then tell ourselves that we've discovered them out there. We're convinced that bad luck "comes in threes," that certain combinations of numbers are more likely than others to win the lottery, or that the time of year we were born tells us something about our personality. (On the day I am writing this, in fact, my morning newspaper quotes a meteorologist explaining yesterday's storms by saying that "we had to pay for all the warm weather" we've enjoyed recently. He may be kidding, but lots of people really think this way.)

Such an inclination to see patterns or purposes where none exist disposes us to overlook the fact that some similarities and streaks occur by chance. If I flip a coin over and over, I may well get four or five heads in a row. This is meaningless: A fifty-fifty chance of heads doesn't mean that I'm supposed to get one head, then one tail, then another head. It means that the longer I flip, the closer to 50 percent my overall ratio of heads will be. And my chance of getting tails after five heads in a row is not one bit higher than my chance of getting tails at any other point in the series.

Where other factors, such as skill, enter the picture, we are even more inclined to believe in patterns. Take the case of "streak shooting" in basketball, sometimes known as the "hot hand" phenomenon. Most fans—and most professional players themselves—believe that someone on the court is more likely to make a shot after having just made his last few shots than after having missed them. After all, he's on a roll, right?

Wrong. Tom Gilovich at Cornell University, along with Robert Vallone and Amos Tversky of Stanford, have shown in a series of experiments that the hot hand is really a product of the observer's cold brain. First, they looked at individual field goal records for forty-eight Philadelphia 76ers games and found that players were no more likely to sink the ball after a hit than after a miss. Then they divided each player's record into clumps of four consecutive shots to see if there were more streaks than would be expected by chance. There weren't. Next they picked a couple of players who are widely thought to have nights when they just couldn't miss. Negative.

Gilovich and his colleagues didn't stop there. They looked specifically at free throws—nice, clean, undefended shots perfect for statistical analysis. Players didn't hit a higher percentage of their second free throws when they had just made their first. Finally, the researchers set up some college athletes on the basketball court to see if these students could predict any of their shots based on how they had been doing up until then. They couldn't.

The problem, it would seem, is that people, including die-hard, statistics-happy sports fans, "tend to perceive chance shooting as streak shooting"—which is rather like reading significance into the fact that a coin comes up heads four times in a row. Of course, basketball is not a game of chance, but Gilovich's group has pretty well established that "contrary to common belief, a player's chances of hitting are largely independent of the outcome of his or her previous shots." The larger problem, they add, is that many of us "tend to 'detect' patterns even where none exist."

More people commit suicide during the holidays

There's a certain plausible perversity to the idea that wide-spread merriment contrasts sharply with the internal state of depressed people and pushes them over the edge. As two University of Virginia psychiatrists remarked a few years ago, "Hauling out discussions of the Christmas depression syndrome has become, in the United States, an annual Christmas custom somewhat like hauling out the decorations, singing carols, and putting on Santa Claus suits." Nevertheless, as they (and other researchers) go on to point out, the idea that more people kill themselves during the holidays is simply false.

First of all, data from the National Center for Health Statistics make it quite clear that April, not December, is the cruelest month. Daily suicide reports from 1950 through 1978, as reviewed by many statisticians, show that suicides peak in the spring. In some years, there is a second, less impressive, rise in the late summer and early fall. But year after year, Americans—and Canadians, too, incidentally—are *least* likely to end it all in December and January.

Even if we look at all the major holidays throughout the year, we find that none is associated with an increase in the suicide rate. In fact, regardless of sex, race, or method of doing oneself in, there are significantly *fewer* suicides on most holidays than on other days. Reviewing data from the 1970s, David Phillips and his colleagues at the University of California at San Diego showed that the suicide rate declines markedly a few days before most of the major holidays and stays low until they're over. There is a rise just afterward, but it is not substantial enough to offset the drop. Not all studies have confirmed the postholiday rebound effect, but every investigation has found that the holidays themselves either lower the suicide rate or, at worst, don't affect it at all.

Of course, just because someone doesn't get to the point of suicide doesn't mean he or she is jolly. But even on less dramatic measures, there is reason to challenge the conventional wisdom. The number of admissions to psychiatric hospitals (and visits to their emergency rooms) typically declines in December. Some psychotherapists report that their depressed clients get worse around Christmas even if they don't need to be hospitalized, but this isn't based on research and, in any case, it might not apply to the population at large. Finally, the idea that folks in the far north suffer from midwinter depression has been challenged by a three-year study in Anchorage, Alaska: Neither suicide attempts nor calls to a crisis hotline increased during the winter months.

Firstborns are different from other children

Some people maintain that just from knowing whether someone is a firstborn, middle-born, or last-born child, they can predict that individual's personality and intelligence.

But then some people also take horoscopes seriously.

The comparison is more appropriate than it might seem at first. Birth order really is "much like astrology," says Toni Falbo, an educational psychologist at the University of Texas at Austin. "People like it. It says, 'I'm not to blame for the way I am.'"

The studies purporting to show that most achievers were

eldest children, or that most sociable people were the babies of the family, have been largely discredited by now. As a rule, the better, the later, and the larger the study, the less likely it is to find that birth order is a useful predictor of almost anything. In fact, when Swiss social scientists Cecile Ernst and Jules Angst reviewed some 1,500 studies in 1983, they concluded that further research in the area would be a waste of money.

Popular magazines continue to make much of birth order,* and some academics have been just as enamored of the idea. It's easy to measure, and the idea that it tells us something about an individual is intuitively plausible. But according to *Family Size and Achievement,* a 1989 book by demographer Judith Blake that reviews data on 150,000 individuals, "Once you control for family background factors, birth order doesn't make any difference" with respect to either cognitive ability or number of years spent in school.

Blake's book contains a detailed refutation of the "confluence theory" offered by University of Michigan psychologist Robert Zajonc in the mid-1970s. Zajonc made headlines with his claims that standardized test scores can be predicted by the number of firstborns, second borns, etc., taking the test. But when Blake looked at birth patterns before 1938 and compared them to SAT scores for that group of children—just as Zajonc had done for a later period—there was no connection.

Even if it is unrelated to achievement, it seems reasonable to assume that birth order might help determine one's personality. The psychoanalyst Alfred Adler argued in the 1920s that the firstborn never recovers from being "dethroned" by the arrival of a brother or sister, and some

*My favorite example is a February 1989 article in one of the better-known women's magazines claiming that Jane Fonda and Tom Hayden's happy marriage was predictable on the basis of their respective birth orders. (The two split up just after the article went to press.)

clinicians still think that self-esteem, empathy, popularity, and other traits are affected by birth order in consistent ways.

But some careful readers started to notice that theories about birth order are suspiciously flexible. They can explain whatever a researcher comes up with, even if it contradicts last week's study. For instance, if it were found that last borns are unusually anxious, that would seem logical because they grew up as the weakest in the family. But if a study associated anxiety with firstborns, this would be said to fit with the fact that eldest children were raised by inexperienced parents. And, of course, middle children were lost in the shuffle growing up, so claims about *their* anxiety, too, seem to make sense.

The plain truth, according to Ernst and Angst, is that "birth order differences in personality . . . are nonexistent in our sample. In particular, there is no evidence for a 'firstborn personality.' " Neither is there any empirical support for the widespread idea that the only child is self-centered, unhappy, and spoiled. Falbo and a colleague reviewed 141 studies in 1987 and found that "only children are not substantially different from other children who are raised with siblings with respect to personality characteristics." Where small differences were found—such as in achievement motivation—they invariably favored the onlies.

Part of the reason for the failure of birth order to tell us much about a person is that even if it did affect children's cognitive skills and personality, these effects tend to get washed out by all the other influences in their lives. The belief in the lifelong impact of birth order, according to Falbo, is just one more example of "a holdover in our psychological theorizing—that your personality is fixed by the time you're six. That assumption is simply incorrect."

So how could so many people, including social scientists, be misled about birth order for so long? First, what seems to be a function of position in the family may really say more about cultural norms or parental beliefs. If firstborns are groomed to take over the family business, they probably will receive more attention and encouragement. Consequently, they may grow up to be different from their sibs. Similarly, if parents *believe* the youngest child is the most sociable and affectionate, they might unconsciously treat him or her in such a way as to make that happen. But neither social arrangements nor self-fulfilling prophecies mean that birth order per se is an important factor.

Second, most of the early studies that seemed to show an effect were plagued by various methodological problems. The most common error was failing to tease apart family size and social class from birth order. For example, plenty of surveys showed that eldest children were overrepresented among high achievers. But that really doesn't tell us anything about being a firstborn—it tells us something about not having many (or any) siblings. After all, any group of firstborns is going to contain a disproportionate number of children from small families: Every family has a firstborn but fewer have a fourth born.

The fact is that children from small families *are* more likely to be high achievers. That's true mostly because small families tend to have relatively higher incomes and better educations. But even if socioeconomic status is held constant, size still matters. "Small families are, on average, much more productive of the kind of intellectual ability that helps people succeed in school," Blake says. The reason is that both financial resources and attention are diluted in larger families.

As for effects on personality, the results are mixed. Some research suggests that you're slightly more likely to be outgoing, well-adjusted, and independent if you had few siblings (or none) growing up. Two newer studies, however, have been unable to find any reliable differences on the basis of family size alone. One thing is clear: No *disadvan-*

tages have ever been shown to follow from growing up in a small family.

Position in the family doesn't seem to control our destiny, then, and size of family has only a limited impact. But what about spacing between children? The relatively scant research on this issue doesn't allow for any definite conclusion. Some psychologists say that children's development improves as spacing between sibs increases. Indeed, when more than 2,000 tenth-grade boys were asked to rate how reasonable and supportive they thought their parents were, those who sounded most positive turned out to be at least four years older or younger than their nearest sibling. But another study found that a firstborn was more likely to have high self-esteem if his or her sib was *less* than two years younger, and a third discovered that spacing made no difference in terms of social competence. Still others have found effects for boys but not for girls.

The consensus seems to be, as one researcher put it, that "a wider spacing creates more 'breathing room' for both children and their parents." But not all psychologists agree, and it isn't clear that any effects persisting into adulthood are terribly significant. This is even more true with respect to birth order, the popular assumptions about which are, in Blake's words, "not worth anything."

Marijuana today, hard drugs tomorrow

The use of marijuana declined during the 1980s, but the controversy over whether it is a "stepping-stone" to drugs like heroin or cocaine hasn't died. Most of the disagreement, though, is not about the facts but about what they mean.

It is undeniably true that the great majority of hard drug users had smoked grass earlier. You'll have to look pretty hard to find any heroin addicts who have never rolled a joint. But was marijuana the *first* drug they tried, the one that started it all? That depends on what you consider a drug. Most of the experts will tell you that hard drug users typically began with alcohol and/or nicotine, yet the authorities are less likely to cluck about beer and cigarettes being "gateway" drugs.

The idea that cigarettes lead to crack strikes us as ludicrous mostly because the overwhelming majority of smokers never go on to use drugs that can kill them more quickly than tobacco. And exactly the same is true of marijuana: Surveys by the National Commission on Marijuana and Drug Abuse have shown that only a tiny proportion of those who have used pot ever move to heroin. (These studies were conducted a while ago, so they don't address the relationship between marijuana and crack.)

This leads us to reflect on the whole idea of causality. Just because more people try marijuana before heroin than the other way around doesn't mean marijuana "leads to" experimenting with heroin. "If we eliminated marijuana totally from the universe, people would still find their way to heroin and cocaine," says Robert B. Millman, director of alcohol and drug abuse programs at New York Hospital—Payne Whitney Clinic.

There is evidence allowing us to predict *which* pot smokers are more likely to try other drugs: those who had a particularly positive experience with pot and those who used it a lot. There are also reasonably good guesses about *why* some marijuana users move to the hard stuff. One is that they want to keep experimenting with mind-altering substances. Another is that they now have greater access to other drugs. James A. Halikas, a psychiatrist who directs the chemical dependency treatment programs at the University of Minnesota, thinks this is the key issue. "Someone who has marijuana available has other drugs available to him as well. That's why we see anesthesiologists or pharmacists at such high risk for abuse of narcotics: It has nothing to do with the specialty itself; it's just that the drugs are at hand."

Yet another reason is that some third factor, having to do with one's life situation or psychological state, could lead to heavy marijuana use *and* to the use of more dangerous drugs. A sense of hopelessness or need to escape might motivate both, which means that smoking marijuana doesn't cause someone to shoot heroin any more than eating a hamburger causes someone to have ice cream for dessert. In fact, says Halikas, statisticians searching for something reliably associated with the use of hard drugs would do better to look for a criminal record: Breaking the law is a more powerful predictor of serious drug use than is smoking marijuana.

Creativity requires a touch of madness

"All who have been famous for their genius . . . have been inclined to insanity," said Aristotle. Twenty-three hundred years later, many of us still assume that truly creative people, particularly in the arts, are a little crazy. After all, the breakdowns or suicides of a number of artists have become legend, including composers such as Robert Schumann and George Frideric Handel and poets like Anne Sexton and Robert Lowell.

Just how widespread is this? Several researchers have looked at groups of creative individuals to see how many were suffering from relatively serious emotional problems. The results have been striking. Of forty-seven leading British artists and writers, Kay Jamison, a psychologist at Johns Hopkins medical school, found that eighteen (38 percent) had been treated for a mood disorder. Fully half of the poets she questioned had been hospitalized or received medication for such a problem.

Meanwhile, University of Iowa psychiatrist Nancy Andreasen has been busy keeping tabs on the faculty members at that school's well-known Writers' Workshop. As of 1987, twenty-four of the thirty creative writers had at some time been diagnosed with a mood disorder—nearly three times the rate of a matched group of thirty professionals in other fields. What's more, Andreasen found that the writers' parents and siblings were also much more likely than the general population to have had a psychological disorder as well as to have reached an impressive level of creative achievement. "The families of the writers were riddled with both creativity and mental illness," says Andreasen.

It's easy to spin out theories about what's going on here. Manic states can heighten the senses, accelerate the flow of ideas, and reduce the need for sleep. "Such people have a higher energy level," Jamison explains. "They think faster." It's also possible that both elation and depression provide good material for creative work—a variety of sensations to be explored artistically. Alternatively, those who are fond of biological explanations may assume (even in the absence of convincing evidence) that it must all be in the genes.

But is mental illness really necessary for art—or even more useful than mental health? Andreasen emphasizes that psychological disorders in themselves do not lead to higher creativity. "It's not the illness that makes people more creative. It's that they have a fundamental cognitive style that makes them more creative and *also* makes them more susceptible to illness." That style could be described as unusual openness, sensitivity, or intensity. Ernest Hartmann, a Tufts University psychiatrist, likes to talk about "thin boundaries." In the course of studying hundreds of nightmare sufferers, he found that those who experienced more than their share of unpleasant dreams also had a history of being easily hurt and were extremely aware of their own feelings and those of others. "They're especially vulnerable to stress, loss, and rejection—which are known as precipitants of mental illness," Hartmann observes. But thin boundaries are also found in people who "would tend to become artists if they had any talent."

Because creativity and manic-depressive disorder seem to be only indirectly related, with each being connected to a third factor, virtually all researchers join Andreasen in denying any necessary connection between madness and art. The great majority of creative people are not psychotic, and the great majority of psychotic people are not creative. Frank Barron, a psychologist at the University of California at Santa Cruz who has studied creativity for nearly three decades, puts it this way: "There are lots of manic depressives who don't manifest any creativity. If you go into a [psychiatric] hospital, you don't find eccentric people, you find apathetic, pathetic sick people."

When Barron gives personality tests to original thinkers, he finds that they sometimes score high on measures of abnormality but also on measures of "ego strength." The latter he translates as "persistence, a sense of reality in the midst of all the confusion, the ability to plan and to right yourself after you've been bounced one way or the other." In other words, mood swings and health are not mutually exclusive. According to Andreasen, creative people "are fundamentally rather healthy, neat, well-put-together people who happen to be vulnerable to mood disorders. Between the episodes [of mania and depression] they are very normal." In fact, she adds, creative people seem to do their best work during these healthy periods. "They don't do well when their mood isn't normal. They're too disorganized when they're high and too despondent when they're depressed."

Psychoanalysts have made this point for many years: Artists must be able to leave the everyday world of rationality and inhibitions behind for a while to tap the primitive, unconscious realm. But they must also be able to return to the real world so as to shape, integrate, and evaluate what they have done. Creative individuals need a reservoir of psychological strength to turn life—even a life pockmarked by emotional difficulties—into something that can move or inspire others.

The studies showing a relationship between psychological problems and creativity may be as interesting for what they don't find as for what they do. First, says Jamison, "There's no evidence for an association with other kinds of mental illness" such as schizophrenia—only for mood disorders. Second, these studies focused only on writers and some visual artists. There's no reason to think that other varieties of creativity, such as original scientific thinking, are statistically related to any kind of psychological problem.

Third, creativity is more likely to be found among people whose mood disorders are relatively mild. "After a certain point in mania, you're not producing," says Jamison. "You're just nuts." Some psychologists go even further, suggesting that the eccentricity of creative people may lead to their being misdiagnosed as manic-depressive. Mood swings don't always imply mental illness. It may be "an intense sensibility rather than psychopathology," says Barron.

In fact, it's possible that being a creator, particularly in a society that doesn't always value the process or the product, can cause—or at least worsen—psychological difficulties. "Artists are often mavericks whose pursuits isolate them from the mainstream," says Peter Ostwald, a San Francisco psychiatrist and author of a study of the composer Robert Schumann. "I see a close relationship between the difficult lifestyle of a person and the development of anger, frustration, and depression."

People are starving because of overpopulation

PLUs (People Like Us) are sometimes inclined to think that if only the third world masses would stop having so many babies, they would have enough food to eat. This explanation has the advantage of easing our guilt because it implies that starving people have only themselves to blame for their predicament.

But data from the United Nations Food and Agriculture Organization show that there is no obvious relation between hunger and population density. Sure, there are countries where people are both crowded and malnourished. But there are also countries where people are starving despite a relatively low ratio of people to farmable land: Honduras and Angola, for instance. And then there are countries with a far higher population density but much *less* hunger, such as China and Japan.

Once again, we find that an apparent cause-and-effect relationship doesn't stand up to close scrutiny. The most likely explanation, according to Frances Moore Lappé and her associates at the Institute for Food and Development Policy, is that when hunger and population growth do go together it is because they are both results of the same thing: powerlessness.

If a tiny number of rich people or multinational corporations control most of the land—as is true in countries like Honduras and the Philippines—then neither the size of the population nor the number of arable acres is the source of the problem. Even relatively few people may be kept poor and hungry if they're working for someone else. And even relatively plentiful cropland isn't going to help if it's being used to raise feed for cows that will be made into American hamburgers.

Having lots of children (potential breadwinners) may be a rational strategy for survival when people live from hand to mouth. By the same token, well-meaning birth control programs can't by themselves improve people's lives. The evidence suggests that starvation is less a function of people having too many mouths to feed than of having too little control over their bodies, their land, their time, and their future.

Like father, like son

With respect to attitudes and personality, it seems to be true that The apple doesn't fall far from the tree. Even during the late 1960s and early 1970s, the famous generation gap was a good deal narrower than most people assumed. One national poll of fifteen through twenty-one year olds taken in 1971, for example, found that about three-quarters of teenagers said they accepted and agreed with their parents' values and ideals.

In a large-scale survey conducted by the sociologist Melvin Kohn and his colleagues at Johns Hopkins University, teenagers and young adults were asked to rank a list of values (good manners, curiosity, obedience, etc.) in order of importance. Their priorities turned out to be remarkably similar to those of their parents, suggesting that we could certainly support the generalization Like parent, like child.

The proverb we are investigating, however, is more specific. The Hopkins researchers did conclude that "fathers play at least as large a role as do mothers" in transmitting values. But they're silent on the question of whether sons in particular are more influenced by their fathers than by their mothers—or whether sons are more similar to their fathers than daughters are. In fact, research on these questions is in short supply, so it's impossible to accept or reject this particular proverb. To some extent it seems that someone who grew up in a two-parent family is especially influenced by the parent of the same sex. But the question to keep in mind here is: influenced with respect to what? Parents and children may resemble each other in problem-solving styles, for example, but not in the ways they relate to other people—or so a Berkeley study suggests.

What about politics? "Around the world the story is much the same," Robert E. Lane of Yale University wrote in the late 1960s. "Father is the source of political orientation, especially for sons." That may have been the conventional wisdom, but it wasn't necessarily supported by good evidence. In a book published in 1974, M. Kent Jennings of the University of Michigan and Richard G. Niemi of Princeton University challenged the view that Dad is the opinion setter of the household. Overall, they found from interviews with 1,669 high-school seniors and their parents, children were especially likely to see eye to eye with their parents when mother and father shared a single political orientation. When they disagreed, however, "mothers [had] the edge, slight though it may be." This was particularly true for daughters, but sons, too, were slightly more likely to side with their moms on the issues of the day.

These findings, however, like those from any future surveys that may be conducted, are limited not only by the sort of questions the researchers happened to ask, but also by the styles of family relationships that defined the particular culture and period of time in which the study took place. As ideas about the proper roles of mothers and fathers change—not to mention the fact that about half of all children in the United States will spend at least part of their childhood with only one parent—the accuracy of folk wisdom about sons taking after fathers will have to be reexamined.

Kids don't read because they're addicted to television

Daniel R. Anderson and his associates at the University of Massachusetts like to spend their time watching children watch TV. They've been churning out studies on the subject since the mid-1970s and their general impression is that television gets blamed for things that aren't its fault. From their investigations, and those of other researchers, it seems clear that there just aren't enough data to justify the sweeping statements one hears about how TV is ruining the next generation and bringing about the downfall of Western Civilization.

This doesn't mean parents can plop their children in front of the electronic baby-sitter with a clear conscience. A good case can be made that most American TV programs are dreadfully demeaning, vapid and violent. Several studies—although not all—have found that children's imaginations are more stimulated when they hear stories on tape than when they see them on video. Violence on television may contribute to kids' aggressiveness. And, according to research published in 1985, TV-watching seems to be associated with childhood obesity.

But if we look at the medium itself rather than at current programming, and if we narrow our focus to its effects on reading and academic achievement, then the case against television may not be as strong as some critics suggest. "There's no evidence that if kids weren't watching TV, they'd be doing something educationally valuable," according to Anderson. "About two-thirds of kids don't read at all—and that was also true before television existed."

In 1988, Susan B. Neuman of the University of Lowell (also in Massachusetts) took a look at survey data from eight states and also at the 1984 National Assessment of Educational Progress. In all, she had access to what more than 2 million children reported about how much they watched and read. She concluded that the two pastimes were rarely substituted for one another. Activities that are "functionally *different* from television tend to remain unaffected by the time spent watching television," she wrote. That means TV viewing doesn't seem to take the place of reading. Seventeen year olds watch less television than nine and thirteen year olds, but not because they've switched from sitcoms to sonnets. Similarly, as Anderson and a colleague point out, "There is no conclusive evidence that television viewing displaces homework."

That leads to another question: Is TV-viewing negatively related to student achievement? To a limited degree, yes— particularly for girls and for children who score high on intelligence tests. That was the finding of a 1982 review of twenty-three studies, which discovered that grades went down as time in front of the tube went up—above ten hours of viewing per week. Interestingly, watching fewer hours than that was actually associated with better performance in school than watching none at all.

But this doesn't mean sitting in front of the TV *caused* a rise or fall in achievement. Viewing habits are more likely a symptom of something else in the child's life that also affects grades. Maybe a limited amount of viewing indicates that students have the sort of parents who set limits on their entertainment and also encourage them to study—while kids who watch constantly have parents who lack ambitious educational goals for their children. In any case, "it appears unlikely that television alone is responsible for a nation-wide decline in measures of achievement," the researchers concluded.

The idea that TV is hypnotic and addictive, a mindless form of entertainment that sucks in viewers and then sucks out their brains, doesn't get much empirical support either. Anderson's research shows that children look away from the set every few seconds while they watch and that they spend about one-third of their TV-viewing time doing other things simultaneously. Preschool-age kids also appear to be using their minds when the TV is on: They remember things selectively, make inferences about the story and characters, and generally stay mentally active. "Young children's attention to television is not passive and involuntary," Anderson and his associates report, "but instead reflects the development, with TV-viewing experience, of sophisticated strategies for optimally distributing visual attention to the most informative parts of the TV program."

Of course, what is informative to a four year old is not necessarily a graduate philosophy seminar for a grown-up. But, again, we shouldn't confuse inane programming with something diabolical about the medium itself. And if self-reports from a self-selected sample mean anything, then consider the results of a survey by researcher Robin Smith of the University of Minnesota. While nearly two-thirds of the 491 adults returning Smith's questionnaire said they thought TV was addictive, they must have been thinking of other people. Significantly, very few of them answered yes to questions meant to signal that they themselves might be addicted (e.g., "I can't walk away from the TV once it is on").

Hooked or not, people who watch a lot of television are bound to be affected by the experience—although perhaps not in predictable ways. Viewers' attitudes are clearly shaped by the sort of programs they see. For more than two decades, George Gerbner and his colleagues at the Annenberg School of Communications at the University of Pennsylvania have been exploring this issue. More striking to them than the customary connection between TV viewing and violence is the finding that "television's mean and dangerous world tends to cultivate a sense of relative danger, mistrust, dependence, and—despite its supposedly 'entertaining' nature—alienation and gloom." Specifically, according to data from questionnaires, the more TV a person watches, the more likely he or she is to believe that most people are just out for themselves and would take advantage of you if given a chance. The stories and characters in one's living room—and let us remember that the average American television set is on for about seven hours a day—support a dismal view of human nature. This may help to explain why so many of us grumble that "people are just no damned good" and assume that selfishness and aggression are more natural than helpfulness and caring.

But there is a big difference between finding that cynicism is reinforced by American television programs and claiming that kids would be reading Dostoevsky if it weren't for the boob tube. The latter represents just the sort of shallow reasoning that TV itself is said to cause.

Women are more empathic (and intuitive) than men

In our society, the sterotypical feminine role calls to mind words like *nurturance, empathy, sympathy, sensitivity,* and even *women's intuition.* It seems likely, therefore, that females would embody these features more than males.

The picture that actually emerges from research, however, is far more complicated. When children are asked to take someone else's point of view—to imagine what another person is thinking or feeling—boys are usually just as skilled as girls. Similarly, a test specifically designed to measure intuitive ability turned up no gender differences when administered to 200 adults in Maryland. On the other hand, a review of studies, published in the mid-1970s, showed that females were usually better able than males to judge the meanings of body posture, facial expression, and tone of voice—although the average difference between the sexes was quite small.

A few years later, Sara Snodgrass decided to examine the question of women's intuition from a fresh perspective. For her doctoral dissertation at Harvard University, she asked thirty-six pairs of undergraduates to work together on a task, with one person assigned to teach something to the other. Both were asked periodically how they were feeling and how they thought the other was feeling. It turned out that women weren't any more sensitive to the other's emotional state than men were—but those playing the role of student were more tuned in to how the "teacher" was feeling than the other way around.

This makes perfect sense, says Snodgrass, because people in subordinate roles need to pay careful attention to their leader's state of mind; their own lives and careers can depend on it. And in real life, men are more likely to hold dominant positions while women have to defer to them. Therefore, she concludes, "it is not surprising that women have become the more sensitive sex. . . . 'Women's intuition' would perhaps more accurately be referred to as 'subordinate's intuition.'"

Other researchers, meanwhile, instead of looking at how well we can figure out someone else's feelings, have investigated how we *respond* to those feelings. Are women more empathic than men, more apt to feel other people's pain or joy?

Some of the answer depends on who is doing the research. Suspiciously, experiments performed by women researchers have been more likely to find that female subjects are especially empathic than experiments conducted by men. But what seems to matter most of all is the way empathy is measured. That was the conclusion of psychologist Nancy Eisenberg and a student of hers after they reviewed more than 100 studies in 1983. "There is a huge sex difference in self-report of empathy as measured with questionnaires . . . [but] little evidence of a sex difference in physiological response to another's emotional distress," they wrote.

In other words, women are more likely than men to *describe* themselves as empathic. But that may reflect how they see and present themselves rather than whether they really do react more strongly than males to someone else's pain. When researchers judge empathy by watching faces or measuring heart rate, men and women usually score about the same. It's hard, then, to make a case that sex differences in empathy are clear-cut—let alone innate—just as it's hard to argue that intuition or sensitivity has more to do with gender than with power.

Grouping students by ability allows them to learn better

Here is the unvarnished, unsettling truth: The practice of separating students into high-, average-, and low-ability groups doesn't respond to differences in what they can learn so much as it *creates* differences in what they *will* learn. Typically, the top-level groups or classes get a stimulating education of the sort that would benefit almost all students, while low-level groups are given mindless exercises and boring assignments that would turn anyone off to learning.

Most public elementary schools and virtually all senior high schools in the United States use some variant of "tracking." The first graders who someone decides are bright get to read interesting stories while the others have to struggle with the modern version of See Dick Run. The sharp high-school sophomores learn analytical geometry; the others slog through endless pages of multiplication problems in Basic Math.

The studies of ability grouping—and there are quite a few by now—lead to these conclusions: Overall school achievement does not go up when students are segregated by ability. While some research shows that kids in the top groups, who enjoy an enriched curriculum, do benefit academically from tracking, the gains typically are quite small. More disturbing, these minimal benefits are achieved at the expense of the kids in the remedial or low-level groups, whose academic performance plummets compared to what it would be in mixed-ability classrooms.

Self-esteem also sags when a child is dumped on what a

student of mine once called "the dummy pile." And if ability grouping is unfair in theory, it is even worse in practice: Promising students who come from poor or minority backgrounds have a particularly hard time getting placed in the advanced classes. A school may look integrated from the outside, but racial and ethnic segregation continue, thanks in large part to tracking.

These findings emerge from what one scholar describes as "virtually mountains of research evidence indicating that homogeneous grouping doesn't consistently help *anyone* learn better." Here's a small taste of that evidence:

Robert Slavin of Johns Hopkins University reviewed thirteen of the best studies he could find in 1987. In light of how many teachers swear by the practice, he concluded, "it is surprising to see how unequivocally the research evidence refutes the assertion that ability-grouped class assignment can increase student achievement in elementary schools." As for high schools, a study of nearly 11,000 students published in 1989 calculated that those who were in the bottom track were more likely to drop out *as a result of being in that track.* In forty-five California middle-school classrooms, meanwhile, "grouping according to ability provides fewer opportunities for learning," researchers found. In England, students placed in the slow groups did worse than kids who came from the identical social background but who had the good fortune to attend schools featuring mixed-ability classrooms. And in Israel, it was discovered that mixing different kids together was much better for low-resource students while presenting no real disadvantage for high-resource students.

Academically speaking, whether or not the rich get slightly richer as a result of tracking systems, the poor clearly get much poorer. Again, some of this is due to the very nature of separating students by ability and some of it is due to the way this separation is carried out in most American schools. The net result, though, is that the children who most need a leg up get a boot in the face instead: poorer teachers, books, and lessons as well as less intellectual stimulation from peers.

What's more, they are likely to live down to predictions about their achievement, thus creating a self-fulfilling prophecy. Psychologically speaking, according to education professor Jeannie Oakes, who is also the author of a powerful book called *Keeping Track,* academic grouping "seems to foster lowered self-esteem, lowered aspirations, and negative attitudes toward school" among students identified as slow learners.

But surely it's easier to teach a group of kids who are all at a similar ability level, isn't it? The problem, replies Oakes, is that "the idea of a homogeneous group is a fallacy to begin with." A bunch of students might have similar scores on one test, but they probably represent a range of abilities when other sorts of measures are used. Tracking may encourage a teacher to overlook these differences and treat everyone in the room as if they were basically the same.

So why does such a counterproductive and unfair arrangement continue to dominate American schools? Oakes, in an article written with pioneering education researcher John I. Goodlad, suggests that the answer may lie in the fact that "teachers of the upper tracks like things this way"—and so do their students' parents. Anyone who cries foul is called a utopian and accused of failing to recognize that kids are different. "Obviously, not all students benefit equally from lessons," Goodlad and Oakes reply. "There is nothing particularly unfair about that. But tracking prejudges how much children will benefit and results in the absence of some children from the places where academically and socially valued subjects are taught."

The solution, according to people who have studied the question, is not simply to put different students together in the same room, but to change how they are taught. Literally hundreds of studies have shown that children who are encouraged to help each other to learn (rather than being forced to work individually or to compete against each other) end up achieving more. This is true for all grade levels, all subjects, and all kinds of schools. Cooperative learning produces kids who like each other more, like themselves more, like school more, and become better learners. When students of different abilities work together in the same small groups, everyone benefits: for the quicker kids, learning can come from the process of explaining the material to someone else.

"None of us is as smart as all of us," says David Johnson, a social psychologist at the University of Minnesota. As far as the benefits of cooperative learning are concerned, he adds, "there's almost nothing that American education has seen with this level of empirical support."

Except maybe the conclusion that grouping students by ability is a terrible idea.

■ ■ ■ Mondays always get me down

Popular songs and comic strips get a lot of mileage out of the idea that Mondays are uniquely depressing. It seems logical enough that if we enjoy weekend recreation more than weekday work—if our attitude matches the bumper sticker that reads Work Sucks But I Need the Bucks—then the first day back on the job is not likely to find us euphoric.

In fact, at least half a dozen studies have found that more suicides in the United States take place on Monday than on any other day of the week. But when we focus instead on how the average person feels, we hear a different story. A group of researchers at the State University of New York at

Stony Brook decided a few years ago that if a blue Monday syndrome really existed, they would have to do more than ask people whether they *believed* their moods were foul on Mondays. When asked, most people do indeed say this. But as we've already seen ("Women's moods change at 'that time of the month,'" pp. 41–46), what we assume is true about our emotional state may say more about internalized assumptions than about what really happens.

Without revealing what they were looking for, the SUNY researchers asked forty-six married men to answer some questions about their moods every day for three months. Then they did the same thing with another fifty-eight men—this time simultaneously getting the men's wives to report on how their husbands were feeling. All the results pointed in the same direction: The men were most cheerful during the weekend, but Mondays didn't depress them more than any other day of the week.

Taking still another tack, the experimenters asked more than 600 men to fill out a questionnaire that was designed to be sensitive to signs of depression. Each subject filled out the form only once, but different people got it at different times of the week. It turned out that Monday's subjects didn't feel any worse on average than those who happened to receive the survey on other days. Overall, then, it looks as if—at least for men—Mondays are really no bluer than the rest of the week.

Marry in haste, repent at leisure

If by "haste" we mean early in life, then there is no question that such marriages are especially likely to fail. Couples who marry in their teens are, by some accounts, *twice* as likely to get divorced as those who marry in their twenties. Some studies have found that the divorce rate edges up again for marriages between people in their thirties—probably because a higher proportion of these are second and third marriages, which don't always last as long—but this statistic isn't accepted by all the experts. In any case, the chances that a teenage marriage will unravel are so high that demographers Teresa Castro Martin and Larry L. Bumpass were able to write in 1989 that "the inverse relationship between age at marriage and the likelihood of marital disruption is among the strongest and most consistently documented in the literature."

On another reading, however, a "hasty" marriage is one that people (of any age) rush into before taking the time to get to know each other. Are these people asking for trouble? Not surprisingly, what little research exists on the question suggests that they are. A large-scale British study from the 1970s found that 20 percent of those who were divorced—as opposed to only 8 percent of those still married—had known their partner for less than a year before tying the knot. A survey of 404 black American women who had become pregnant during adolescence revealed that those who reported frequent and intensive contact with their husbands for at least a year before marriage were only half as likely to have separated from them.

Even short of divorce, it seems that rushing into marriage does indeed lead a disproportionate number of people—at least women—to repent at leisure. Of fifty-one wives who described the state of their marriages to Kansas State University researchers, it turned out that those who had dated their husbands for at least two years before marching up the aisle were more likely than other women to say they were satisfied with married life. (Of course these fifty-one, who chose to fill out the questionnaire, may not have been representative of the other forty-nine who threw it away, just as the people who take the trouble to complete and return magazine surveys are not necessarily typical of the population at large.)

We all know of exceptions, of course, but it would appear that marrying younger and marrying faster don't exactly maximize the chances of a happy, lifelong relationship. Still, this doesn't mean that living together before marriage is a surefire recipe for wedded bliss. A 1981 survey of Swedish women and a 1987–1988 survey of U.S. citizens both showed that those who had set up housekeeping before the wedding gifts arrived were more likely to divorce than those who hadn't.

Don't read too much into this, though. It doesn't mean that a given couple is less likely to have a satisfying marriage if they move in together first. It probably reflects the fact that those who live together are the sort of people who, when they do get married, will be more receptive to the idea of divorce if their relationship should turn sour. People who jump right into marriage, on the other hand, might be the type who view wedding vows as absolutely binding (or who shrink from the prospect of living alone) and thus would stay together no matter what.

Don't have sex before the big game

There's a scene in *Annie Hall* in which Woody Allen's character rolls over in bed after making love and sighs, "As Balzac said, 'There goes another novel.'"

Freud helped to popularize the idea that each of us has a fixed amount of energy and that draining it one way leaves less for other activities. Although it has since been discredited, this model may help to account for the assumption that people (by which is usually meant men) become dulled and dried out from sex. Other possible sources of this belief include religious teachings that frown on pleasure, particularly pleasure of a physical sort,* and simple misogyny, with men fearing that women will sap their life force, domesticating and emasculating them in the bargain.

Whatever its source, the idea that sex is draining pops up again in locker rooms where athletes are solemnly instructed that celibacy is the best policy. Is this view still heard today? A 1988 survey of baseball and basketball coaches found that only 9 percent admitted to believing that sex before a game adversely affects performance— athletic performance, that is—but that another 41 percent weren't sure. Maybe an even larger proportion of football coaches and boxing trainers continue to insist on abstinence.

Anyone who tries to evaluate the value of this practice soon realizes that hard data on sex and sports aren't easy to come by. One occasionally hears some anecdotal evi-

*Interestingly, the Puritans themselves were not really puritanical, according to historical documents reviewed by Richard Shenkman.

dence from an Olympic athlete who scored before he scored, but what seems to be the only published study on the question appeared in 1968. Not exactly a model of excellence in experimental design, it consisted of giving a grip-strength–endurance test to fourteen ex-jocks who had had sex either the previous night or six days earlier. Would you be astonished to learn there weren't any differences?

No studies support the folklore, and no researcher seems to take it seriously. Julian Stein, professor of physical education at George Mason University, suggests that it's "another example of coaches trying to completely dominate their players." Frank Katch, chairman of the department of exercise science at the University of Massachusetts, says he couldn't imagine that sex would have any effect at all— "unless it were a pleasurable experience, in which case it could help." Of course, the loss of sleep from interminable intercourse or the anxiety involved with trying to *find* a sexual partner might not leave an athlete in peak condition. (Casey Stengel reportedly said that it's not the catchin' that causes problems—it's the chasin'.) But as for sex itself, there's no reason why athletes shouldn't be creative with their warm-up exercises.

Adoption cures infertility

I have a friend who tried for three years to have a child and, finally conceding defeat, decided to adopt. Within a matter of days she was pregnant. The chances are good you know of a similar story. The question is: do we just hear about these incidents out of proportion to their actual numbers or is it conceivable that the decision to adopt actually affects fertility?

Such a connection would seem to make sense. Adopting means giving up on pregnancy, which in turn means "no more monthly temperature charts, no more medical tests, and no more pressure to perform sexually on cue," as one group of social workers wrote in 1985. Thus would-be parents whose infertility has no clear-cut, physiological cause, such as her blocked fallopian tubes or his low sperm count, may be victims of a kind of stress that is literally unbearable—and that is also relieved by the decision to stop trying.

That's the theory. What does the research say? The studies have to be interpreted with caution: They are fairly old (mostly from the early 1960s) and, in some cases, guilty of mixing together couples whose infertility is due to different causes. Still, after having reviewed fourteen of them I think it can be said that another piece of folk wisdom bites the dust. Couples who adopt aren't any more likely to conceive than those who don't adopt. In fact, they often seem a good deal *less* likely to conceive, although not too much significance should be attached to this fact.

Most of the good studies are set up in pretty much the same way: People who show up at an infertility clinic are tested to rule out obvious problems. Those whose inability to become pregnant remains a mystery to the doctors are then followed for several years. In the controlled studies, the subsequent pregnancy rate for couples who adopt is compared to the rate for nonadopters. One study, the most optimistic of the bunch, reported in 1965 that eighteen of twenty-seven couples who adopted eventually conceived. Oddly, the researchers took this as proof that adoption works even though they also reported the same conception rate for couples whose infertility was due to "emotional stress" but who didn't adopt.

Up until then, none of the studies used control groups to put the numbers in perspective. In any case, most of them were pretty discouraging, with conception rates for adopting couples ranging from 0 to 14 percent. Then a controlled British study was published that showed a 10 percent rate for adopters—and a 40 percent rate for everyone else. A Cleveland clinic found that only 5 adopting couples out of 197 became pregnant during the first two years; after five years, the rate was around 17 percent, which was just about the same as for the nonadopters. In another study, the rate was 23 percent for adopters and 35 percent for nonadopters.

Two more experiments, both published in the 1970s, should be sufficient to clinch the point. Of couples who appeared at a Montreal clinic but who didn't seem irreversibly sterile, 29 percent who adopted eventually got pregnant, as compared to a whopping 90 percent of those who didn't adopt. (At the end of the first year, the numbers were 2 or 3 percent versus nearly 50 percent, respectively.) Five years later, researchers at a California clinic estimated that about one-third of adopters and two-thirds of nonadopters would eventually conceive.

Is there any reason that adoption should *reduce* the probability of conception? It's possible that couples with a baby around the house have sex less often. Or maybe the adopting couples had physiological problems that the tests failed to pick up. Surveys often find that these women had spent more time than nonadopters trying to get pregnant before showing up at a clinic, which means their infertility may be due to something more serious. But these theories aside, the fact remains that not one well-designed study has been able to show that adoption significantly increases the chances of getting pregnant for any group of people who have been having trouble.

Blind people are blessed with supersensitive hearing

The idea that people deprived of one faculty must be gifted in other ways probably caught on because of our need to believe that the universe is ordered and just, that everything ultimately works out for the best. Thus the blind are often assumed to have a naturally acute sense of hearing or touch or even some mysterious sixth sense.

Alas, studies generally fail to support these claims. Blind people simply "learn to listen more carefully to compensate, and to be more sensitive to the feel of an object," says Mark Uslan at the American Foundation for the Blind. Those who cannot see pay close attention to details that sighted people rarely notice—the feel of a sidewalk underfoot, for example. Some studies have shown that when people with normal vision are kept in the dark for a week or two, their auditory and tactile senses seem to improve, too, due to their newly increased attentiveness.

In practice, it's often difficult to "differentiate between 'true' sensory sensitivity" and just paying closer attention, according to Michael Bross and Myra Borenstein, two Canadian researchers. In 1982, they used an audiometer to test how well people could pick out very brief tones from background noise. Blind and sighted individuals did equally well.

Like most such studies, this one involved very few subjects. But when all the research is added up, the pattern that emerges is one in which no differences exist on the sort of basic sensitivity that reflects the equipment we're born with. And even on the "higher order" skills that are affected by motivation and experience, the data are mixed. In a study reported by Charles E. Rice of the Stanford Research Institute, for instance, people who were blind from infancy tended to do better on a test of echo perception than either those who were sighted or those who became blind later in life. However, one of the subjects with normal vision was so good at the task that Rice had to rule out a hypothesis of "sensory compensation"—that is, the idea that "the congenitally blind have abilities beyond those possessed by the normal sighted."

Echo perception, and not some magical "facial vision," accounts for the ability of certain blind people to detect the presence or distance of objects, according to University of Louisville researcher Emerson Foulke. It's a matter of listening for how sound bounces off things in the room—"demonstrably an auditory phenomenon. Sighted people aren't aware they have this ability because they have no reason to use it," he says. In fact, when it comes to honing in on a target, children who have been blind from birth often are *less* skilled than those who lost their vision later in life.

For hearing and touch alike, writes David Warren, a psychologist at the University of California at Riverside who has conducted a thorough review of the literature, "the sensory compensation notion, which has been advanced with mystical awe in the past, cannot be supported: the visually handicapped child (or adult) does not have keener senses than the sighted."

Adolescence is a time of turmoil and alienation

You can almost hear Daniel Offer shaking his head over the phone. "Whatever adolescents do, their parents dismiss it with, 'Ach, these are teenagers!'—as if this explains everything. The public seems to want to hold on to the idea that the teenage years are more difficult than any other period in life."

Well, aren't they? Absolutely not, says Offer, who is a professor of psychiatry at the University of Chicago and author of eight books on the subject. From his first interviews with more than a hundred high-school boys two decades ago, Offer noticed that he wasn't finding much to support the idea that adolescence is inherently a pathological period. By now, he and his colleagues have interviewed about 2,000 adolescents, and his specially designed questionnaire has been filled out by another 50,000 of them around the world. The results suggest that perhaps 15 or 20 percent of American teens seem to be chronically depressed or anxious—a rate not very different from that for other age groups. These troubled teens, he found, were "far outnumbered by those who were relatively happy, coped well with their lives, and made a relatively smooth transition to adulthood."

Of course, you don't hear about these well-adjusted adolescents on the evening news. Instead you hear about teenage suicide. While this is certainly a serious problem—and one that became even more serious during the 1960s—the suicide rate for teens is still "lower than that for almost all other age groups in the U.S.," Offer writes. Similarly, you hear so much about drug abuse that you may not realize it has been declining over the last few years. It's easy to forget that drugs aren't a problem for the overwhelming majority of high-school students.

In a recent paper, Offer takes pains to distinguish disturbed adolescents from disturbing adolescents. While someone is in the process of finding (or, more accurately, creating) his or her identity, that person may be regarded as a pain by adults. But that doesn't mean the teenager is *in* pain. Moreover, Offer has found that a large number of teenagers don't fit into either category: "They sail through adolescence with little effort."

Naturally, fewer sail through when they must confront real misery every day. Teenagers whose lives are scarred by violence or warped by hunger don't have an easy time of it, and parents or teachers of these kids may scoff at Offer's optimism. But his point is that there is nothing about adolescence *itself* that makes someone miserable. If nearly half of the teenagers in Bangladesh seem depressed, which is what his colleagues there found, the villain is poverty, not some abstraction called "life-cycle transition."

Offer says he would be more tentative about his conclusions if he were the only one coming up with these sort of reassuring findings. But he isn't. While clinicians—people who see mostly disturbed youths—continue to publish papers on the storminess of the adolescent years, researchers who look at a broader population are a lot less glum.

Take the work of psychiatrist Michael Rutter and his colleagues, who studied a random sample of 200 fourteen and fifteen year olds living in small towns in England. The proportion of these teens who showed evidence of some psychiatric disorder was only marginally higher than the rate for adults, and the nature of those disorders didn't indicate problems unique to adolescence. Inner turmoil was relatively common among these teens, but surprisingly few of them were alienated from their parents.

On the subject of mood swings, for which adolescents are famous, take at a look at an intriguing study conducted in 1977 by Mihaly Csikszentmihalyi (whom his friends understandably prefer to call "Mike") and Reed Larson. They gave beepers to seventy-five suburban high-school students and then paged them at random intervals over the course of a week. Each time they were beeped, the subjects wrote down what they were doing and how they were feeling about it—collectively offering a subjective portrait of adolescence.

Their moods were indeed more variable than adults', but their feelings weren't really unpredictable once you looked at what was going on around them at the time. Moreover, these emotional shifts didn't indicate that something was seriously wrong: Those whose moods were most variable were just as "happy and as much in control as their steadier peers, and they appear[ed] to be as well adjusted on other measures." There seems little empirical support, then, for the widespread idea that adolescence is one long nightmare with occasional breaks for pizza.

There's safety in numbers

There's no question that a stroll through the city streets is less risky if you're walking with someone, just as it makes sense to stick to well-traveled areas. In this sense the saying is true. But if you are concerned about whether people will rescue you if you should need assistance, then higher numbers may actually mean *less* security. In their book, *The Unresponsive Bystander,* psychologists Bibb Latane and John Darley sum up the findings of their research:

It may be that people are less likely to find themselves in trouble if there are others present. But if a person does find himself in trouble, safety in numbers may be illusory. . . . A victim may be more likely to get help or an emergency to be reported, the fewer people who are available to take action.

This research grew out of the infamous Kitty Genovese murder of 1964: Thirty-eight neighbors heard this woman scream for help over the course of more than half an hour while she was being stabbed to death; none came to her aid or even called the police. By now, more than 100 studies have confirmed Latane and Darley's conclusion that more witnesses means less of a chance of helping. Someone is more likely to come to your aid if he or she believes no one else can do so.

In a typical study, college students were led, one at a time, into a room where they were invited to have a conversation over an intercom with either one or five other people. When a voice over the speaker began stuttering and choking as if he was having an epileptic seizure, 85 percent of the students who thought they were the only person listening left their room to get help. But a mere 31 percent of those who believed that other subjects could hear the victim bothered to do anything.

Why? Apart from the obvious fact that a bystander may assume someone else has already done something, Latane and Darley offer several reasons. (1) The fact that other people are not helping may lead us to conclude that nothing serious is happening. (2) We fear appearing foolish in the eyes of others if it turns out no help was actually needed. (3) The duty to act is shared by everyone present, diffusing the responsibility and thereby reducing our own obligation. (4) If it becomes clear later on that something should have been done, there will be other people to share the blame.

Stress is bad for you

"ARE YOU OVERSTRESSED? TAKE THIS SIMPLE QUIZ." Better yet, don't. Popular magazines warn that stressful life events will make you sick, but the hard data suggest it's not that simple. The statistical relationship between stress and illness is higher than would be expected by chance, but not all that impressive as statistical relationships go. Specifically, lots of people lead very stressful lives yet somehow manage to stay healthy.

This means that we need to look not at some objective entity called Stress, but at how different individuals perceive and react to particular strains in life. And we need to ask what separates people who are adversely affected by stress from those who let it roll off their backs. Among the factors that have been identified are physiology, early childhood experience, social support, and personality patterns.

Suzanne Oullette Kobasa, a psychologist at the City University of New York, has spent more than ten years identifying the cluster of traits that add up to "hardiness"—a disposition that protects people from the negative effects of stress. In her first major study, more than 800 executives were asked to describe stressful events in their lives and also illnesses they'd had recently. As other researchers before her had found, the correlation was weak. So Kobasa focused on 161 people who had lived through very stressful events. The idea was to see what distinguished those who had been sick a lot from those who hadn't let the stress get them down.

Three central traits emerged, which she refers to as control, commitment, and challenge. Control means that people are confident in their ability to affect their own lives rather than seeing themselves as victims of fate. Commitment refers to a clear sense of what their own values are— and the importance of these values—as well as a vigorous involvement with their environment. Challenge suggests that such people are more likely to see change as offering a new set of opportunities rather than as being threatening.

Subsequent studies of other executives confirmed this basic picture of hardiness and its importance in keeping people healthy. Neither social support nor exercise was as powerful a source of resistance to illness as hardiness was, Kobasa and her colleagues found. But more to the point, she noted that "any blanket conclusion about the debilitating effects of stressful events is an overgeneralization."

Kobasa's research probably focused on high-powered executives because as a group they are thought to be at high risk. Okay, the people who iron their shirts and empty their wastebaskets tell themselves: Maybe these guys do make obscene amounts of money in their cushy, corporate careers, but at least they pay for it in stress-induced heart attacks. It's not much of a consolation, but it's something.

As it happens, it's also wrong. Robert A. Karasek at the University of Southern California argues that job stress is a function of two separate elements: the psychological demands of the work and the ability to make decisions about how those demands are handled. Strain results "when individuals have insufficient control over their work situation to be able to satisfactorily deal with the level of demands being placed on them," he and his colleagues wrote in the *American Journal of Public Health* in 1988.

The emphasis on control, of course, echoes Kobasa's work. But these researchers go on to point out that the concept has important implications for calculating what sorts of jobs are most dangerous. Their large-scale study of workers in the United States and Sweden found that the incidence of heart disease does not necessarily increase as you move up the job ladder. In many cases, the people stuck with less lucrative and prestigious work once again get a bum deal.

"It is not in high status, presumably 'success oriented,' managerial or professional occupations (where Type A and high incomes are most prevalent) that we record the highest level" of heart disease, they report. "Instead, the peak prevalence occurs in a subset of lower status jobs with high psychological 'work load' and low job decision latitude." It's the men and women who sew clothes in factories or cook meals in restaurants who deserve your sympathy, then, not the people passing papers in downtown skyscrapers.

Birds of a feather flock together vs. Opposites attract

Psychologists and sociologists have wrestled with this question for decades, trying to decide whether attraction is usually based on similarity or complementarity. By now the results are in and, in a word, the birds have it.

"The theory of complementary needs, as a factor governing mate choice, has received a lot of attention, but empirical evidence does not substantiate it," Richard W. Lewak and his coauthors wrote in 1985. "Marriage partners tend to be more alike than different." When two people notice and can appreciate things that distinguish them, it is usually against a background of more fundamental similarities.

Lewak's own work shows that we tend to marry people whose IQs are more or less similar to our own. Other research demonstrates that those of the same racial, religious, and economic backgrounds usually flock together, as do those with similar political views. (Some of this, of course, is less a matter of conscious preference than of simple availability: If we associate more with those who are like us, we will tend to pair up with someone from that pool.) As far as physical attractiveness is concerned, people may indicate a preference for the most appealing person possible. But surveys of couples show that here, too, like eventually finds like. As University of Michigan psychologist David M. Buss says, the principle that we are attracted to those similar to ourselves is "one of the most well established replicable findings in the psychology and biology of human mating."

To make things even more interesting, there is some evidence to suggest that couples *become* more similar over time. Researchers followed 175 married couples for anywhere from seven to twenty-one years. As the years went by, the wives' scores on tests of intelligence, perception, and motor skills came to resemble the scores their husbands had received sometime earlier. Another study, meanwhile, found that husbands and wives tended to have similar cholesterol and blood-pressure levels and also reported about the same level of satisfaction with life. It would seem, then, that when sufficient similarity isn't discovered, it may simply be created.

■ ■ ■ **A** woman's work is never done

It's obviously difficult to conclude anything about actual work behavior from a laboratory experiment, but one 1984 study did find an interesting gender difference in work habits. Forty female and forty male college students were given several pages of dots to count and told to work as long as they thought appropriate for the $4 they were being paid. The women worked 38 percent longer than the men (fifty-nine minutes versus forty-three minutes), and they also got more accomplished and did it more accurately.

But even more revealing is the fact that when men and women in the real world finish working from sun to sun, it's the women who then go on to do most of the housework. In 1975, according to Thomas Juster and Frank Stafford at the University of Michigan, full-time working women put in about twenty-five hours a week around the house, while their husbands did less than half that much work. Even that figure overstates the men's contribution because it counts outdoor chores. When only laundry, bed making, and similar indoor drudgery is tallied, men averaged about one hour a week.

According to many observers, even when the average man does wash the dishes or clean the toilet, he assumes he is "helping out" his wife—doing her a favor—as if these tasks were naturally her primary responsibility. The same goes for child care: It isn't unusual to hear men talk about "baby-sitting" their own children. Husbands may play with their kids or discipline them, according to a group of University of Nevada researchers, but they leave it to their wives to handle the bulk of "maintenance tasks such as feeding, changing and bathing."

By 1981, says Juster, the Michigan data showed that working women were doing a little less housework and men were doing a little more. But even a decade later the gap hasn't narrowed nearly enough to compensate for the fact that more than half of American women are now in the labor force, two-thirds of them working at full-time paying jobs. "Most women work one shift at the office or factory and a 'second shift' at home," the sociologist Arlie Hochschild wrote in 1989. No wonder the women she interviewed kept talking about how much they needed sleep. When paid work and housework were combined, another study found, employed women labored about two hours more every day than did employed men.

And speaking of labor, a study conducted in 1986 by Ohio State University's Margaret Sanik suggested that working women continue doing most of the homemaking even when they are in the last few months of pregnancy. Husbands in her survey put in about fifteen hours a week around the house; the employed mothers-to-be logged nearly twice that.

Men are doing more family work than they used to, acknowledges Wheaton College researcher Joseph Pleck, but "it will clearly be a long time—if ever—before they reach parity."

Blondes have more fun

One of the chief purposes of advertising is to create a demand for stuff that might otherwise be regarded as a waste of money. Thus, since most American women have dark hair, the manufacturers of hair coloring figured they had better plant the idea that any given woman is more likely to have fun, and be preferred by gentlemen, if she lightens up.

Still, one's view of oneself and one's enjoyment of life can be affected by widespread beliefs and preferences, however irrational or artificially induced they may be. If most people in the United States strongly prefer spending time with blond people, this would be a fact worth noticing. As it happens, a handful of studies on the topic have been published—enough to suggest that, as usual, the issue isn't as straightforward as it might appear. Keep in mind that almost all of these reports are based on the judgments of undergraduates, who (as we have already seen in the case of attitudes toward sex) might not be representative of the population at large.

It is true that people with blond hair are more likely than others to be seen as attractive—and this has been found regardless of whether men or women are asked to do the rating. However, two studies published in the 1970s showed that when people are asked to look beyond beauty, dark-haired males and females were preferred overall and were perceived as more intelligent, sincere, and "valuable." If blondes have more fun, then—or are seen as fun-loving—it may be at the expense of being taken seriously.

Hollywood both plays on and perpetuates these stereotypes by casting women with blond hair in the role of the temptress—the sexpot who is perfect for a fling but is then flung aside when the man finally returns to his senses and his reliable dark-haired wife or girlfriend. (*Fatal Attraction* is only one of many films that fit this description.) Blond men, too, are more likely to be presented as vacuous, but the disparity is less pronounced here because male movie-makers are more likely to emphasize appearance where women are concerned. In fact, the nouns *brunette* and *blonde* are applied almost exclusively to women, suggesting that something as trivial as hair color doesn't matter where men are concerned.

A recent unpublished study complicates the picture further by suggesting that attributions may not reflect hair color by itself but hair color as it interacts with attractiveness. Photos of women were tinted so that some raters would see a given woman with light hair while others saw her with dark. It turned out that hair color mostly affected the students' judgments about women who were independently perceived as pretty. "It's only attractive blondes who are seen as having more fun," says Michael Cunningham, the psychologist who did the experiment.

Perhaps the most surprising and consistent finding in this line of research is the extremely negative view of red-heads. Blondes may be dismissed as ditzy, but more than 80 percent of male and female students at one college said they disliked red hair in someone of the opposite sex. Eight years later, another group of undergraduates said they found redheads unattractive—and went on to characterize red-haired men as effeminate and unlikely to be successful. In still another study, a man with strawberry blond hair was introduced to one group of people as having just joined the university faculty, while others were told he was a janitor. Half an hour later, most people who thought the man was a professor remembered him as being blond, while the majority of those who thought he was a janitor described him as a redhead.

Even hundreds of years B.C. (Before Clairol), the writers of fairy tales and the likes of Ovid and Virgil were waxing poetic over the magical powers of golden hair. But this is a matter of taste, a taste strongly influenced by where one happens to live: Blondes are regarded quite differently in Copenhagen, Rome, Nairobi, and Tokyo. It should be obvious that there is nothing about hair color—or, for that matter, skin color—that is intrinsically connected to fun or to sexual potency or intelligence. If redheads are seen as being short-tempered, the belief may have originated in the equation of red with fire and then been perpetuated due to selective perception and memory. We are more likely to notice and remember a hotheaded person with red hair while ignoring all the emotional brunettes (or the placid redheads) we come across. But where behavior is concerned, there is always the possibility of a self-fulfilling prophecy with hair color, just as there is with overall attractiveness (see "Beauty is only skin deep," pp. 25–27): If enough people treat someone as unstable or intelligent or sociable, he or she may eventually live up to this expectation.

Necessity is the mother of invention

When it comes to art, necessity pretty clearly doesn't explain very much: There is no "need" for another painting or symphony. In the more theoretical sciences, too, no one is clamoring for new theories to explain the origin of the universe (with the possible exception of other astrophysicists).

The proverb would seem to have more to do with medical research or applied technology. Someone is more likely to work on, and to find, a vaccine for AIDS when there is a pressing need for it. But even here appearances may be deceiving. A social demand for a discovery may be only an indirect cause: It frees up lots of money for research and is responsible for putting inventive people together to share ideas. "Societal necessity may provide the means," says Teresa Amabile, author of *The Social Psychology of Creativity* and *Growing Up Creative*, "but it doesn't make people think more creatively."*

Howard Gardner, too, has spent years thinking about creativity, and he acknowledges that "for the average person, it's when you're stuck that you can do something you hadn't thought of before." But while pragmatic considerations may unleash an inventiveness you never knew you were capable of, "that doesn't show that in general the desire for the new is based on an externally generated compulsion."

At a conference in England featuring some of the greatest living scientists, Gardner recalls hearing them say over and over that the real motivation for their work was how enjoyable they found it. In fact, these researchers admitted to inventing practical justifications for what they did—giving it the appearance of necessity—in order to be allowed to keep doing what they really wanted to do anyway. Fun— "that's what allows people to return to their lab day after day after day, or compose when society doesn't appreciate their compositions," says Gardner.

If social necessity doesn't explain most instances of in-

*Sometimes particular programs and institutions get the credit for sponsoring innovations they actually had nothing to do with. It's part of American folklore, for example, that Tang (an artificial, mock–orange-flavored drinklike substance), Teflon, and Velcro were invented as part of the space program. Not so. "It was a myth that the public bought," Thomas O. Paine, NASA administrator in the late 1960s, told a reporter in 1989.

ventiveness, *financial* necessity (on the part of the inventor) is an even poorer hypothesis. Incentives such as money are more likely to kill creativity than to enhance it, as Amabile's experiments have clearly shown (see "Rewards motivate people," pp. 31–35). "People will be most creative when they feel motivated primarily by the interest, enjoyment, satisfaction, and challenge of the work itself—and not by external pressures," she says.

Ignorance is bliss

The English poet Thomas Gray said it in 1747: "Where ignorance is bliss / 'Tis folly to be wise." He didn't specify the conditions under which ignorance actually *is* bliss, but other writers have made the point unconditionally. "A person is never happy except at the price of some ignorance" is how Anatole France put it.

Is this true in its widest interpretation? Do people who know less in general tend to say they are especially happy? The answer seems to be no, but neither do researchers find consistent evidence for the reverse proposition—that more education makes for contentment, all else being equal. A study of more than 2,000 adults in the 1970s, for example, showed no clear pattern. The people who reported the *lowest* overall life satisfaction were those in the second-*highest* category of education: They had spent some time in college but never graduated.

Other surveys also fail to support a straightforward relationship. Norval Glenn, a sociologist, and Charles Weaver, a professor of management, could find virtually no connection between the number of years of schooling people had under their belts and how happy they said their marriages were. On various other measures of well-being, they reported in a later article, education mattered slightly—but the association was weaker for men than for women and weakest of all for black men. While the effects of education are "predominantly positive, the data do not provide the strong and consistent evidence for positive effects on psychological well-being that the supporters of American education would like to see"—although, of course, they provide no support at all for the idea that ignorance is bliss. Glenn and Weaver went on to speculate that our happiness may be more affected by our *mother's* level of education than by our own.

A political scientist at the University of Kentucky did find that "intelligence" (actually, a score on a vocabulary test) seemed to go hand in hand with self-reports of both happiness and satisfaction with different aspects of life. But such associations can be misleading. What appears to be the result of a particular variable—vocabulary skills, in this case—might really be produced by other features that overlap with it. Sure enough, once this researcher used statistical corrections to eliminate the effects of things like age, gender, income, race, physical condition, marital status, and so forth, he found that test scores by themselves had almost nothing to do with happiness or satisfaction. Someone's age, gender, and so forth said more about how happy that person was than how many words he or she knew.* Again, neither ignorance nor knowledge was a reliable predictor of bliss.

Here, as with so many other attitudes and behaviors, it's useful to keep in mind that what is true of Americans is not necessarily true of the rest of the world. In the United States, more school meant slightly more enjoyment of life but no more happiness, political scientist Doh C. Shinn

---

*This study did find, though, that people with less education were somewhat more likely to sound hopeless about life and agree with statements such as "nothing seems to be worthwhile any more."

found. But a similar survey discovered that education had a much stronger effect on both measures in Korea. There, about half the people whose education went no further than elementary school said they were happy and that they enjoyed life, while 70 percent of Korean college graduates indicated they were happy and 62 percent said they were enjoying their lives. In both countries, income was more closely related to happiness than schooling was, but "a life of well-being has more to do with educational attainment in Korea than in America," Shinn concluded.

All of these studies, of course, are based on a rather different meaning of *ignorance* than the one we generally have in mind when we paraphrase Thomas Gray. More relevant are the people who seem to believe that what they don't know won't hurt them—or perhaps that knowing unpleasant things will hurt them more. If their spouse is having an affair, they'd rather not know about it; if they have a terminal disease, they'd prefer not to be told.

It's hard to know how to prove or disprove the assumptions underlying these choices: A crude measure such as "Would you say you are very happy / somewhat happy / not at all happy with your life?" doesn't really get at the meaning of bliss; similarly, not knowing about one thing may not have the same effect on you as not knowing about another. In the long run, ignorance of many kinds often seems to be foolish because it only delays a confrontation with something disagreeable or dangerous that will make its presence felt eventually.

But maybe it's silly to try to justify awareness of things about oneself or one's environment in terms of how much happiness it will buy. The premise of this book, after all, has been that we ought to live without illusions—or at least that it is better to know when a cherished belief isn't true. Remember that Socrates didn't say we can maximize our *pleasure* by being introspective; he said "the unexamined life isn't worth living." And Robert Frost didn't say it's *easiest* to tackle a problem head on; he said "the best way out is always through." We may decide to live life with our eyes open, in other words, regardless of whether this makes us happier.

COMMONLY MISUSED WORDS

Even people who pride themselves on being supremely literate often use words incorrectly. Here are a dozen words and phrases that don't mean what a lot of folks seem to think they mean.

BEMUSE   It suggests confusion, not amusement.

DEVOLVE   Responsibility for something may devolve to (or on) you, but situations do not "devolve" into anarchy. The word does not denote the opposite of "evolve."

DISINTERESTED   Although the more tolerant language authorities and dictionaries are bowing to popular usage, most continue to insist that the word means "impartial." It isn't a synonym for "uninterested."

DROLL   A droll sense of humor is playful or whimsical, not dry.

ENORMITY   Strictly speaking, *enormity* is used only to describe the extent to which something is evil or outrageous. *Enormousness* refers simply to size.

FORTUITOUS   Again, lenient linguists are starting to allow *fortuitous* and *fortunate* to be used interchangeably, but purists get huffy over this one. To call a meeting "fortuitous" is to suggest only that it happened by chance; it doesn't imply that there was anything desirable about it.

I.E. This is a way of introducing an explanation or equivalent description, not an example. The latter is signified by "e.g." The two expressions are often confused—i.e., one is used when the other is intended. Many people do so—e.g., my high-school English teacher.

IMMACULATE CONCEPTION The term does not refer to the belief that Mary was still a virgin when she gave birth to Jesus. It concerns the belief that Mary was free of original sin when she herself was conceived.

IN LIEU OF This means "instead of," not "in light of."

SCAN The allowable usage on this one, too, is changing, but the preferred meaning is to scrutinize, not to skim.

SCHIZOPHRENIA The problem here is less a matter of improper usage than of faulty understanding of psychiatry. Schizophrenics do not have multiple personalities; that's another disorder altogether. They are characterized instead by such things as delusions (faulty beliefs), hallucinations (seeing or hearing things that aren't there), disorganized thinking and language, various disturbances of emotion, and other symptoms. The metaphorical use of the word (e.g., "Voters are schizophrenic; they want more services but lower taxes") only serves to reinforce the confusion about the psychiatric diagnosis.

WILLY-NILLY It means "whether you want it or not"; it does not mean "in a confused state."

REFERENCES

If quotations in the text are not cited here, it is because they come from personal communication rather than from published material.

INTRODUCTION

Teigen's study, "Old Truths or Fresh Insights," appeared in the *British Journal of Social Psychology* (25:43–49, 1986).

SWIMMING AND EATING

The only written source I'm aware of is Arthur H. Steinhaus's article "Evidence and Opinions Related to Swimming after Meals," first published in the *Journal of Health, Physical Education, Recreation* (Apr.:59, 1961), and reprinted in his book, *Toward an Understanding of Health and Physical Education* (Dubuque, IA: William C. Brown, 1963).

GENDER DIFFERENCES IN SEXUAL MOTIVATION

Person-centered versus body-centered: E. Hatfield et al., "Gender Differences in What Is Desired in the Sexual Relationship," *Journal of Psychology and Human Sexuality* (1:39–52, 1988). Hyde's study: J. Carroll,

K. Volk, and J. Hyde, "Differences between Males and Females in Motives for Engaging in Sexual Intercourse," *Archives of Sexual Behavior* (14:131–39, 1985). Allgeier's study is described in an unpublished 1987 paper, "Policies, Perceptions, and Motivations Surrounding Sexual Interactions." Ideal versus usual motive (and age differences): J. Sprague and D. Quadagno, "Gender and Sexual Motivation," *Journal of Psychology and Human Sexuality* (2:57–76, 1989). Quadagno's Florida replication hasn't yet been published. Cross-cultural data: R. Endleman, *Love and Sex in Twelve Cultures* (New York: Psyche Press, 1989, 84, 116).

CHOCOLATE

For the famous chocolate/acne study, see J. Fulton et al., "Effect of Chocolate on Acne Vulgaris," *Journal of the American Medical Association* (*JAMA*) (210:2071–74, 1969) and also follow-up letters on the subject in a later edition of *JAMA* (211:1956, 1970).

No one has bothered to publish any research debunking the recent, but popular, assumptions about chocolate's unique effects on mood. For a few general references on the subject, though, see M. Schuman, M. J. Gitlin, and L. Fairbanks, "Sweets, Chocolate, and Atypical Depressive Traits," *Journal of Nervous and Mental Disease* (175:491–95, 1987).

AGING AND CONSERVATISM

The Bennington College study was published in T. M. Newcomb et al., *Persistence and Change* (New York: Wiley, 1967); an update will be out soon, with Duane Alwin as the first author. The 1965/1973/1982 study is by M. K. Jennings and G. B. Markus, "Partisan Orientations over the Long Haul," *American Political Science Review* (78:1000–18, 1984). David Sears's report is called "Life-Stage Effects on Attitude Change, Especially among the Elderly" and appears in *Aging: Social Change,* edited by S. B. Kiesler et al. (New York: Academic Press, 1981). For the 1956/1958/1960 and 1972/1974/1976 study, see J. A. Krosnick and D. F. Alwin, "Aging and Susceptibility to Attitude Change," *Journal of Personality and Social Psychology* (*JPSP*) (57:416–25, 1989). For a clear and accessible introduction to the whole topic, I recommend N. D. Glenn, "Aging and Conservatism," *Annals of the American Academy of Political and Social Science* (415:176–86, 1974). For a lengthier treatment by Glenn, see "Values, Attitudes, and Beliefs," in *Constancy and Change in Human Development,* edited by O. G. Brim, Jr., and J. Kagan (Cambridge, MA: Harvard University Press, 1980). Finally, for evidence that older adults may be more generous than younger folks, see E. Midlarsky and M. E. Hannah, "The Generous Elderly," *Psychology and Aging* (4:346–51, 1989).

LEMMINGS

There are several interesting papers about lemmings, including J. H. Myers and C. J. Krebs, "Population Cycles in Rodents," *Scientific American* (June:38–46, 1974); K. Curry-Lindahl, "New Theory on a Fabled Exodus," *Natural History* (Aug.–Sept.:47–53, 1963); and L. Hansson, "The Lemming Phenomenon," *Natural History* (Dec.:39–42, 1989), but don't expect to find very much on the suicide question. The Howard quotation appears in *Verbatim* (Spring:5, 1979).

CAPITAL PUNISHMENT

Here are just a few of the many sources on the death penalty, with special emphasis on deterrence: H. Bedau, ed., *The Death Penalty in America,* 3d ed. (New York: Oxford University Press, 1982) (Ehrlich's article is reprinted here); W. J. Bowers, *Legal Homicide* (Boston: Northeastern University Press, 1984); F. E. Zimring and G. Hawkins, *Capital Punishment and the American Agenda* (Cambridge, UK: Cambridge University Press, 1986); A. Blumstein, J. Cohen, and D. Nagin, eds., *Deterrence and Incapacitation* (Washington, DC: National Academy of Sciences, 1978); and W. J. Bowers and G. L. Pierce, "Deterrence or Brutalization," *Crime and Delinquency* (26:453–84, 1980).

All of issue number 3 of the *Journal of Criminal Law and Criminology* (74, 1983) is devoted to this topic. (See especially B. Forst, "Capital Punishment and Deterrence," 927–42 [the "do as we do" quotation appears here, on p. 939], and D. Archer, R. Gartner, and M. Beittel, "Homicide and the Death Penalty," 991–1013.) For a broader perspective on crime in the United States, see E. Currie, *Confronting Crime* (New York: Pantheon, 1975). The Currie quotation in the footnote is from his article "Crimes of Violence and Public Policy," in *American Violence and Public Policy,* edited by L. A. Curtis (New Haven, CT: Yale University Press, 1985, 45–46).

BEAUTY IS SKIN DEEP

For a comprehensive review of the relevant literature, see E. Hatfield and S. Sprecher, *Mirror, Mirror* (Albany, NY: State University of New

York Press, 1986). The 1972 study by K. Dion, E. Berscheid, and E. Walster, "What Is Beautiful Is Good," was published in *JPSP* (24:259–90, 1972). Warren Jones's paper (with R. O. Hansson and A. L. Phillips) is called "Physical Attractiveness and Judgments of Psychopathology," and was published in *Journal of Social Psychology* (105:79–84, 1978). Also on mental disorder and appearance: A. Farina et al., "Physical Attractiveness and Mental Illness," *Journal of Abnormal Psychology* (86:510–17, 1977); T. Napoleon, L. Chassin, and R. D. Young, "A Replication and Extension of 'Physical Attractiveness and Mental Illness,' " *Journal of Abnormal Psychology* (89:250–53, 1980); and K. E. O'Grady, "Sex, Physical Attractiveness, and Perceived Risk for Mental Illness," *JPSP* (43:1064–71, 1982). Also see the many publications of Thomas F. Cash.

CATHERINE THE GREAT

John Alexander's book *Catherine the Great: Life and Legend* (New York: Oxford University Press, 1989) should be enough.

TONE DEAFNESS

3The 1930s study: M. Wolner and W. H. Pyle, "An Experiment in Individual Training of Pitch-Deficient Children," *Journal of Educational Psychology* (24:602–608, 1933). Behavioral study: C. C. Dennis, "The Conditioning of a Pitch Response Using Uncertain Singers," in *Research in Music Behavior,* edited by C. K. Madsen et al. (New York: Teachers College Press, 1975). Teaching oneself perfect pitch: P. T. Brady, "Fixed-Scale Mechanism of Absolute Pitch," *Journal of the Acoustical Society of America* (48:883–87, 1970). Also see Frank R. Wilson, *Tone Deaf and All Thumbs?* (New York: Viking-Penguin, 1986) and C. R. Hoffer and M. L. Hoffer, *Teaching Music in the Elementary Classroom* (New York: Harcourt Brace Jovanovich, 1982).

SNOWFLAKES

N. C. Knight, "No Two Alike?" *Bulletin of the American Meteorological Society* (69:496, 1988).

REWARDS

First the references for the specific studies described here. Tutoring experiment: J. Garbarino, "The Impact of Anticipated Reward upon Cross-Aged Tutoring," *JPSP* (32:421–28, 1975). Collages and stories: T. M. Amabile, B. A. Hennessey, and B. S. Grossman, "Social Influences on Creativity," *JPSP* (50:14–23, 1986). Seat belts: E. S. Geller et al., "Employer-Based Programs to Motivate Safety Belt Use," *Journal of Safety Research* (18:1–17, 1987). Neill quotation: M. Morgan, "Reward-Induced Decrements and Increments in Intrinsic Motivation," *Review of Educational Research* (54:5, 1984). Crayons and markers: M. R. Lepper et al., "Consequences of Superfluous Social Constraints," *JPSP* (42:51–65, 1982). Altruism and mothers' rewards: R. A. Fabes et al., "Effects of Rewards on Children's Prosocial Motivation," *Developmental Psychology* (25:509–15, 1989). Blood donors: D. L. Paulhus, D. R. Shaffer, and L. L. Downing, "Effects of Making Blood Donor Motives Salient upon Donor Retention," *Personality and Social Psychology Bulletin (PSPB)* (3:99–102, 1977). Puzzle competition: E. L. Deci et al., "When Trying to Win," *PSPB* (7:79–83, 1981). Collage competition: T. M. Amabile, "Children's Artistic Creativity," *PSPB* (8:573–78, 1982).

Now some further reading on the subject in case you're feeling ambitious. On intrinsic motivation and rewards, the two most important books are M. R. Lepper and D. Greene, eds., *The Hidden Costs of Rewards* (Hillsdale, NJ: Lawrence Erlbaum, 1978) and E. L. Deci and R. M. Ryan, *Intrinsic Motivation and Self-Determination in Human Behavior* (New York: Plenum, 1985). Other names to look for in the journals: John Condry, Judith M. Harackiewicz, Ruth Butler, and Mark Morgan. On creativity and rewards, see primarily the work of Teresa Amabile: her academic book, *The Social Psychology of Creativity* (New York: Springer-Verlag, 1983) and her popular book, *Growing Up Creative* (New York: Crown, 1989). For a quick introduction, see my profile of her, A. Kohn, "Art for Art's Sake," *Psychology Today* (Sept. 1987, 52–57). For evidence that competition is inherently counterproductive, see A. Kohn, *No Contest* (Boston: Houghton Mifflin, 1986).

SPICY FOOD

No damage from jalapeños: D. Y. Graham, J. L. Smith, and A. R. Opekun, "Spicy Food and the Stomach," *JAMA* (260:3473–75, 1988). Chili powder and ulcers: N. Kumar et al., "Do Chillies Influence Healing of Duodenal Ulcer?" *British Medical Journal (BMJ)* (288:1803–1804,

1984). Milk: K. McArthur, D. Hogan, and J. I. Isenberg, "Relative Stimulatory Effects of Commonly Ingested Beverages on Gastric Acid Secretion in Humans," *Gastroenterology* (83:199–203, 1982). Spicy food and nightmares: E. Hartmann, *The Nightmare* (New York: Basic Books, 1984, 255–56).

SEVEN-YEAR ITCH

See various publications of the National Center for Health Statistics, including "National Estimates of Marriage Dissolution and Survivorship: United States" (1980) and "Duration of Marriage Before Divorce" (1981). Also see K. A. London and B. F. Wilson, "D-I-V-O-R-C-E," *American Demographics* (Oct.:22–26, 1988) and T. C. Martin and L. L. Bumpass, "Recent Trends in Marital Disruption," *Demography* (26:37–51, 1989) (the University of Wisconsin study).

RICHER AND POORER

On income, see "Background Material and Data on Programs within the Jurisdiction of the Committee on Ways and Means" (Washington, DC: Committee on Ways and Means, 1989), which is every bit as lively as the title suggests (see pp. 983ff). Also see Table 12 of "Money Income of Households, Families, and Persons in the United States: 1987," *Current Population Reports* (Consumer Income Series P-60, no. 162, Washington, DC: U.S. Bureau of the Census). The Sheldon Danziger and Peter Gottschalk quotation is from their article, "Increasing Inequality in the United States," *Journal of Post Keynesian Economics* (11:177, 1988–89). On assets and financial assets: L. Mishel and J. Simon, *The State of Working America* (Washington, DC: Economic Policy Institute, 1988). Galbraith quotation: J. K. Galbraith, "When Capitalism Meets Communism, Credos Are Shakier," *Boston Globe* (Dec. 3, 1989, A3).

FAMILIARITY

The original article is R. B. Zajonc, "Attitudinal Effects of Mere Exposure," *JPSP Monographs* (9, no. 2, pt. 2:1–27, 1968). The new review is R. F. Bornstein, "Exposure and Affect," *Psychological Bulletin (Psych Bull)* (106:265–89, 1989).

MENSTRUATION

Let's start with the studies on mood. One hundred and fifty-eight high-school girls: S. Golub and D. M. Harrington, "Premenstrual and Menstrual Mood Changes in Adolescent Women," *JPSP* (41:961–65, 1981). Forty-six college students: P. Englander-Golden, M. R. Whitmore, and R. A. Dienstbier, "Menstrual Cycle as Focus of Study and Self-Reports of Moods and Behaviors," *Motivation and Emotion* (2:75–86, 1978). Slade's study: P. Slade, "Premenstrual Emotional Changes in Normal Women," *Journal of Psychosomatic Research* (28:1–7, 1984). McFarland's study: C. McFarland, M. Ross, and N. DeCourville, "Women's Theories of Menstruation and Biases in Recall of Menstrual Symptoms," *JPSP* (57:522–31, 1989). Ruble and Brooks-Gunn quotation: D. N. Ruble and J. Brooks-Gunn, "Menstrual Symptoms," *Journal of Behavioral Medicine* (2:181, 1979). PMS estimate: M. J. Gitlin and R. O. Pasnau, "Psychiatric Syndromes Linked to Reproductive Function in Women," *American Journal of Psychiatry (AJP)* (146:1413–22, 1989). Parlee quotation: M. B. Parlee, "The Psychology of the Menstrual Cycle," in *Behavior and the Menstrual Cycle,* edited by R. C. Friedman (New York: Marcel Dekker, 1982). These sources will lead you to other studies that also found little or no evidence of emotional change as a result of the menstrual cycle.

On task performance, I have cited B. Sommer, "Cognitive Behavior and the Menstrual Cycle," in *Behavior and the Menstrual Cycle,* edited by R. C. Friedman (New York: Marcel Dekker, 1982, 101). You may also want to check out J. T. E. Richardson, "Student Learning and the Menstrual Cycle," *Studies in Higher Education* (13:303–14, 1988); B. E. Bernstein, "Effect of Menstruation on Academic Performance among College Women," *Archives of Sexual Behavior* (6:289–96, 1977); M. A. Schuckit et al., "Premenstrual Symptoms and Depression in a University Population," *Diseases of the Nervous System* (36:516–17, 1975); R. N. Walsh et al., "The Menstrual Cycle, Personality, and Academic Performance," *Archives of General Psychiatry* (38:219–21, 1981); and B. Sommer, "Menstrual Cycle Changes and Intellectual Performance," *Psychosomatic Medicine* (34:263–69, 1972). The only section of the widely publicized Kimura study that has been published at this writing is E. Hampson and D. Kimura, "Reciprocal Effects of Hormonal Fluctuations on Human Motor and Perceptual-Spatial Skills," *Behavioral Neuroscience* (102:456–59, 1988). I have criticized this research (and the press coverage it received) in A. Kohn, "Why Sex and Research Don't Mix," *Boston Globe* (Nov. 27, 1988, A21).

On menopause, see Gitlin and Pasnau's *AJP* article cited above (p.

1419). Pasnau's quotation appears in D. Goleman, "Wide Beliefs on Depression in Women Contradicted," *The New York Times* (Jan. 9, 1990, C8). The cross-cultural evidence is reported in Y. Beyene, "Cultural Significance and Physiological Manifestations of Menopause," *Culture, Medicine, and Psychiatry* (10:47–71, 1986).

ALUMNI CONTRIBUTIONS

In order, the three studies are L. Sigelman and R. Carter, "Win One for the Giver?" *Social Science Quarterly* (60:284–94, 1979); G. Brooker and T. D. Klastorin, "To the Victors Belong the Spoils?" *Social Science Quarterly* (62:744–50, 1981); and J. F. Gaski and M. J. Etzel, "Collegiate Athletic Success and Alumni Generosity," *Social Behavior and Personality* (12:29–38, 1984).

ABSENCE VS. OUT OF SIGHT

See many of Abraham Tesser's writings, including "Self-Generated Attitude Change," *Advances in Experimental Social Psychology* (11:289–338, 1978) and "Attitude Polarization as a Function of Thought and Reality Constraints," *Journal of Research in Personality* (10:183–94, 1976). The college study is P. Shaver, W. Furman, and D. Buhrmester, "Transition to College," in *Understanding Personal Relationships,* edited by S. Duck and D. Perlman (London: Sage, 1985).

SALT

The 1988 editorial was titled "Salt Saga Continued," in *BMJ* (297: 307–08, 1988). Scottish study: W. C. S. Smith et al., "Urinary Electrolyte Excretion, Alcohol Consumption, and Blood Pressure in the Scottish Heart Health Study," on pp. 329–30 of the same (July 30, 1988) issue of *BMJ*. The cross-cultural study, "Intersalt," was written by the Intersalt Cooperative Research Group and also appeared in this issue, on pp. 319–28. The review of salt reduction studies was by D. E. Grobbee and A. Hofman, "Does Sodium Restriction Lower Blood Pressure," *BMJ* (293:27–29, 1986). For a good, if slightly dated, introduction to the controversy, see F. O. Simpson, "Salt and Hypertension," *Clinical Science* (57:463s–80s, 1979).

Full Moon

1972 article: A. L. Lieber and C. R. Sherin, "Homicides and the Lunar Cycle," *AJP* (129:101–6, 1972). Rebuttal to this article: A. D. Pokorny and J. Jachimczyk, "The Questionable Relationship between Homicides and the Lunar Cycle," *AJP* (131:827–29, 1974). Crow-munching researchers: D. I. Templer, R. K. Broomer, and M. D. Corgiart, "Lunar Phase and Crime," *Perceptual and Motor Skills* (57:993–94, 1983). Review of thirty-seven studies: J. Rotton and I. W. Kelly, "Much Ado about the Full Moon," *Psych Bull* (97:286–306, 1985). There's no point in listing most of the other references because you can find them cited in the Rotton and Kelly article. One published more recently is G. L. Little, R. Bowers, and L. H. Little, "Lack of Relationship between Moon Phase and Incidents of Disruptive Behavior in Inmates with Psychiatric Problems," *Perceptual and Motor Skills* (64:1212, 1987). For a critical analysis of the various mechanisms proposed to explain the alleged effect of the moon on behavior, see R. Culver, J. Rotton, and I. W. Kelly, "Moon Mechanisms and Myths," *Psychological Reports* (62:683–710, 1988).

Finally, the moon's lack of effect on births. New York study: M. Osley, D. Summerville, and L. B. Borst, "Natality and the Moon," *American Journal of Obstetrics and Gynecology* (117:413–15, 1973). Ohio study: C. D. Nalepka et al., "Time Variations, Births, and Lunar Association," *Issues in Comprehensive Pediatric Nursing* (6:81–89, 1983). Los Angeles study: G. O. Abell and B. Greenspan, "Human Births and the Phase of the Moon," *New England Journal of Medicine (NEJM)* (300:96, 1979). Review of twenty-one studies: R. Martens, I. W. Kelly, and D. H. Saklofske, "Lunar Phase and Birthrate," *Psychological Reports* (63:923–34, 1988).

Squeaky Wheel

Pay study: B. Major, V. Vanderslice, and D. B. McFarlin, "Effects of Pay Expected on Pay Received," *Journal of Applied Social Psychology* (14: 399–412, 1984). Bargaining quotation: J. Z. Rubin and B. R. Brown, *The Social Psychology of Bargaining and Negotiation* (New York: Academic Press, 1975, 267). R. Fisher and W. Ury, *Getting to Yes* (New York: Penguin, 1983).

Abuse

Cathy Spatz Widom published three key articles in 1989 that described her findings on the relation between abuse and crime and also reviewed the literature on the broader implications of abuse. See "Does Violence Beget Violence?" *Psych Bull* (106:3–28, 1989); "Child Abuse, Neglect, and Adult Behavior," *American Journal of Orthopsychiatry* (59:355–67, 1989); and "The Cycle of Violence," *Science* (244:160–66, 1989). The other article cited here is J. Kaufman and E. Zigler, "Do Abused Children Become Abusive Parents?" *American Journal of Orthopsychiatry* (57:186–92, 1987).

TIME FLIES

The 1933 study (and reference to 1904 study): S. Rosenzweig and A. G. Koht, "The Experience of Duration as Affected by Need–Tension," *Journal of Experimental Psychology* (16:745–74, 1933). Have fun if believe time flew: S. Gupta and L. L. Cummings, "Perceived Speed of Time and Task Affect," *Perceptual and Motor Skills* (63:971–80, 1986). Watched pots: D. Cahoon and E. M. Edmonds, "The Watched Pot Still Won't Boil," *Bulletin of the Psychonomic Society* (16:115–16, 1980) and R. A. Block, E. J. George, and M. A. Reed, "A Watched Pot Sometimes Boils," *Acta Psychologica* (46:81–94, 1980). For a good introduction to the topic, see S. Coren, C. Porac, and L. M. Ward, *Sensation and Perception,* 2d ed. (Orlando, FL: Academic Press, 1984).

HIROSHIMA

On invasion casualty estimates: B. J. Bernstein, "A Postwar Myth," *Bulletin of the Atomic Scientists* (June/July:38–40, 1986) and R. E. Miles, Jr., "Hiroshima," *International Security* (10:121–40, 1985). On extent of damage to Japan: W. Reissner, "Why Truman Used the Atom Bomb," *Intercontinental Press* (Aug. 19, 1985, 501–503). On Strategic Bombing Survey report: a good library should have the original on microfilm (look for "Japan's Struggle to End the War," M-1013, roll 18, report dated July 1, 1946). National Archives Document: see G. Alperovitz, "Did We Have to Drop the Bomb?" *The New York Times* (Aug. 3, 1989, A23). Various quotations and evidence on Japan's readiness to surrender: see R. J. C. Butow, *Japan's Decision to Surrender* (Stanford, CA: Stanford University Press, 1954, esp. 130–35) and G. Alperovitz, *Atomic Diplomacy,* 2d ed. (New York: Penguin, 1985) (which will lead you to hundreds of other sources). Erikson's analysis: K. Erikson, "Of Accidental Judgments and Casual Slaughters," *The Nation* (Aug. 3/10, 1985, 65, 80–85).

Boys and Math

J. S. Hyde, E. Fennema, and S. J. Lamon's article, "Gender Differences in Mathematics Performance," *Psych Bull* (107:139–55, 1990). On girls' superiority on classroom grades, see M. M. Kimball, "A New Perspective on Women's Math Achievement," *Psych Bull* (105:198–214, 1989). On the general trend of gender differences in performance, see A. Feingold, "Cognitive Gender Differences Are Disappearing," *American Psychologist* (43:95–103, 1988). On verbal ability, see J. S. Hyde and M. C. Linn, "Gender Differences in Verbal Ability," *Psych Bull* (104:53–69, 1988). On reading tests and mothers' beliefs, see M. Lummis and H. W. Stevenson, "Gender Differences in Beliefs and Achievement," *Developmental Psychology* (26:254–63, 1990).

Laughter

Cousins, 1976: N. Cousins, "Anatomy of an Illness (as Perceived by the Patient)," *NEJM* (295:1458–63, 1976). Cousins, 1989: N. Cousins, *Head First* (New York: Dutton, 1989). First Dillon study: K. M. Dillon, B. Minchoff, and K. H. Baker, "Positive Emotional States and Enhancement of the Immune System," *International Journal of Psychiatry in Medicine* (15:13–17, 1985–86). Berk studies: L. S. Berk et al., "Neuroendocrine and Stress Hormone Changes during Mirthful Laughter," *American Journal of the Medical Sciences* (298:390–96, 1989) and "Mirth Modulates Adreno-corticomedullary Activity," *Clinical Research* (36:121A, 1988). Second Dillon study: K. M. Dillon and M. C. Totten, "Psychological Factors, Immunocompetence, and Health of Breast-Feeding Mothers and Their Infants," *Journal of Genetic Psychology* (150:155–62, 1989). Coping with pain: R. Cogan et al., "Effects of Laughter and Relaxation on Discomfort Thresholds," *Journal of Behavioral Medicine* (10:139–44, 1987). Letter from Sweden: L. Ljungdahl, "Laugh If This Is a Joke," *JAMA* (261:558, 1989). Letter from Tennessee: J. K. Neumann, "Humor Therapy," *JAMA* (262:2540–41, 1989). Illinois study: R. Safranek and T. Schill, "Coping with Stress," *Psychological Reports* (51:222, 1982). Canadian study: R. A. Martin and H. M. Lefcourt, "Sense of Humor as a Moderator of the Relation between Stressors and Moods," *JPSP* (45:1313–24, 1983). Ohio study: A. L. Porterfield, "Does Sense of Humor Moderate the Impact of Life Stress on Psychological and Physical Well-Being?" *Journal of Research in Personality* (21:306–17, 1987). Also see J. H. Goldstein, "A Laugh a Day," *The Sciences* (Aug.–Sept.:21–25, 1982).

Reading in the Dark

Ophthalmology Study Guide for Students and Practitioners of Medicine, 5th ed., is produced by the American Academy of Ophthalmology and the Association of University Professors of Ophthalmology.

Aggression

The text of the Seville Statement is reprinted as the appendix to my book, *The Brighter Side of Human Nature* (New York: Basic Books, 1990). Chapter 2 of that book contains a more thorough treatment of the whole issue, as well as lots of references.

Baron's review: R. A. Baron, *Human Aggression* (New York: Plenum, 1977). Fromm quotation: E. Fromm, *The Anatomy of Human Destructiveness* (New York: Fawcett Crest, 1975, 174–75). Moyer quotation: K. E. Moyer, *Violence and Aggression* (New York: Paragon House, 1987, 24, 34). Rousseau quotation: M. Sahlins, *The Use and Abuse of Biology* (Ann Arbor: University of Michigan Press, 1976, 9).

Subliminal Ads

Among the studies failing to find any effect from subliminal stimuli: J. R. Vokey and J. D. Read, "Subliminal Messages: Between the Devil and the Media," *American Psychologist* (40:1233, 1985); M. Gable et al., "An Evaluation of Subliminally Embedded Sexual Stimuli in Graphics," *Journal of Advertising* (16:26–29, 1987); and S. G. George and L. B. Jennings, "Effect of Subliminal Stimuli on Consumer Behavior," *Perceptual and Motor Skills* (41:847–54, 1975). The best single source I know of is T. E. Moore, "Subliminal Advertising," *Journal of Marketing* (46:38–47, 1982).

On the other side, there is Wilson Bryan Key, *Subliminal Seduction* (Englewood Cliffs, NJ: Prentice–Hall, 1973). Caveat lector.

Breakfast

Dickie and Bender quotation: N. H. Dickie and A. E. Bender, "Breakfast and Performance," *Human Nutrition: Applied Nutrition* (36A:46, 55, 1982). The Iowa Studies are all by W. W. Tuttle et al. See, for example, "Effect of Altered Breakfast Habits on Physiologic Response," *Journal of Applied Physiology* (1:545–59, 1949); "Effect of Omitting Breakfast on the Physiologic Response of Men," *Journal of the American Dietetic Association*

(*JADA*) (26:332–35, 1950); and "Effect on School Boys of Omitting Breakfast," *JADA* (30:674–77, 1954). The 1965 California survey: N. B. Belloc and L. Breslow, "Relationship of Physical Health Status and Health Practices," *Preventive Medicine* (1:409–21, 1972). Los Angeles study: H. M. Lieberman et al., "Evaluation of a Ghetto School Breakfast Program," *JADA* (68:132–38, 1976). Lawrence study: A. F. Meyers et al., "School Breakfast Program and School Performance," *American Journal of Diseases of Children* (143:1234–39, 1989).

Other studies on children: N. H. Dickie and A. E. Bender, "Breakfast and Performance in Schoolchildren," *British Journal of Nutrition* (48:483–96, 1982); E. Pollitt et al., "Fasting and Cognitive Function," *Journal of Psychiatric Research* (17:169–74, 1982–83); Angus Craig, "Acute Effects of Meals on Perceptual and Cognitive Efficiency," *Nutrition Reviews* (44 suppl.:163–71, 1986); E. Pollitt, R. L. Leibel, and D. Greenfield, "Brief Fasting, Stress, and Cognition in Children," *American Journal of Clinical Nutrition* (34:1526–33, 1981).

Jamaican studies: D. Simeon and S. Grantham-McGregor, "Cognitive Function, Undernutrition, and Missed Breakfast," *Lancet* (Sept. 26, 1987, 737–38); D. T. Simeon and S. Grantham-McGregor, "Effects of Missing Breakfast on the Cognitive Functions of School Children of Differing Nutritional Status," *American Journal of Clinical Nutrition* (49:646–53, 1989); and C. Powell, S. Grantham-McGregor, and M. Elston, "An Evaluation of Giving the Jamaican Government School Meal to a Class of Children," *Human Nutrition: Clinical Nutrition* (37C:381–88, 1983).

ACTIONS VS. WORDS

The two studies cited are T. M. Amabile and L. G. Kabat, "When Self-Descriptions Contradict Behavior," *Social Cognition* (1:311–35, 1982) and J. H. Bryan and N. Walbek, "Preaching and Practicing Generosity," *Child Development* (41:329–53, 1970). The Hume quotation is from *A Treatise of Human Nature* (Oxford: Clarendon Press, 1888, bk. III, pt. III, sec. 1).

POSTPARTUM BLUES

Birth vs. surgery: V. Levy, "The Maternity Blues in Post-partum and Post-operative Women," *British Journal of Psychiatry (BJP)* (151:368–72, 1987). Canadian study: I. H. Gotlib et al., "Prevalence Rates and Demographic Characteristics Associated with Depression in Pregnancy and the Postpartum," *Journal of Consulting and Clinical Psychology* (57:269–74, 1989). British study: P. J. Cooper et al., "Non-psychotic Psychiatric Disorder after Childbirth," *BJP* (152:799–806, 1988). Iowa study: M. W. O'Hara et al., "A Controlled Prospective Study of Postpartum Mood Disorders," *Journal of Abnormal Psychology* (in press). A few more studies and reviews for good measure: B. Pitt, " 'Maternity Blues,' " *BJP* (122:431–33, 1973); M. J. Gitlin and R. O. Pasnau, "Psychiatric Syndromes Linked to Reproductive Function in Women," *AJP* (146:1413–22, 1989); C. E. Cutrona, "Nonpsychotic Postpartum Depression," *Clinical Psychology Review* (2:487–503, 1982); and M. W. O'Hara and E. M. Zekoski, "Postpartum Depression," in *Motherhood and Mental Illness 2,* edited by R. Kumar and I. F. Brockington (London: Wright, 1988).

COMPETITION AND CHARACTER

Butt quote: D. S. Butt, *Psychology of Sport* (New York: Van Nostrand Reinhold, 1976, 54). Ogilvie and Tutko study: B. C. Ogilvie and T. A. Tutko, "Sport: If You Want to Build Character, Try Something Else," *Psychology Today* (Oct. 1971, 61–63). Self-concept: A. A. Norem-Hebeisen and D. W. Johnson, "The Relationship between Cooperative, Competitive, and Individualistic Attitudes and Differentiated Aspects of Self-Esteem," *Journal of Personality* (49:415–26, 1981). Sense of control: See, for example, C. Ames, "Children's Achievement Attributions and Self-Reinforcement," *Journal of Educational Psychology* (70:345–55, 1978). The 1989 self-esteem review: D. W. Johnson and R. T. Johnson, *Cooperation and Competition* (Edina, MN: Interaction Book Co., 1989, esp. 156–60).

For more references and a more detailed argument about the consequences of competition, see A. Kohn, *No Contest* (Boston: Houghton Mifflin, 1986, esp. chaps. 5 and 6).

ELEPHANTS

B. Rensch, "The Intelligence of Elephants," *Scientific American* (Feb.:44–49, 1957).

GREAT MINDS

Simonton book (including James quotation): D. K. Simonton, *Scientific Genius* (Cambridge, UK: Cambridge University Press, 1988).

INSANITY DEFENSE

Alaska: M. R. Phillips, A. S. Wolf, and D. J. Coons, "Psychiatry and the Criminal Justice System," *AJP* (145:605–10, 1988). Oregon: J. L. Rogers, J. D. Bloom, and S. M. Manson, "Oregon's New Insanity Defense System," *Bulletin of the American Academy of Psychiatry and the Law* (12:383–402, 1984). Massachusetts: B. F. Phillips and J. A. Hornik, *The Insanity Defense in Massachusetts* (published under the auspices of the state's Department of Mental Health in 1984). Steadman's multistate study has not yet been published.

On the exclusionary rule, see T. Y. Davies, "A Hard Look at What We Know (and Still Need to Learn) about the 'Costs' of the Exclusionary Rule," *American Bar Foundation Research Journal* (Summer:611–90, 1983). More popular treatments include K. N. Wright, *The Great American Crime Myth* (Westport, CT: Greenwood Press, 1985, esp. 136ff) and S. Walker, *Sense and Nonsense about Crime* (Monterey, CA: Brooks/Cole, 1985, esp. 94–97).

PLAYING HARD TO GET

Romeo and Juliet effect: R. Driscoll, K. E. Davis, and M. E. Lipetz, "Parental Interference and Romantic Love," *JPSP* (24:1–10, 1972). The other studies, in order, are E. Walster et al., " 'Playing Hard to Get,' " *JPSP* (26:113–21, 1973); K. A. Matthews, D. Rosenfield, and W. G. Stephan, "Playing Hard-to-Get," *Journal of Research in Personality* (13: 234–44, 1979); and R. A. Wright and R. J. Contrada, "Dating Selectivity and Interpersonal Attraction," *Journal of Social and Personal Relationships* (3:131–48, 1986).

COLDS

Temperature: H. F. Dowling et al., "Transmission of the Common Cold to Volunteers under Controlled Conditions," *American Journal of Hygiene* (68:59–65, 1958) and R. G. Douglas, Jr., K. M. Lindgren, and R.

B. Couch, "Exposure to Cold Environment and Rhinovirus Common Cold," *NEJM* (279:742–47, 1968).

Routes of transmission: J. M. Gwaltney, P. B. Moskalski, and J. O. Hendley, "Hand-to-hand Transmission of Rhinovirus Colds," *Annals of Internal Medicine* (88:463–67, 1978); S. E. Reed, "An Investigation of the Possible Transmission of Rhinovirus Colds through Indirect Contact," *Journal of Hygiene* (75:249–58, 1975); E. C. Dick et al., "Aerosol Transmission of Rhinovirus Colds," *Journal of Infectious Diseases* (156:442–48, 1987); and L. C. Jennings et al., "Near Disappearance of Rhinovirus along a Fomite Transmission Chain," *Journal of Infectious Diseases* (158:888–92, 1988). *Lancet* editorial: Feb. 6, 1988, 277–78. Kissing with impunity: D. J. D'Alessio et al., "Short-Duration Exposure and the Transmission of Rhinoviral Colds," *Journal of Infectious Diseases* (150:189–94, 1984). For a review of the research, see J. O. Hendley and J. M. Gwaltney, Jr., "Mechanisms of Transmission of Rhinovirus Infections," *Epidemiologic Reviews* (10:242–58, 1988).

Chicken soup: K. Saketkhoo, A. Januszkiewicz, and M. A. Sackner, "Effects of Drinking Hot Water, Cold Water, and Chicken Soup on Nasal Mucus Velocity and Nasal Airflow Resistance," *Chest* (74:408–10, 1978).

SPOILING BABIES

J. Liedloff, *The Continuum Concept,* rev. ed. (Reading, MA: Addison-Wesley, 1977) and S. M. Bell and M. D. S. Ainsworth, "Infant Crying and Maternal Responsiveness," *Child Development* (43:1171–90, 1972).

POWER CORRUPTS

P. G. Zimbardo et al., "The Psychology of Imprisonment," in *Theory and Research in Abnormal Psychology,* 2d ed., edited by D. Rosenhan and P. London (New York: Holt, Rinehart and Winston, 1975).

BOSTON DRIVING

The 1983 data were incorporated in A. Kohn, "Stop!" *Boston Magazine* (Sept. 1985, 109–17). The new data are from the Insurance Services Office and the Automobile Insurers Bureau of Massachusetts. For a tongue-in-cheek treatment of the problem, see I. Gershkoff and R. Trachtman, *Wild in the Streets* (Reading, MA: Addison-Wesley, 1982).

NEVER TOO OLD VS. OLD DOG

Studies cited on intelligence, memory, and aging: K. W. Schaie and C. Hertzog, "Fourteen-Year Cohort-Sequential Analyses of Adult Intellectual Development," *Developmental Psychology* (19:531–43, 1983); P. B. Baltes, F. Dittmann-Kohli, and R. Kliegl, "Reserve Capacity of the Elderly in Aging-Sensitive Tests of Fluid Intelligence," *Psychology and Aging* (1:172–77, 1986); and K. W. Schaie and S. L. Willis, "Can Decline in Adult Intellectual Functioning Be Reversed?" *Developmental Psychology* (22:223–32, 1986).

More reading on the same topic: G. Labouvie-Vief, "Intelligence and Cognition," in *Handbook of the Psychology of Aging*, 2d ed., edited by J. E. Birren and K. W. Schaie (New York: Van Nostrand Reinhold, 1985); J. L. Horn and G. Donaldson, "On the Myth of Intellectual Decline in Adulthood," *American Psychologist* (31:701–19, 1976); R. E. Guttentag, "Memory and Aging," *Developmental Review* (5:56–82, 1985); R. A. Dixon et al., "Text Recall in Adulthood as a Function of Level of Information, Input Modality, and Delay Interval," *Journal of Gerontology* (37:358–64, 1982); L. M. Giambra and D. Arenberg, "Problem Solving, Concept Learning, and Aging," in *Aging in the 1980s,* edited by L. W. Poon (Washington, DC: American Psychological Association, 1980); and L. W. Poon, "Memory Training for Older Adults," in *Geriatric Mental Health,* edited by J. P. Abrams and V. J. Crooks (New York: Grune and Stratton, 1984).

Aging and depression: M. C. Feinson, "Aging and Mental Health," *Research on Aging* (7:155–74, 1985).

INBREEDING

On the effects of consanguinity: M. J. Khoury et al., "An Epidemiologic Approach to the Evaluation of the Effect of Inbreeding on Prereproductive Mortality," *American Journal of Epidemiology* (125:251–62, 1987); F. C. Fraser and C. J. Biddle, "Estimating the Risks for Offspring of First-Cousin Matings," *American Journal of Human Genetics* (28:522–26, 1976); N. Freire-Maia, "Effects of Consanguineous Marriages on Morbidity and Precocious Mortality," *American Journal of Medical Genetics (AJMG)* (18:401–6, 1984); and N. Freire-Maia et al., "Inbreeding Studies in Brasilian Schoolchildren," *AJMG* (16:331–55, 1983).

On the prevalence of consanguinity: R. R. Lebel, "Consanguinity Studies in Wisconsin," *AJMG* (15:543–60, 1983); M. Khlat, "Consanguineous Marriages in Beirut," *Social Biology* (35:324–30, 1988); M.

Khlat, "Consanguineous Marriage and Reproduction in Beirut, Lebanon," *American Journal of Human Genetics* (43:188–96, 1988).

PRAYING MANTISES

E. Liske and W. J. Davis, "Sexual Behavior of the Chinese Praying Mantis," *Animal Behaviour* (32:916–17, 1984).

BEAUTY AND THE BEHOLDER

A. E. Gross and C. Crofton, "What Is Good Is Beautiful," *Sociometry* (40:85–90, 1977); G. Owens and J. G. Ford, "Further Consideration of the 'What Is Good Is Beautiful' Finding," *Social Psychology* (41:73–75, 1978); and J. W. Pennebaker et al., "Don't the Girls Get Prettier at Closing Time," *PSPB* (5:122–25, 1979).

EXPRESSING HOSTILITY

Boxing study: T. Orlick, *Winning through Cooperation* (Washington, DC: Acropolis Books, 1978, 92–93). Aerospace employees study: E. B. Ebbesen, B. Duncan, and V. J. Konečni, "Effects of Content of Verbal Aggression on Future Verbal Aggression," *Journal of Experimental Social Psychology* (11:192–204, 1975). Shocking study: R. G. Geen, D. Stonner, and G. L. Shope, "The Facilitation of Aggression by Aggression," *JPSP* (31:721–26, 1975). Pennebaker's grief studies: See, for example, J. W. Pennebaker and R. C. O'Heeron, "Confiding in Others and Illness Rate among Spouses of Suicide and Accidental-Death Victims," *Journal of Abnormal Psychology* (93:473–76, 1984) and J. W. Pennebaker, C. F. Hughes, and R. C. O'Heeron, "The Psychophysiology of Confession," *JPSP* (52:781–93, 1987). Konečni quotation: V. J. Konečni, "Annoyance, Type and Duration of Postannoyance Activity, and Aggression," *Journal of Experimental Psychology: General* (104:100, 1975). Screaming and hitting couples: M. A. Straus, "Leveling, Civility, and Violence in the Family," *Journal of Marriage and the Family* (36:13–29, 1974). Sports and war: R. G. Sipes, "War, Sports and Aggression," *American Anthropologist* (75:64–86, 1973). Tavris: C. Tavris, "On the Wisdom of Counting to Ten," *Review of Personality and Social Psychology* (5:170–91, 1984) and *Anger* (New York: Simon & Schuster, 1982).

Want more? Try S. K. Mallick and B. R. McCandless's frequently cited "A Study of Catharsis of Aggression," *JPSP* (4:591–96, 1966); any of

Leonard Berkowitz's many writings on aggression; and, on sports, M. B. Quanty, "Aggression Catharsis," in *Perspectives on Aggression,* edited by R. G. Geen and E. C. O'Neal (New York: Academic Press, 1976).

White Hair

All I could find were A. J. Ephraim, "On Sudden or Rapid Whitening of the Hair," *Archives of Dermatology* (79:142–49, 1959) and F. Helm and H. Milgrom, "Can Scalp Hair Suddenly Turn White?" *Archives of Dermatology* (102:102–3, 1970). Maybe you'll have better luck.

Nearsighted and Smart

Let's start with the studies that establish a correlation. Israeli soldiers: M. Rosner and M. Belkin, "Intelligence, Education, and Myopia in Males," *Archives of Ophthalmology* (105:1508–11, 1987). Danish soldiers: T. W. Teasdale, J. Fuchs, and E. Goldschmidt, "Degree of Myopia in Relation to Intelligence and Educational Level," *Lancet* (Dec. 10, 1988, 1351–54). U.S. Public Health survey: J. Angle and D. A. Wissmann, "The Epidemiology of Myopia," *American Journal of Epidemiology* (111:220–28, 1980). Precocious SAT scorers: C. P. Benbow, "Physiological Correlates of Extreme Intellectual Precocity," *Neuropsychologia* (24:719–25, 1986).

Now, onto the meaning of the correlation. Even myopes play games: C. S. Peckham, P. A. Gardiner, and H. Goldstein, "Acquired Myopia in Eleven-Year-Old Children," *BMJ* (274:542–44, 1977). High scores precede myopia: See Peckham, Gardiner, and Goldstein; and J. W. B. Douglas, J. M. Ross, and H. R. Simpson, "The Ability and Attainment of Short-Sighted Pupils," *Journal of the Royal Statistical Society* (130:479–503, 1967). Young's monkeys: See, for example, F. A. Young, "The Nature and Control of Myopia," *Journal of the American Optometric Association* (48: 451–57, 1977) and "The Development of Myopia," *Contacto* (15:36–42, 1971). Eskimos: F. A. Young et al., "The Transmission of Refractive Errors within Eskimo Families," *American Journal of Optometry* (46:676–85, 1969). Baldwin quotation: W. R. Baldwin, "A Review of Statistical Studies of Relations between Myopia and Ethnic, Behavioral, and Physiological Characteristics," *American Journal of Optometry and Physiological Optics* (58:523, 1981). Advantage only on verbal tests: See Douglas, Ross, and Simpson; and F. A. Young, "Reading, Measures of Intelligence and Refractive Errors," *American Journal of Optometry Monograph* (May, no. 314, 1963).

Dying by the Sword

Seattle: A. L. Kellermann and D. T. Reay, "Protection or Peril?" *NEJM* (314:1557–60, 1986). Detroit: F. E. Zimring and G. Hawkins, *The Citizen's Guide to Gun Control* (New York: Macmillan, 1987, 30).

No Pain, No Gain

Fitness: S. N. Blair et al., "Physical Fitness and All-Cause Mortality," *JAMA* (262:2395–2401, 1989). Stamford quotation: B. Stamford, "No Pain, No Gain?" *Physician and Sportsmedicine* (Sept.:244, 1987). Swimming study: D. L. Costill, "Practical Problems in Exercise Physiology Research," *Research Quarterly for Exercise and Sport* (56:378–84, 1985).
For information on how exercise can be positively dangerous, see H. A. Solomon, *The Exercise Myth* (San Diego: Harcourt Brace Jovanovich, 1984, esp. chap. 7) and L. H. Opie, "Sudden Death and Sport," *Lancet* (Feb. 1, 1975, 263–66).

Laugh/Cry

Laughter as contagious: J. Morrison, "A Note Concerning Investigations on the Constancy of Audience Laughter," *Sociometry* (3:179–85, 1940) and A. J. Chapman, "Social Facilitation of Laughter in Children," *Journal of Experimental Social Psychology* (9:528–41, 1973).
Avoiding depressed people: J. C. Coyne, "Depression and the Response of Others," *Journal of Abnormal Psychology* (85:186–93, 1976) and other writings by Coyne; research by T. Elliott and R. Umlauf reported in H. Hall, "Weep and You Weep Alone," *Psychology Today* (June 1989, 18); I. H. Gotlib and L. A. Robinson, "Responses to Depressed Individuals," *Journal of Abnormal Psychology* (91:231–40, 1982); and K. L. Yarkin, J. H. Harvey, and B. M. Bloxom, "Cognitive Sets, Attribution, and Social Interaction," *JPSP* (41:243–52, 1981).

Homeless Mentally Ill

The New York Times estimate: G. Kolata, "Twins of the Streets," *NYT* (May 22, 1989, A1). *AJP* estimate: H. Herrman et al., "Prevalence of Severe Mental Disorders in Disaffiliated and Homeless People in Inner Melbourne," *AJP* (146:1179, 1989). Austin study: D. A. Snow et al., "The Myth of Pervasive Mental Illness among the Homeless," *Social*

Problems (33:407–23, 1986). Los Angeles study: P. Koegel, A. Burnam, and R. K. Farr, "The Prevalence of Specific Psychiatric Disorders among Homeless Individuals in the Inner City of Los Angeles," *Archives of General Psychiatry* (45:1085–92, 1988). Conference of Mayors estimate reported in J. Schmalz, "Belying Popular Stereotypes, Many of Homeless Have Jobs," *The New York Times* (Dec. 19, 1988, A1, B7). Kozol quotation: J. Kozol, "Are the Homeless Crazy?" *Harper's* (Sept. 1988, 17–18).

RELIGION AND ALTRUISM

Churchgoers' intolerance: G. W. Allport and J. M. Ross, "Personal Religious Orientation and Prejudice," *JPSP* (5:432, 1967). Episcopalians: C. Y. Glock, B. B. Ringer, and E. R. Babbie, *To Comfort and to Challenge* (Berkeley: University of California Press, 1967, 182–83). College males: R. W. Friedrichs, "Alter versus Ego," *American Sociological Review* (25:496–508, 1960). The 1965 interviews: V. B. Cline and J. M. Richards, Jr., "A Factor-Analytic Study of Religious Belief and Behaviors," *JPSP* (1:577, 1965). Biblical literalists: L. V. Annis, "Emergency Helping and Religious Behavior," *Psychological Reports* (39:151–58, 1976). Volunteering and cheating: R. E. Smith, G. Wheeler, and E. Diener, "Faith without Works," *Journal of Applied Social Psychology* (5:320–30, 1975). Neighborhood involvement: S. Georgianna, "Is a Religious Neighborhood a Good Neighborhood?" *Humboldt Journal of Social Relations* (11:1–16, 1984). Rescuers: S. P. Oliner and P. M. Oliner, *The Altruistic Personality* (New York: Free Press, 1988, 156).

SEXUAL PEAKS

The only remotely relevant published material I could find were H. S. Kaplan, *The New Sex Therapy* (New York: Brunner/Mazel, 1974, chap. 6); B. Goldstein, *Human Sexuality* (New York: McGraw-Hill, 1976, 107); and L. K. George and S. J. Weiler, "Sexuality in Middle and Late Life," *Archives of General Psychiatry* (38:919–23, 1981); and R. C. Schiari et al., "Healthy Aging and Male Sexual Function," *AJP* (147: 766–771, 1990).

SPARE THE ROD

Sample of early studies on effects of physical punishment: W. C. Becker, "Consequences of Different Kinds of Parental Discipline," in

Review of Child Development Research, vol. 1, edited by M. L. Hoffman and L. W. Hoffman (New York: Russell Sage Foundation, 1964); R. R. Sears, E. E. Maccoby, and H. Levin, *Patterns of Child Rearing* (Evanston, IL: Row, Peterson, 1957); and M. M. Lefkowitz, L. O. Walder, and L. D. Eron, "Punishment, Identification, and Aggression," *Merrill-Palmer Quarterly* (9:159–74, 1963). Twenty-two-year follow-up: L. D. Eron et al., "Aggression and Its Correlates over 22 Years," in *Childhood Aggression and Violence,* edited by D. H. Crowell, I. M. Evans, and C. R. O'Donnell (New York: Plenum, 1987).

Straus study: M. A. Straus, R. J. Gelles, and S. K. Steinmetz, *Behind Closed Doors* (Garden City, NY: Doubleday Anchor, 1980, esp. 110). St. Louis study: S. J. Holmes and L. N. Robins, "The Role of Parental Disciplinary Practices in the Development of Depression and Alcoholism," *Psychiatry* (51:24–35, 1988). Brandeis study: not yet published, conducted by Ying Peng and Malcolm W. Watson. Hitting toddlers: T. G. Power and M. L. Chapieski, "Childbearing and Impulse Control in Toddlers," *Developmental Psychology* (22:271–75, 1986). California study: M. Heinstein, *Behavior Problems of Young Children in California* (Berkeley: Calif. Department of Public Health, 1969, 125). Poll of parents: reported in B. A. Lehman, "Spanking Teaches the Wrong Lesson," *Boston Globe* (Mar. 13, 1989, 27, 29). Miller: A. Miller, *For Your Own Good* (New York: Farrar, Straus and Giroux, 1984, passim).

KNUCKLE CRACKING

The early articles: J. B. Roston and R. Wheeler-Haines, "Cracking in the Metacarpophalangeal Joint," *Journal of Anatomy* (81:165–73, 1947) and A. Unsworth, D. Dowson, and V. Wright, "Cracking Joints," *Annals of Rheumatic Diseases* (30:348–58, 1971). The two case studies were reported by Morris Ziff in an editorial in *Lancet* (Sept. 18, 1971, 649).

Survey of elderly crackers: R. L. Swezey and S. E. Swezey, "The Consequences of Habitual Knuckle Cracking," *Western Journal of Medicine* (122:377–79, 1975). The new work by Watson: P. Watson, W. G. Kernohan, and R. A. B. Mollan, "The Effect of Ultrasonically Induced Cavitation on Articular Cartilage," *Clinical Orthopaedics and Related Research* (no. 245:288–96, 1989); P. Watson, A. Hamilton, and R. Mollan, "Habitual Joint Cracking and Radiological Damage," *BMJ* (299:1566, 1989); P. Watson, W. G. Kernohan, and R. A. B. Mollan, "A Study of the Cracking Sounds from the Metacarpophalangeal Joint," *Proceedings of the Institution of Mechanical Engineers* (203:109–18, 1989); and P. Watson and R. A. B.

Mollan, "The Effect of Suction Cavitation on Articular Cartilage," *Journal of Orthopaedic Rheumatology* (1:209–18, 1988).

STREAK SHOOTING

T. Gilovich, R. Vallone, and A. Tversky, "The Hot Hand in Basketball," *Cognitive Psychology* (17:295–314, 1985).

SUICIDES

University of Virginia quotation: J. R. Hillard and J. Buckman, "Christmas Depression," *JAMA* (248:3175–76, 1982). Suicide rates by month: S. M. Kevan, "Perspectives on Season of Suicide," *Social Science and Medicine* (14D:369–78, 1980); K. MacMahon, "Short-Term Temporal Cycles in the Frequency of Suicide, United States, 1972–1978," *American Journal of Epidemiology* (117:744–50, 1983); H. Gabennesch, "When Promises Fail," *Social Forces* (67:129–45, 1988); D. Lester, "Temporal Variation in Suicide and Homicide," *American Journal of Epidemiology* (109:517–20, 1979).

Suicide rates and holidays: D. P. Phillips and J. Liu, "The Frequency of Suicides around Major Public Holidays," *Suicide and Life-Threatening Behavior* (10:41–50, 1980); D. P. Phillips and J. S. Wills, "A Drop in Suicides around Major National Holidays," *Suicide and Life-Threatening Behavior* (17:1–12, 1987); T. G. Sparhawk, "Traditional Holidays and Suicide," *Psychological Reports* (60:245–46, 1987); D. Lester, "Suicide and Homicide Rates on National Holidays," *Psychological Reports* (60:414, 1987).

Winter depression in Alaska: R. Christensen and P. W. Dowrick, "Myths of Mid-Winter Depression," *Community Mental Health Journal* (19:177–86, 1983).

BIRTH ORDER

The most important books are C. Ernst and J. Angst, *Birth Order* (Berlin: Springer-Verlag, 1983) and J. Blake, *Family Size and Achievement* (Berkeley: University of California Press, 1989). On only children, see D. F. Polit and T. Falbo, "Only Children and Personality Development," *Journal of Marriage and the Family* (49:309–25, 1987). For a statement of Zajonc's "confluence theory," see R. B. Zajonc, "The Decline and Rise of Scholastic Aptitude Scores," *American Psychologist* (41:862–67, 1986). Other good studies: R. M. Hauser and W. H. Sewell, "Birth Order and Educational Attainment in Full Sibships," *American Educational Research Journal (AERJ)* (22:1–23, 1985); L. C. Steelman and B. Powell, "The Social and Academic Consequences of Birth Order," *Journal of Marriage and the Family* (47:117–24, 1985); and B. R. Mednick, R. L. Baker, and D. Hocevar, "Family Size and Birth Order Correlates of Intellectual, Psychosocial, and Physical Growth," *Merrill-Palmer Quarterly* (31:67–84, 1985).

On spacing: J. S. Kidwell, "Number of Siblings, Sibling-Spacing, Sex, and Birth Order," *Journal of Marriage and the Family* (43:315–32, 1981); L. J. Bloom, S. Anderson, and S. Hazaleus, "Personality Correlates of Age-Spacing in First-Borns," *Child Study Journal* (13:247–57, 1984); N. J. Bell et al., "Family Constellation, Social Competence, and Sex-Role Development," *Journal of Genetic Psychology* (146:273–75, 1985); and J. A. Hoffman and E. C. Teyber, "Some Relationships between Sibling Age Spacing and Personality," *Merrill-Palmer Quarterly* (25:77–80, 1979). The quotation is from Kidwell (p. 317).

MARIJUANA

D. F. Duncan, "Marijuana and Heroin," *British Journal of Addiction* (70:192–97, 1975); R. B. Millman and R. Sbriglio, "Patterns of Use and Psychopathology in Chronic Marijuana Users," *Psychiatric Clinics of North America* (9:533–45, 1986); and W. McGlothlin, "Epidemiology of Marihuana Use," research monograph no. 14, in *Marihuana Research Findings: 1976,* edited by R. C. Petersen (Rockville, MD: National Institute on Drug Abuse, 1977).

CREATIVITY AND MADNESS

Establishing a correlation: K. R. Jamison, "Manic-Depressive Illness and Accomplishment," in *Manic-Depressive Illness,* edited by F. K. Goodwin and K. R. Jamison (New York: Oxford University Press, in press) and N. C. Andreasen, "Creativity and Mental Illness," *AJP* (144:1288–92, 1987). For other studies, see R. Richards et al., "Creativity in Manic-Depressives, Cyclothymes, Their Normal Relatives, and Control Subjects," *Journal of Abnormal Psychology* (97:281–88, 1988); R. Richards, "Relationships between Creativity and Psychopathology," *Genetic Psychology Monographs* (103:261–324, 1981); and the work of Hagop S. Akiskal at the University of Tennessee, Memphis.

Figuring out what the correlation means: F. Barron, *Creativity and Psychological Health* (Princeton, NJ: D. Van Nostrand, 1963); R. A. Prentky, *Creativity and Psychopathology* (New York: Praeger, 1980); and E. Hartmann, *The Nightmare* (New York: Basic Books, 1984, esp. chaps. 5 and 6).

OVERPOPULATION

The UN data appear in a 1984 Department of Agriculture report, which is cited in F. M. Lappé and R. Schurman, *The Missing Piece in the Population Puzzle* (published in 1988 by the Institute for Food and Development Policy, Food First Development Report No. 4). Also see F. M. Lappé and J. Collins, *World Hunger: Twelve Myths* (New York: Grove Press, 1986).

FATHER AND SON

The 1971 survey: Harris poll reported in *Life* magazine (Jan. 8, 1971, 22–30). Johns Hopkins study: M. L. Kohn et al., "Social Stratification and the Transmission of Values in the Family," *Sociological Forum* (1:73–102, 1986). Berkeley study: J. A. Clausen, P. H. Mussen, and J. Kuypers, "Involvement, Warmth, and Parent-Child Resemblance in Three Generations," in *Present and Past in Middle Life*, edited by D. H. Eichorn et al. (New York: Academic Press, 1981). Lane quotation: R. E. Lane, "Political Education in the Midst of Life's Struggles," *Harvard Educational Review* (38:481, 1968). High-school seniors and parents study: M. K. Jennings and R. Niemi, *The Political Character of Adolescence* (Princeton, NJ: Princeton University Press, 1974).

TELEVISION

Children's imagination: P. Greenfield, D. Farrar, and J. Beagles-Roos, "Is the Medium the Message?" *Journal of Applied Developmental Psychology* (7:201–18, 1986); P. Greenfield and J. Beagles-Roos, "Radio vs. Television," *Journal of Communication* (38:71–92, 1988); M. A. Runco and K. Pezdek, "The Effect of Television and Radio on Children's Creativity," *Human Communication Research* (11:109–20, 1984).

Children's obesity: W. H. Dietz and S. L. Gortmaker, "Do We Fatten Our Children at the Television Set?" *Pediatrics* (75:807–12, 1985).

Reading and achievement: S. B. Neuman, "The Displacement Effect,"

Reading Research Quarterly (23:414–40, 1988) and P. A. Williams et al., "The Impact of Leisure-Time Television on School Learning," AERJ (19:19–50, 1982). Addictiveness and mindlessness: D. R. Anderson et al., "The Effects of TV Program Comprehensibility on Preschool Children's Visual Attention to Television," Child Development (52:151–57, 1981) and R. Smith, "Television Addiction," in Perspectives on Media Effects, edited by J. Bryant and D. Zillmann (Hillsdale, NJ: Lawrence Erlbaum, 1986). On these issues, as well as on reading, achievement, and creativity, the most comprehensive review of the research is D. R. Anderson and P. A. Collins, "The Impact on Children's Education" (published in 1988 as Working Paper No. 2 of the Office of Educational Research and Improvement of the U.S. Department of Education). Perception of danger: G. Gerbner et al., "Television's Mean World" (mimeographed by the Annenberg School of Communications at the University of Pennsylvania in 1986), which is part of an ongoing series of studies of the effects of TV viewing.

EMPATHY AND INTUITION

Taking others' points of view: D. Krebs and B. Sturrup, "Role-Taking Ability and Altruistic Behaviour in Elementary School Children," Journal of Moral Education (11:94–100, 1982) and M. L. Hoffman, "Sex Differences in Empathy and Related Behaviors," Psych Bull (84:712–22, 1977). Maryland study: B. D. Fallik, "Relative Association between Intuition, Two Cognitive Style Dimensions, Visual and Aural Dominance and Gender," Dissertation Abstracts International (46, no. 1-B:107, 1985). Judging nonverbal cues: J. A. Hall, "Gender Effects in Decoding Nonverbal Cues," Psych Bull (85:845–57, 1978). Dominance vs. gender: S. E. Snodgrass, "Women's Intuition," JPSP (49:146–55, 1985). Sex of experimenter: N. Eisenberg and R. Lennon, "Sex Differences in Empathy and Related Capacities," Psych Bull (94:109, 1983) and N. Feshbach, "Studies of Empathic Behavior in Children," in Progress in Experimental Personality Research, vol. 8, edited by B. A. Maher (New York: Academic Press, 1978, 24–25). Depends how you measure: See Eisenberg and Lennon; R. Lennon and N. Eisenberg, "Gender and Age Differences in Empathy and Sympathy," in Empathy and Its Development, edited by N. Eisenberg and J. Strayer (Cambridge, UK: Cambridge University Press, 1987).

ABILITY GROUPING

The first stop for anyone looking into this topic is Jeannie Oakes's book *Keeping Track* (New Haven, CT: Yale University Press, 1985). Also see her chapter "Tracking in Secondary Schools," in *School and Classroom Organization,* edited by R. E. Slavin (Hillsdale, NJ: Lawrence Erlbaum, 1989); and J. I. Goodlad and J. Oakes, "We Must Offer Equal Access to Knowledge," *Educational Leadership* (Feb. 1988, 16–22). For other review articles, see M. M. Dawson, "Beyond Ability Grouping," *School Psychology Review* (16:348–69, 1987); C. C. Kulik and J. A. Kulik, "Effects of Ability Grouping on Secondary School Students," *AERJ* (19:415–28, 1982); and T. L. Good and S. Marshall, "Do Students Learn More in Heterogeneous or Homogeneous Groups?" in *The Social Context of Instruction,* edited by P. L. Peterson, L. C. Wilkinson, and M. Hallinan (Orlando, FL: Academic Press, 1984).

Now for the research cited here. Slavin study: R. E. Slavin, "Ability Grouping and Student Achievement in Elementary Schools," *Review of Educational Research* (57:293–336, 1987). Eleven thousand high-school students: A. Gamoran and R. D. Mare, "Secondary School Tracking and Educational Inequality," *American Journal of Sociology* (94:1146–83, 1989). California middle schools: A. B. Sørensen and M. T. Hallinan, "Effects of Ability Grouping on Growth in Academic Achievement," *AERJ* (23: 519–42, 1986). British study: A. C. Kerckhoff, "Effects of Ability Grouping in British Secondary Schools," *American Sociological Review* (51:842–58, 1986). Israeli study: Y. Dar and N. Resh, "Classroom Intellectual Composition and Academic Achievement," *AERJ* (23:357–74, 1986).

Finally, Johnson is quoted in A. Kohn, "It's Hard to Get Left Out of a Pair," *Psychology Today* (Oct. 1987, 52–57).

MONDAYS

Suicides: D. Lester, "Temporal Variation in Suicide and Homicide," *American Journal of Epidemiology* (109:517–20, 1979); E. Rogot, R. Fabsitz, and M. Feinleib, "Daily Variation in USA Mortality," *American Journal of Epidemiology* (103:198–211, 1976); and H. Gabennesch, "When Promises Fail," *Social Forces* (67:129–45, 1988). SUNY research: A. A. Stone et al., "Prospective and Cross-Sectional Mood Reports Offer No Evidence of a 'Blue Monday' Phenomenon," *JPSP* (49:129–34, 1985).

HASTY MARRIAGES

Marrying early in life: G. C. Kitson et al., "Who Divorces and Why?" *Journal of Family Issues* (6:285–93, 1985); N. D. Glenn and M. Supancic, "The Social and Demographic Correlates of Divorce and Separation in the United States," *Journal of Marriage and the Family* (46:563–75, 1984); and T. C. Martin and L. L. Bumpass, "Recent Trends in Marital Disruption," *Demography* (26:41, 1989).

Jumping into marriage: B. Thornes and J. Collard, *Who Divorces?* (London: Routledge & Kegan Paul, 1979, esp. 68, 78); F. F. Furstenberg, Jr., "Premarital Pregnancy and Marital Instability," in *Divorce and Separation*, edited by G. Levinger and O. C. Moles (New York: Basic Books, 1979); and K. J. Grover et al., "Mate Selection Processes and Marital Satisfaction," *Family Relations* (34:383–86, 1985).

Cohabitation: The Swedish and U.S. studies, respectively, are reported in an Associated Press story, "Ex-Unwed Couples Found More Likely to Divorce," *The New York Times* (Dec. 7, 1987, A25) and F. Barringer, "Doubt on 'Trial Marriage' Raised by Divorce Rates," *The New York Times* (June 9, 1989, A1, A28).

SEX AND SPORTS

Shenkman in footnote: R. Shenkman, *Legends, Lies, and Cherished Myths of American History* (New York: Harper & Row, 1989, 61). Survey of coaches: M. Gordon, "College Coaches' Attitudes Toward Pregame Sex," *Journal of Sex Research* (24:256–62, 1988). Grip-test study: W. R. Johnson, "Muscular Performance Following Coitus," *Journal of Sex Research* (4:247–48, 1968). A couple of other guys' thoughts on the matter: M. H. Anshel, "Effects of Sexual Activity on Athletic Performance," *Physician and Sportsmedicine* (Aug. 1981, 65–68); and D. L. Cooper, "Can Scoring Influence Athletic Performance?" *Journal of the American College Health Association* (23:197–99, 1975).

ADOPTION AND INFERTILITY

Social workers' quotation: R. K. Katz et al., "Is the Adoption Process an Aid to Achieving Pregnancy?" *Social Work* (30:66, 1985). The studies, in order of appearance: B. Sandler, "Conception After Adoption," *Fertility and Sterility (F&S)* (16:313–22, 1965); M. Humphrey and K. M. Mackenzie, "Infertility and Adoption," *British Journal of Preventive and Social Medicine* (21:90–96, 1967); W. C. Weir and D. R. Weir, "Adoption and

Subsequent Conceptions," *F&S* (17:283–88, 1966); J. Rock, C. Tietze, and H. B. McLaughlin, "Effect of Adoption on Infertility," *F&S* (16:305–12, 1965); G. H. Arronet, C. A. Bergquist, and M. C. Parekh, "The Influence of Adoption on Subsequent Pregnancy in Infertile Marriage," *International Journal of Fertility* (19:159–62, 1974); and E. J. Lamb and S. Leurgans, "Does Adoption Affect Subsequent Fertility?" *American Journal of Obstetrics and Gynecology* (134:138–44, 1979). Citations for other studies that found the same thing will be supplied on request.

BLINDNESS

M. Bross and M. Borenstein, "Temporal Auditory Acuity in Blind and Sighted Subjects," *Perceptual and Motor Skills* (55:963–66, 1982); C. E. Rice, "Early Blindness, Early Experience, and Perceptual Enhancement," *American Foundation for the Blind Research Bulletin* (no. 22, Dec.:1–22, 1970); and D. H. Warren, "Implications of Visual Impairments for Child Development," in *Low Incidence Conditions*, vol. 3 of *Handbook of Special Education*, edited by M. C. Wang, M. C. Reynolds, and H. J. Walberg (Oxford, UK: Pergamon Press, 1989).

A few more sources for the truly motivated: D. H. Warren, *Blindness and Early Childhood Development*, 2d ed. (New York: American Foundation for the Blind, 1984); L. Stankov and G. Spilsbury, "The Measurement of Auditory Abilities of Blind, Partially Sighted, and Sighted Children," *Applied Psychological Measurement* (2:491–503, 1978); and W. Niemeyer and I. Starlinger, "Do the Blind Hear Better?" *Audiology* (20:503–515, 1981).

ADOLESCENCE

For more on normal teenagers, find anything with Daniel Offer's name on it. He is the lead author, most recently, of *The Teenage World* (New York: Plenum Medical Book Co., 1988) and, perhaps most famously, of *The Psychological World of the Teenager* (New York: Basic Books, 1969). Also cited here: M. Rutter et al., "Adolescent Turmoil," *Journal of Child Psychology and Psychiatry* (17:35–56, 1976) and M. Csikszentmihalyi and R. Larson, *Being Adolescent* (New York: Basic Books, 1984). Also worthwhile is D. G. Oldham, "Adolescent Turmoil: A Myth Revisited," in *Adolescent Psychiatry*, vol. 6, edited by S. C. Feinstein and P. L. Giovacchini (Chicago: University of Chicago Press, 1978).

SAFETY IN NUMBERS

Quotation: B. Latane and J. Darley, *The Unresponsive Bystander* (New York: Appleton-Century-Crofts, 1970, 127). Epileptic study: J. Darley and B. Latane, "Bystander Intervention in Emergencies," *JPSP* (8:377–83, 1968).

STRESS

Among Kobasa's studies: S. C. Kobasa, "Stressful Life Events, Personality, and Health," *JPSP* (37:1–10, 1979); S. C. Kobasa, S. R. Maddi, and S. Kahn, "Hardiness and Health," *JPSP* (42: 168–77, 1982); and S. C. O. Kobasa et al., "Effectiveness of Hardiness, Exercise and Social Support as Resources against Illness," *Journal of Psychosomatic Research* (29: 525–33, 1985).

Jobs and stress: R. A. Karasek et al., "Job Characteristics in Relation to the Prevalence of Myocardial Infarction in the US Health Examination Survey (HES) and the Health and Nutrition Examination Survey (HANES)," *American Journal of Public Health* (78:910–16, 1988).

BIRDS VS. OPPOSITES

Lewak quotation: R. W. Lewak, J. A. Wakefield, Jr., and P. F. Briggs, "Intelligence and Personality in Mate Choice and Marital Satisfaction," *Personality and Individual Differences* (6:471, 1985). Some other studies: B. I. Murstein, "Mate Selection in the 1970s," *Journal of Marriage and the Family* (42:51–66, 1980) and A. B. Hollingshead, "Cultural Factors in the Selection of Marriage Mates," *American Sociological Review* (15:619–27, 1950). Couples becoming more similar: A. L. Gruber-Baldini and K. W. Schaie, "Longitudinal-Sequential Studies of Marital Assortativity" (paper presented at the annual meeting of the Gerontological Society of America in Chicago, Nov. 1986) and research of D. Edington and L. Yen described in V. Bozzi, "In Sickness and in Health," *Psychology Today* (Apr. 1989, 22). Buss quotation: D. M. Buss and M. Barnes, "Preferences in Human Mate Selection," *JPSP* (50:560, 1986).

A WOMAN'S WORK

Dot-counting experiment: B. Major, D. B. McFarlin, and D. Gagnon, "Overworked and Underpaid," *JPSP* (47:1399–1412, 1984). Michigan study: described in J. H. Pleck, *Working Wives/Working Husbands* (Beverly Hills, CA: Sage Publications, 1985). Nevada researchers' quotation: R. Stafford, E. Backman, and P. Dibona, "The Division of Labor among Cohabiting and Married Couples," *Journal of Marriage and the Family* (39:44, 1977). Hochschild quotation: A. Hochschild, *The Second Shift* (New York: Viking, 1989, 4). Women do more total work: This study, too, is described in Pleck. Sanik's study hasn't yet been published.

BLONDES

Preference for dark hair: E. D. Lawson, "Hair Color, Personality, and the Observer," *Psychological Reports* (28:311–22, 1971) and S. Feinman and G. W. Gill, "Sex Differences in Physical Attractiveness Preferences," *Journal of Social Psychology* (105:43–52, 1978). Red hair: see Feinman and Gill; D. E. Clayson and M. R. C. Maughan, "Redheads and Blonds," *Psychological Reports* (59:811–16, 1986). Professor/janitor study is quoted in Clayson and Maughan (p. 811).

NECESSITY

Paine quotation in footnote: R. Rosenberg, "Spinoffs: A Myth Is Born," *Boston Globe* (July 17, 1989, 21, 23).

IGNORANCE IS BLISS

The studies, in order: A. Campbell, P. E. Converse, and W. L. Rodgers, *The Quality of American Life* (New York: Russell Sage Foundation, 1976, esp. 136–38); N. D. Glenn and C. N. Weaver, "A Multivariate, Multisurvey Study of Marital Happiness," *Journal of Marriage and the Family* (40:269–82, 1978); N. D. Glenn and C. N. Weaver, "Education's Effects on Psychological Well-Being," *Public Opinion Quarterly* (45:22–39, 1981); L. Sigelman, "Is Ignorance Bliss?" *Human Relations* (34:965–74, 1981); D. C. Shinn, "Education and the Quality of Life in Korea and the United States," *Public Opinion Quarterly* (50:360–70, 1986).

INDEX

ability grouping, students' learning
and, 163–166
absence, heart made fonder by,
48–49
abused children, as future child
abusers, 54–56
acne, chocolate as cause of, 15–17
actions, as louder than words, 78–79
Adler, Alfred, 145
adolescence, turmoil in, 176–178
adoption, infertility cured by,
171–173
advertising, subliminal, 72–74
aggression:
and human nature, 69–72
sparing the rod and, 135–138
aging:
conservatism and, 17–19
depression and, 108
learning abilities and, 106–108
Ainsworth, Mary, 100–101
Alexander, John, 27–28
alienation, adolescence as time of,
176–178
Allen, Woody, 11
Allgeier, Elizabeth, 12, 133
Allport, Gordon, 130

Alperovitz, Gar, 62
altruism:
behavioral example and, 79
of religious people, 129–131
rewards and, 34
alumni donations, athletic success
and, 46–47
Alwin, Duane, 19
Amabile, Teresa, 33, 34, 78, 189,
190
Anderson, Daniel R., 157, 158,
159
Andreasen, Nancy, 151, 152
Anger (Tavris), 117
Angst, Jules, 145, 146
Archer, Dane, 24
Aristotle, 115, 150
Art, Mind, and Brain (Gardner), 87
arthritis, as result of
knuckle-cracking, 138–140
athletic success:
alumni generosity and, 46–47
atomic bombing of Hiroshima, lives
saved by, 58–62
Atomic Diplomacy (Alperovitz), 62
attractiveness, attraction:
of opposites, 182–183

attractiveness *(cont.)*
  playing hard to get and, 91–94
  see also beauty

baby:
  mother's blues after birth of,
    79–81
  spoiling of, by picking up, 99–101
Baldwin, William R., 122
Baltes, Paul, 107
Baron, Robert A., 69
Barron, Frank, 152
basketball players, shooting streaks
    of, 141–142
beauty:
  in eye of beholder, 112–113
  as skin deep, 25–27
  see also attractiveness, attraction
Bedau, Hugo, 22
Bell, Silvia, 100–101
Bender, A. E., 75, 76
Berk, Lee, 66
Bernstein, Barton, 59
Berscheid, Ellen, 25
Bible, 129, 130, 135
birds of a feather, flocking together
    of, 182–183
birth order, 144–148
birthrate, full moon and, 52–53
Blake, Judith, 145, 147, 148
blind people, supersensitive hearing
    of, 174–175
bliss, ignorance as, 190–193
blondes, more fun had by, 186–188
blood pressure, salt and, 49–50
blues, *see* depression
Borenstein, Myra, 174
Bornstein, Robert F., 41
Boston drivers, 104–106
Bowers, William J., 23, 24
boys, mathematical abilities of, 63–64
breakfast, importance of, 75–78
Brooks-Gunn, Jeanne, 43
Bross, Michael, 174
Bryan, James H., 79
Bumpass, Larry L., 168
Buss, David M., 183

Butt, Dorcas Susan, 81
Byrnes, James, 62
bystanders, assistance given by,
    178–179

Candid Camera, 65
capital punishment, as deterrent to
    murder, 21–24
carrots, eyesight and, 88
Catherine the Great, death of, 27–28
Catherine the Great: Life and Legend
    (Alexander), 27
Chapieski, M. Lynn, 137
character, competition as builder of,
    81–83
chicken soup, as cold remedy, 94–98
childbirth, sexual desire and, 132
children:
  abused, as future child abusers,
    54–56
  birth order of, 144–148
  spoiled from sparing the rod,
    135–138
  television and, 157–160
Chitty, Dennis, 20–21
chocolate, acne caused by, 15–17
Christmas depression syndrome, 143
Churchill, Winston, 60
colds, catching and curing of, 94–98
college teams, alumni donations and,
    46–47
competition:
  as character-building, 81–83
  productivity and, 34
Conference of Mayors, U.S., 128–129
conservatism, age and, 17–19
contempt, as bred by familiarity,
    40–41
Continuum Concept, The (Liedloff), 99
corruption, as effect of power,
    102–104
Costill, David, 125
couples:
  Seven-Year Itch and, 36–37
  see also love; marriage
cousins, marriage between, 109–111
Cousins, Norman, 64–65

Coyne, James C., 126
cracking of knuckles, arthritis as
    result of, 138–140
craziness:
    creativity and, 150–154
    full moon-induced, 50–53
    of homeless people, 127–129
creativity, 86–87
    madness linked to, 150–154
    necessity and, 188, 189–190
    rewards and, 33
Crofton, Christine, 112
crying:
    of babies, spoiling and, 99–101
    as solitary activity, 126–127
Csikszentmihalyi, Mihaly, 178
Cunningham, Michael, 187
Currie, Elliott, 22n

Danziger, Sheldon, 39
Darley, John, 178–179
Davis, W. Jackson, 111
death:
    of Catherine the Great, 27–28
    Hiroshima atomic bombing and,
        58–62
    by the "sword," 123
death penalty, murder rate and,
    21–24
Deci, Edward, 32, 34
depression:
    aging and, 108
    emotional support and, 126–127
    during holidays, 143–144
    on Mondays, 166–167
    postpartum, 79–81
    stress and, 67
    in teenagers, 176
Dick, Elliot C., 96, 97
Dickie, N. H., 75, 76
digestion:
    spicy foods and, 35–36
    swimming and, 9–10
Dillon, Kathleen, 65, 66
Dion, Karen, 25
dreams, spicy foods and, 36
drivers, Boston, 104–106

drugs, hard, marijuana as leading to,
    148–150

eating, swimming after, 9–10
Ehrlich, Isaac, 23, 24
Eisenberg, John, 84
Eisenberg, Nancy, 162
Eisenhower, Dwight D., 60
elephants:
    memory in, 84–85
    mice feared by, 84
empathy, in women vs. men,
    161–162
Endleman, Robert, 14
Englander-Golden, Paula, 42
Erikson, Kai, 61
Ernst, Cecile, 145, 146
Eron, Leonard, 135
eyesight:
    carrots as good for, 88
    intelligence and, 119–123
    reading as damaging to, 68, 120,
        121
eyes of beholder, beauty in, 112–113

Falbo, Toni, 144, 146
familiarity, contempt bred by, 40–41
Family Size and Achievement (Blake),
    145
fathers, sons' similarity to, 155–157
Feingold, Alan, 63–64
Feinson, Marjorie Chary, 108
Females, Males, and Sexuality (Kelley),
    133
firstborns, as different from other
    children, 144–148
Fisher, Roger, 54
fondness, absence as fostering,
    48–49
food, spicy, 35–36
forgetting, see memory
Foulke, Emerson, 175
Frames of Mind (Gardner), 87
France, Anatole, 190
Freeman, Millard, 10
Freud, Sigmund, 170
fright, white hair caused by, 118–119

Fromm, Erich, 70
Frost, Robert, xi, 193
Fry, William, 64, 67
full moon, craziness caused by,
    50–53
Fulton, James, 15
fun:
    had by blondes, 186–188
    time made to fly by having, 56–58

Gagnon, John, 134
gain, pain as companion to, 124–125
Galbraith, John Kenneth, 40
Gardner, Howard, 87, 189
gender differences:
    in empathy and intuition, 161–162
    in mathematical abilities, 63–64
    in motives for sex, 11–14
    in sexual peaks, 131–134
    in work habits, 184–185
Gerbner, George, 160
Getting to Yes (Fisher and Ury), 54
Gilovich, Tom, 142
girls, mathematical abilities of, 63–64
Glenn, Norval, 19, 190–191
Goldstein, Bernard, 133
Goldstein, Jeffrey, 67–68
Goodlad, John I., 165
Gottschalk, Peter, 39
Graham, David, 35
Grantham-McGregor, Sally, 77, 78
Gray, Thomas, 190, 192
grease, squeaky wheel and, 53
great minds, thinking of, 85–87
Gross, Alan E., 112
Growing Up Creative (Amabile), 189
Gwaltney, Jack M., Jr., 95–96, 97

hair:
    cutting as fostering growth of, 119
    turning white from fright, 118–119
Halikas, James A., 149
Hallett, John, 30–31
hard to get, playing, 91–94
Hartmann, Ernest, 36, 151–152
hasty marriages, repentance after,
    168–169

Hatfield, Elaine, 27
Hazan, Cindy, 48–49
health:
    laughter as agent in, 64–68
    stress and, 180–182
hearing, of blind people, 174–175
heart, made fonder by absence,
    48–49
Helson, Ravenna, 86–87
Hertzog, Christopher, 106
Hiroshima, atomic bombing of,
    58–62
Hochschild, Arlie, 185
holidays, suicides during, 143–144
homeless people, as crazy, 127–129
hormones, sexual desire and,
    132–133
horse, as Catherine the Great's last
    love, 27–28
hostility:
    aggression and, 115
    venting of, 113–117
Howard, Philip, 20
Hume, David, 79
humor, healing effects of, 64–68
Hyde, Janet Shibley, 11, 12, 63, 64
hypertension, salt and, 49–50

ignorance, as bliss, 190–193
inbreeding, 109–111
infertility, adoption as cure for,
    171–173
insanity:
    plea of, in murder cases, 88–91
    see also craziness
intelligence:
    of great minds, 85–87
    happiness and, 191
    nearsightedness and, 119–123
intuition, in women vs. men,
    161–162
invention, necessity as mother of,
    188–190

James, William, 85, 86
Jamison, Kay, 151, 153
Jennings, M. Kent, 156

Johnson, David, 83, 166
Johnson, Roger, 83
Jones, Warren H., 26
judging a book by its cover, 25–27
Juster, Thomas, 184, 185

Karasek, Robert A., 181
Katch, Frank, 171
Kaufman, Joan, 55, 56
Keeping Track (Oakes), 165
Kelley, Kathryn, 133
Kelly, Ivan, 52
Key, Wilson Bryan, 72, 73
Khoury, Muin J., 110
Kimura, Doreen, 44, 45
Kinsey Reports on Human Sexuality,
   131–132, 134
kissing, colds caught from, 97
Knight, Nancy, 30, 31
knuckle-cracking, arthritis as result
   of, 138–140
Kobasa, Suzanne Oullette, 180–181
Kohn, Melvin, 155
Konečni, Vladimir J., 116
Kozol, Jonathan, 129

Lane, Robert E., 156
Langbauer, Bill, 84
Lappé, Frances Moore, 154
Larson, Reed, 178
Latane, Bibb, 178–179
laughter:
   as best medicine, 64–68
   contagion of, 126–127
Leahy, William D., 60
learning:
   aging and, 106–108
   breakfast and, 75–78
   grouping students by ability and,
      163–166
lemmings, mass suicide of, 20–21
Lepper, Mark, 33
Levy, Valerie, 79–80
Lewak, Richard W., 182
Lewontin, Richard, 71
Lieberman, Harris, 16
Liebowitz, Michael, 17

Liedloff, Jean, 99–100
Liske, Eckehard, 111
living and dying by the sword, 123
love:
   absence's effect on, 48–49
   Romeo and Juliet effect in, 92
   sex and, 11–14
Love and Sex in Twelve Cultures
   (Endleman), 14
Lown, Bernard, 71–72

madness, see craziness
Maimonides, 98
Major, Brenda, 53
Malatak, John, 10
marijuana, as leading to hard drugs,
   148–150
marriage:
   between birds of a feather vs.
      opposites, 182–183
   between cousins, 109–111
   repentance following haste in,
      168–169
   seven-year itch and, 36–37
Martin, Teresa Castro, 168
mathematical abilities, in boys vs.
   girls, 63–64
Matthews, Karen A., 93
medicine, laughter as, 64–68
memory:
   aging and, 107
   of elephants, 84–85
menopause, depression and, 45–46
men's traits vs. women's, see gender
   differences
menstrual periods:
   cognitive performance and, 45
   mood swings and, 41–46
mental illness, see craziness
mice:
   elephants' fear of, 84
   favorite foods of, 85
milk, 36n
Miller, Alice, 137
Millman, Robert B., 149
Mollan, Raymond, 139
Mondays, depression on, 166–167

Money, John, 132
mood swings:
  in adolescence, 178
  menstrual periods and, 41–46
  on Mondays, 167
moon, full, alleged effects of,
  50–53
Moore, Timothy E., 74
motivation:
  rewards and, 31–35
  sexual, of men vs. women, 11–14
Moyer, K. E., 70
murder:
  capital punishment as deterrent to,
    21–24
  full moon and, 51–52
  insanity plea and, 88–91
music, tone-deafness and, 28–29
Myers, David, 4
myopia, intelligence linked to,
  119–123

Nadeau, Joe, 85
nearsightedness, intelligence linked
  to, 119–123
necessity, as mother of invention,
  188–190
Neill, A. S., 32
Neuman, Susan B., 158
Niemi, Richard G., 156
nightmares, from spicy foods, 36
Nordlund, James J., 118

Oakes, Jeannie, 165
Offer, Daniel, 176–177
Ogilvie, Bruce, 81–82
old dog, teaching new tricks to,
  106–108
opposites, attraction between,
  182–183
Ostwald, Peter, 153
overpopulation, starvation as result
  of, 154–155

pain, gain impossible without,
  124–125
Paine, Thomas O., 189n

parenting:
  children's romances and, 92
  of crying babies, 99–101
  of firstborn children, 146–147
  physical punishment in, 135–138
  television viewing and, 157–159
Parlee, Mary Brown, 43, 44
Pasnau, Robert O., 45
Pennebaker, James, 112, 115
Phillips, David, 143
physical punishment, 135–138
Pierce, Glenn L., 23, 24
Pleck, Joseph, 185
Pochi, Peter, 15
Pollitt, Ernesto, 77
poor, as getting poorer while rich
  get richer, 38–40
postpartum blues, 79–81
pots, watched, boiling of, 57–58
power, corrupting effect of, 102–104
Power, Thomas G., 137
praying mantises, sex life of,
  111–112
Prentky, Robert, 87
Priest, Louise, 10

Quadagno, David, 13, 14

reading:
  eyes harmed by, 68, 120, 121
  television viewing vs., 157–160
Reed, Sylvia, 96
religious people, altruism of,
  129–131
Rensch, B., 84
repentance, hasty marriage followed
  by, 168–169
rewards:
  altruism and, 34
  creativity and, 33
  motivation and, 31–35
Rice, Charles E., 175
rich, as getting richer while poor get
  poorer, 38–40
rod, spared, child spoiled from,
  135–138
Roosevelt, Franklin, 62

Rotton, James, 52
Rousseau, Jean-Jacques, 71
Rubin, Melvin, 122
Ruble, Diane N., 43
Rutter, Michael, 177
Ryan, Richard, 32

Sackner, Marvin A., 98
Sadock, Virginia, 132
safety in numbers, 178–179
salt, blood pressure raised by, 49–50
Sanik, Margaret, 185
Schaie, Warner, 106, 107–108
Scholastic Aptitude Tests (SATs), 120, 145
Schull, William, 110
Scientific Genius (Simonton), 86
Sears, David, 18
self-fulfilling prophecies, 25, 26
sensory compensation, in blind people, 174–175
seven-year itch, 36–37
Seville Statement on Violence, 69, 71, 72
sex:
  before the big game, 170–171
  Catherine the Great's appetite for, 27–28
  men's vs. women's motivations in, 11–14
  men's vs. women's peaks in, 131–134
  between praying mantises, 111–112
  in subliminal advertising, 72–73, 74
sex differences, see gender differences
Shaver, Phillip, 48
Shenkman, Richard, 170n
Shinn, Doh C., 191–192
Shreiner-Engel, Patricia, 132, 133–134
Simonton, Dean Keith, 86
Sipes, Richard G., 117
Skinner, B. F., 31
Slade, Pauline, 42

Slavin, Robert, 164
Smith, Robin, 159
Snodgrass, Sara, 161–162
Snow, David A., 128
snowflakes, uniqueness of, 30–31
Social Psychology (Myers), 4
Social Psychology of Creativity, The (Amabile), 189
Sommer, Barbara, 45
sons, as similar to their fathers, 155–157
spicy foods, bad effects of, 35–36
spoiling:
  of babies, by picking them up when they cry, 99–101
  of children, by sparing the rod, 135–138
sports:
  competition in, 81–83
  sexual activity and, 170–171
Sprague, Joey, 13
squeaky wheel, grease gotten by, 53–54
Stafford, Frank, 184
Stamford, Bryant, 125
starvation, overpopulation as cause of, 154–155
Steadman, Henry J., 90
Stein, Julian, 171
Steinhaus, Arthur, 9, 10
Stengel, Casey, 171
stomach:
  spicy foods and, 35–36
  swimming and, 9–10
Straus, Murray, 116, 136
streak shooting, in basketball, 141–142
stress:
  chocolate and, 16
  effects of, 180–182
students, ability grouping of, 163–166
subliminal advertising, 72–74
Subliminal Seduction (Key), 72
suicide:
  during full moon, 51
  during holidays, 143–144

suicide *(cont.)*
    of lemmings, 20–21
    on Mondays, 166
    by teenagers, 176–177
    swimming, after eating, 9–10
    sword, living and dying by, 123

Tarde, Gabriel, 21
Tavris, Carol, 117
teenagers, alienation in, 176–178
television, 124
    children's reading habits and,
        157–160
Tesser, Abraham, 48–49
thinking, of great minds, 85–87
time, flying of, 56–58
Togo, Shigenori, 60–61
Tone Deaf and All Thumbs? (Wilson),
    29
tone-deafness, 28–29
tracking, *see* ability grouping
Truman, Harry S, 58, 61, 62
Tutko, Thomas, 82
Tversky, Amos, 142

United Nations Food and Agriculture
    Organization, 154
Unresponsive Bystander, The (Bibb and
    Latane), 178
Ury, William, 54
U.S. Conference of Mayors,
    128–129
Uslan, Mark, 174

Vallone, Robert, 142
venting of hostility, 113–117

violence, 69–72
    physical punishment and, 135–138

Walbek, Nancy Hodges, 79
Walster, Elaine, 25, 92–93
Warren, David, 175
watched pots, boiling of, 57–58
Watson, Peter, 138–139
Weaver, Charles, 190–191
Weitzman, Michael, 77
wheel, squeaky, grease gotten by,
    53–54
white hair, fright as cause of,
    118–119
Widom, Cathy Spatz, 55
Willis, Sherry L., 107–108
Wilson, Frank, 29
women:
    menstrual mood swings of, 41–46
    postpartum blues in, 79–81
    work of, as never done, 184–185
    see also gender differences
words:
    actions vs., 78–79
    misused, 195–196
work, woman's, as never done,
    184–185
Wright, Rex A., 93

Young, Bill, 134
Young, Francis, 121–122

Zajonc, Robert, 40–41, 145
Ziff, Morris, 139
Zigler, Edward, 55, 56
Zilbergeld, Bernie, 117
Zimbardo, Philip, 102–104

A NOTE TO READERS

Has it ever occurred to you how much time you waste every day in your car and in the shower? Here's an ideal opportunity to put all those hours to good use: Spend them thinking up more examples of common beliefs like the ones examined in this book. If you come up with a bit of folk wisdom that is (1) so widely accepted as to be virtually proverbial and (2) capable of being proved or disproved in an interesting way, I'd like to hear about it. I'll be even more enthusiastic if you can supply a citation to the data that prove or disprove it. If your suggestion is included in an eventual sequel, you'll receive a complimentary copy of the book, autographed by the author. If two suggestions of yours are used, you'll be eligible to receive a nonautographed copy.

Write to:

> Alfie Kohn
> c/o HarperCollins Publishers
> 10 East 53rd Street
> New York, NY 10022

(This offer void where authors' attempts to cut corners on their research is prohibited by law.)